MW00830511

Teaching History
Then and Now

Teaching History Then and Now

A Story of Stability and Change in Schools

LARRY CUBAN

HARVARD EDUCATION PRESS
Cambridge, Massachusetts

Copyright © 2016 by the President and Fellows of Harvard College

All rights reserved. No part of this publication may be reproduced or transmitted in any form or by any means, electronic or mechanical, including photocopy, recording, or any information storage and retrieval systems, without permission in writing from the publisher.

Library of Congress Control Number 2015950419
Paperback ISBN 978-1-61250-886-3
Library Edition ISBN 978-1-61250-887-0

Published by Harvard Education Press,
an imprint of the Harvard Education Publishing Group

Harvard Education Press
8 Story Street
Cambridge, MA 02138

Cover Design: Wilcox Design
Cover Photos: © Gloda/iStock/Getty Images (classroom);
                        © prosot-photography/iStock/Getty Images (questions on blackboard)
The typefaces used in this book are ITC Legacy Serif and Frutiger

I dedicate this book to

Lillian Kubrick Miller
(1937–2013)

She gave and received the gift of love

Contents

Introduction

As a historian of education, I have been fortunate in having a career in public school teaching and administration before entering academia. Between the mid-1950s and early 1970s, I taught history in Cleveland and Washington, DC, high schools. In this book, I return to those minority and poor high schools—then and now—and, through the eyes of a historian using the concepts and tools of my craft, answer a core question central to informing contemporary policies aimed at getting students to learn more, faster, and better, especially in urban districts: over the past-half-century: *What has changed and what has remained the same in the content and pedagogy of high school history over the past half-century?*

The academic subject of history is taught in elementary and secondary schools and required for graduation across the nation. Policymakers, teachers, parents, and taxpayers tell students: learn about the Founding Fathers, the Constitution, principles and practices of democracy, and the wars fought for those principles and then cherish that knowledge and those principles. Conserving the past is vital. Historians and social scientists call this the *heritage* approach to the teaching of history.[1]

Yet at the same time, those very same policymakers, teachers, parents, and taxpayers want students not only to imbibe and appreciate their heritage but also to learn critical thinking skills such as problem solving, questioning, and analyzing ideas. They want students to apply the knowledge and skills they have acquired to both the past (e.g., Founding Fathers, slavery, the Civil War, immigration) and the present in both their communities and the nation. Students can then alter the present. Historians and social scientists call this the *historical*

1

approach to the teaching of the subject (I take up both in more detail in chapter 3).

The paradox of teaching history to conserve the past and change the present is wrapped up in the larger issue of continually reforming public schools over the past century in governance, organization, curriculum, and instruction. The chronic impulse to preserve the status quo in schooling smacks up against the recurring impulse to change—no, *improve*—what goes on daily in classrooms. Like the tension between the heritage and historical approaches to teaching, there is strain between stability and change at the very core of tax-supported public schools in a democracy. Why is that?

STABILITY AND CHANGE IN SCHOOL REFORM

Taxpayers, voters, and parents expect their public schools to conserve both national and local traditions, beliefs, and values. Consider the historic goals for tax-supported public schools. Educators are expected to mold "good" citizens, prepare the next generation for the workplace, and promote the well-being of individual students and society. Schools socialize the young into community and national values embedded in these multiple goals.[2]

Inculcating habits, beliefs, and values so that children can behave as responsible adults in a community requires more than answering teachers' questions, reading textbooks, answering multiple-choice questions, and doing Internet searches. Look into a kindergarten classroom for the most obvious evidence of the school's function: to absorb the norms of a community, five-year-olds learn to take turns; not to push, hit, or bite others; work independently; and cooperate with others who look and act different. Yes, learning numbers and decoding words are important, but only the shortsighted could miss the critical social lessons taught here.

Similarly, throughout elementary and secondary schools, as knowledge demands escalate, the goal of socializing children and youth persists quietly and forcefully in posted classroom rules, report cards that evaluate proper behaviors, and what gets rewarded or punished in school. Conserving values rooted in these historic goals for public schools is essential in a democracy.

Yet public schools are expected to also make changes. Taxpayers, policymakers, and parents expect public schools to change students by getting them to think critically. These thinking skills are embedded in history, math, science, and English content and from kindergarten through Advanced Placement courses. In the classroom and later as adults, students are expected to apply those skills to make changes in themselves and improve their community.

Understanding the paradox facing practitioners of how to enact two opposite and prized values—stability and change—through daily lessons is a first step in grasping the complexity of both schooling and teaching in a democracy. And that is why the core question of about what has changed in teaching history then and now is important to anyone concerned about public schools.

GOING FROM POLICY TO CLASSROOM PRACTICE

There is another reason this question about the teaching of history past and present is significant. The answer traces what occurs in policymakers' offices and the subsequent journey of adopted policies into classrooms. That policy-to-practice journey is filled with potholes that leave dings in even the best ideas before they arrive at the classroom door. Since the early 1980s, for example, US students' mediocre performance on international tests, middling graduation rates, and low numbers of graduates entering and completing college have led policymakers to worry about the nation's future economic growth.

Following the publication of the *Nation at Risk* report in 1983, state and federal policies to improve US schooling increasingly treated public schooling as a marketplace. Expanding parental options to include charters and vouchers, for example, created new schools that competed with traditional neighborhood schools and produced innovations that spread through districts, states, and the nation, according to reformers.

And as in competitive markets, effective schools were rewarded and ineffective ones punished. Using a market-based approach to improve schools depended on adopting policies that would raise curriculum standards and test students to see if they reached those standards. Schools, teachers, and students were held accountable for results, and rewards and penalties were applied accordingly. The current state adoption of Common Core Curriculum Standards, with accompanying online tests, is the most recent incarnation of that underlying belief that public schools should behave more like a marketplace. Both market- and standards-based policies have driven reforms in the past thirty years to tie together more closely an educational system in dire need of repair to the production of "human capital" for a growing economy.[3]

These reforms, of course, are based on a set of assumptions—a theory of change. Reform-minded policymakers assume that adopting higher standards and high-stakes testing will improve classroom practices, and that improved teaching practices will then lead to students acquiring the necessary content and skills to enter college and career. It is further assumed that there is a smooth path from policy to classroom practice. These assumptions have dominated US policy thinking about improving public schools in recent decades. Taking a longer view, however, say over a half-century, of what policies and practices have remained the same and what has changed in the teaching of one academic subject—I examine two efforts, based on similar assumptions, to alter practice in the 1960s and 1990s. This inquiry offers an uncommon way of testing the dominant theory of change.

Thus, in the following chapters, I will describe and analyze changes in history content and pedagogy over the past half-century. I first reconstruct what I did in Glenville High School and Cardozo High School decades ago, offering a uniquely intimate view of classroom practices at that time. I then look at history teaching as it is occurs today in those same high schools. In comparing and contrasting the past and present, I can determine whether the assumptions reformers hold about policies as they wend their way into classrooms turn out as intended and which practices remain the same and which ones have changed.[4]

I have already written widely over the years about the schools I have taught in, the content of my teaching, and how I taught between the mid-1950s and early-1970s. What I have not done in these earlier writings, however, is connect the teaching of history to the "wars" that occurred in the social studies in the 1930s, 1960s, and 1990s and continue in the current squabbles over whose notion of the past should be taught. The record is clear that the content of history in schools—heritage versus historical—has continually split Americans into different political camps.[5]

Look back, for instance, at post–World War I campaigns to ban US history texts with an "unpatriotic" slant. In the 1940s, a national movement to rid public schools of so-called "socialistic" biases in a popular social studies textbook series prompted Mrs. Ellwood Turner, secretary of the Daughters of Colonial Wars, to speak out:

> All the old histories taught my country right or wrong. That's the point of view we want our children to adopt. We can't afford to teach them to be unbiased and let them make up their own minds.[6]

Sharp criticism of history teachers and school boards periodically flared throughout the twentieth century after history tests revealed that most youth knew little about the Declaration of Independence, Abraham Lincoln, and whether the Civil War came before or after the Revolutionary War. Then in the 1960s, again in the 1990s, and a quarter-century later, history "wars" flared anew over what history and social studies content should be taught children and youth. Those recurring battles capture the inherent contradiction within the mission of US public schools to both conserve and change.[7]

In short, this book contains two policy-to-practice case studies of Cleveland and Washington, DC, complete with national, city, district, and classroom contexts. For both cities, I describe a half-century of political, social, and economic changes triggered by the Civil Rights movement, subsequent fiscal crises, revolving-door superintendencies, and mayoral control of schools.

I take up also a series of curricular, instructional, and organizational policy-driven reforms between the 1950s and 1960s (e.g., the appearance of black history materials, battles over the New Social Studies, expanding use of new technologies) and the 1990s to the present (e.g., new curriculum standards, increased testing, and regulatory accountability). I note where these connections between larger societal changes and policy-driven reforms may have touched the actual classroom lessons that fellow teachers and I taught.

CLARIFYING STABILITY AND CHANGE

The key part of the analysis of both time periods and answering the central question I ask requires parsing what the words *change* and *stability* mean.

There are, for example, different kinds of institutional, organizational, and individual change over time (e.g., incremental and fundamental).[8] Are the planned changes occurring over the past five decades mostly *incremental* (e.g., adding new high school courses in ethnic studies and dropping others such as ancient history, new textbooks, adopting a different way of teaching the Gettysburg Address)? Or were there also some fundamental changes in organizing the school, curriculum, and instruction (e.g., introducing project-based learning, trying a new instructional technology, creating schools-within-a-school)—that is, were there changes in the *grammar of schooling* (the deep structures of schooling such as the age-graded school with self-contained classrooms, daily schedules comprising forty-minute to hour-long periods of instruction, and a system in which students progress or regress from year to year depending upon their academic performance and behavior)?[9] Or were these changes mixes of both?

Sorting out both policy and practice changes gets complicated when, for example, policymakers make decisions that end up in practice reinforcing traditional patterns of teaching (e.g., more tests and accountability policies result in teachers spending more instructional time in preparing students for exams). Moreover, school structures and cultures that affect what is taught and how it is taught shift over time within schools. For instance, over time, school enrollments expand

and shrink, daily schedules shorten and lengthen class periods, and big schools get split into smaller ones and then get reorganized back into big ones.

I consider these distinctions between incremental and fundamental planned changes when determining whether my colleagues and I have altered daily teaching practices under repeated reform movements. Thus, the complexity of the concept of change (and reform) has to be unpacked, analyzed, and fit to the contexts and teaching over time. In doing so, the current dominant theory of change propelling reform policies in 2015 can be examined and assessed.[10]

To sum up, the question *What has changed and what has remained the same in the content and pedagogy in high school history over the past half-century?* illuminates the core function of public schools in a democracy, which is to both conserve traditions, values, and beliefs and at the same time to alter them. It is not an easy question to answer but vital to current decision makers, researchers, and practitioners involved in making and implementing policy to improve teaching practices and student learning not only in history but also in other academic subjects as well.[11]

SCHOLARS WRITING AUTOBIOGRAPHICALLY

What will complicate answering the question I have posed is that I combine the personal with the scholarly. I value my fourteen years as a teacher and remember so much of the highs and lows of that experience. Yet a scholar writing autobiographically is uncommon and when it does occur, precarious. Memory can be unreliable.[12] Psychologists, lawyers, social scientists, and novelists (who have their place here as keen social observers) have written extensively about how memory is selective and distorted. For example, one of Ward Just's characters observes: "There were gaps in Andre's memory, things omitted or forgotten, glossed over, redacted and invented. Memories bore the same relation to the facts as distant cousins to a common grandfather."[13] As Cormac McCarthy describes the phenomenon, "You forget what you want to remember and remember what you want to forget."[14] Mark

Twain's take: "It isn't so astonishing, the number of things that I can remember, as the number of things I can remember that aren't so."[15]

Yet summoning up facts from one's past is even trickier than what these writers suggest. As Elizabeth Loftus, an expert on memory, especially eyewitness testimony in trials, puts it: "Truth and reality, when seen through the filter of our memories, are not objective facts, but subjective, interpretative realities. We interpret the past, correcting ourselves, adding bits and pieces, deleting uncomplimentary or disturbing recollections, sweeping, dusting, and tidying things up . . . We are innocent victims of our mind's manipulations."[16]

And here is where conflict inevitably enters. I value my training as a historian who is highly aware that the sources available to me about how I taught a half-century ago are not only fragmentary (e.g., my recollections, actual homework assignments, gradebooks, teacher diaries) but are also selective and necessarily biased. The same is true of former students' recollections and what appears in high school yearbooks and other school documents. I have learned to be cautious with certain primary sources, especially autobiographies describing classrooms, reports from former students, and retired teachers' reminiscences. So I know that writing a personal account means that some things are accurately recorded, some unintentionally misrepresented, and some left unsaid.

I want to recapture faithfully what happened in my classes and at the same time maintain a historian's skepticism of biased sources inherent to any inquiry into the past. Thus, writing about how others and I taught history a half-century ago, scholarly objectivity—that "noble dream"—is very difficult to attain.[17] In writing autobiographically about my seven years at Glenville High School (1956–1963) and four at Cardozo High School (1963–1967), I will portray the truth as I see it, knowing full well the limitations of memory.[18]

Given these truths, the historian-autobiographer faces questions about the facts and style of writing. How will I document my statements? What will my experiences reveal about the micro-history of teaching at Glenville high school in the late 1950s and early 1960s and

Cardozo High School in the mid- to late 1960s? How did the macro-history—those larger trends in these cities, their schools and policies, the spreading civil rights movement, and the national struggle over what history should be taught and how—touch room 235 at Glenville and room 101 at Cardozo? Documenting the macro- and micro-history of teaching history does not erase the dilemma I face; it does, however, present an ongoing challenge to any historian-autobiographer—one that I accept in writing this book.

THE OUTLINE OF THIS BOOK

In chapters 1 and 2, I reconstruct how I taught at Glenville and Cardozo high schools. In each chapter, I describe the respective city and its school systems, as well as national social and political context, to offer a macro view in which I locate my teaching.

Chapter 3 captures the significant national debates that occurred in the 1960s and 1990s on the importance of history within the social studies and its impact on students' ideas and values. The chapter looks at policy changes in curriculum at two different points in time and estimates to what degree policy changes in history content and instruction permeated classroom lessons.

Chapters 4 and 5 return to Glenville and Cardozo high schools a half-century later. As a historian-autobiographer, sitting in classrooms in 2013–2014 and watching history teachers teach lessons was more than a déjà vu moment. Sorting out what I remembered of teaching history a half-century earlier from what I observed now was a task that could easily become a trap—seeing similarities in content and pedagogy and rushing to judgment that little has changed in over five decades. Thus, noting the differences in external and internal contexts (e.g., demographics, city and district politics, school organization) between then and now becomes crucial. Changes have, indeed, occurred in the city, district, schools, and classrooms, but there has been continuity in school structures and regularities in teacher and student behaviors. These two chapters describe and analyze how history teachers teach today in those schools and the macro- and micro-influences that shape their classroom decisions.

Finally, chapter 6 compares and contrasts the two case studies of urban high schools and summarizes the data at two different points in time to answer that central question: *Over the past-half-century, what has changed and what has remained the same in the content and pedagogy of high school history?* I then go beyond answering that question by asking a final one: *So what?*

ONE

Teaching at Glenville High School, 1956–1963

In 1956, a few days before Glenville High School opened, I met with Oliver Deex, the school's brand-new principal, at a local deli. It was a novel experience for me. I had never met with a principal one-on-one since I was a student in high school, and the reasons then had nothing to do with my teaching responsibilities.

As I talked with Deex, I was startled to find out that Glenville student body was over 90 percent black—the word then was *Negro*—and that he was a tad nervous moving into his first high school principalship after leading a nearby junior high school. He gave me a once-over-lightly about segregated schools in Cleveland, the differences between the increasingly black East Side and the all-white West Side, separated by the Cuyahoga River. He began my education in Cleveland's residential segregation and the growth of ethnic and racial ghettos.[1]

SEGREGATED CLEVELAND

Patterns of ethnic and racial segregation in Cleveland had developed early in the twentieth century, when neighborhoods became easily identifiable as Italian, German, Polish, Jewish, and black. In the late nineteenth and early twentieth centuries, upwardly striving immigrant Jewish families clustered in the Central, Scovill, and Woodland Avenue neighborhoods close to downtown. By the 1920s, many of these families began to move eastward into the Glenville area in response to an influx of Southern black migrant families seeking better housing. The result was the gradual transformation of these areas into a black ghetto. By the 1930s, Jewish businesses, synagogues, hospitals, and charitable institutions services dotted 105th Street, one of Glenville's main thoroughfares, and Glenville High School became nearly 90 percent Jewish in that decade.[2]

Residential segregation and in-migration of blacks after World War II again created overcrowded housing in the already racially segregated Central, Scovill, and Woodland neighborhoods, and upwardly mobile black families entered the Glenville area in the late 1940s and early 1950s. As that occurred, more and more Jewish families moved into the eastern suburbs of Cleveland Heights, University Heights, South Euclid, and Beachwood. Middle-class black families increased their presence in the Glenville area, so that by the time I arrived, Glenville High School and the adjacent junior highs and elementary schools, were already over 90 percent black.[3]

I had grown up in Pittsburgh's black ghetto—then called the Hill District—and my memories of being one of a handful of white children in our neighborhood elementary school were unpleasant and not calculated to instill sensitivity. Moreover, in 1955, the popular film *Blackboard Jungle*, featuring Glenn Ford as an idealistic white high school teacher—yes, I identified with Ford—and Vic Morrow and Sidney Poitier as cunning white and black adolescents smoking in bathrooms and attacking their teachers shook me up, as did the film's loud and persistent beat of Bill Haley's "Rock Around the Clock."

Deex asked me about myself and I told him that I had finished the University of Pittsburgh with a major in history and minor in biology. The previous year, I had taught biology at McKeesport Technical High School outside of Pittsburgh. Wanting to teach history, I had applied for posts in Ohio and elsewhere. The week before I reported to McKeesport Tech, I had heard from the Cleveland schools' personnel department that my application to teach social studies had been approved and that I had been assigned to Glenville High School. Haltingly, I asked him how many classes I would be teaching—five, he said. How large were the classes? Around thirty. I told him how eager I was to teach history.

In return, Deex shared a little of his own background. A former stockbroker who after the crash of 1929 lost much of what he had accumulated in the market, he had turned to education to support his family. He got his education credentials, taught, and then became a principal. Oliver Deex was a voracious reader, charming conversationalist, and skeptic when it came to school district policies and politics. I was a college graduate but had never heard of the *Saturday Review of Literature*, *Harper's*, *The Atlantic*, *The Nation*, and dozens of other magazines of the day that he shared with me. Why he took this interest in me, I still have no idea. But he did. From that initial long lunch conversation with Deex, a working relationship evolved between a middle-aged principal and a twenty-one-year-old novice teacher.

Deex's insistent questioning of my beliefs and ideas and gentle prodding stirred a great and life-long hunger for ideas. He encouraged me as I worked toward a master's degree in history, applied successfully for a one-year fellowship at Yale, and actively scrounged funds from the school budget and downtown officials to advance what I was doing in my classes.

Deex also had a vision of a school community and worked hard to build one. He often invited to his home a small group of teachers committed to helping more Glenville students go to college. In his wood-paneled library, a room that looked like a movie set, he would urge my fellow teachers and me to take this or that book. This group of about a dozen teachers and one counselor stayed together as an informal group for the seven years I taught at Glenville and even morphed into a social group, including spouses. I guess today that group of like-minded Glenville teachers would be labeled a "professional learning community."

DAILY TEACHING AT GLENVILLE

Within six months of arriving in room 235, I discovered that being responsible for a homeroom and teaching five classes a day that involved different lessons (I taught world history and US history), grading the homework of over 150 students, and learning the ropes of managing groups a few years younger than me not only wore me out (I was also taking graduate history courses at Western Reserve University—now Case Western Reserve—in the evenings) but drove me to rely on lectures and the textbook in daily lessons far more than I had anticipated, given the progressive education courses I had taken at the University of Pittsburgh.

By mid-year, I had become dissatisfied with my teaching. I routinely lectured, watched maybe half of the students take notes and the other half stare into the distance or try to look attentive. Some fell asleep. I asked students questions about the assigned textbook readings and got one-word answers. Occasionally, a student would ask a question and I would improvise an answer that would trigger a few more students to enter what would become a full-blown back-and-forth discussion. These discussions were unplanned and all too brief—mysteriously disappearing in the blink of an eye. Periodic quizzes and weekly current events discussions altered my routines, but restless and disengaged students persisted. I was not practicing the student-centered instruction I had absorbed at the University of Pittsburgh. I was wholly teacher-centered in my instruction—lecturing, assigning textbook pages, and teaching the whole group as I concentrated on history content.[4]

I was, as I learned in later years, teaching history in the way that it had been taught for decades: the *heritage* approach. Yet before the school year was half-over, I realized that I did not want to teach history mechanically, drowning students in forgettable facts that left me (and probably them) drained and dissatisfied at the end of a long day. I wanted to break out of that pattern. But I didn't know how.[5]

These were the years just after *Brown v. Board of Education*—a decision that had not, as I recall, registered in my memory at the time that

FIGURE 1.1   Homeroom 235 in 1961.

it was announced in 1954 (I was then a college junior working at the US Post Office at night and preparing to be a student teacher). Martin Luther King, Jr. was in the midst of his ministry and took leadership of the Montgomery (ALA) bus boycott of Jim Crow buses. The civil rights movement had traveled northward, although I was not fully aware of the changes taking place. But I was reading more widely now, thanks to Oliver Deex, and was immersed in my evening graduate courses. I followed the slow progress of desegregation in the country, the Little Rock standoff in 1957 between Arkansas governor Orval Faubus and US president Dwight Eisenhower, as well as the emergence of different activist groups in the North and South opposing segregated facilities and schools.[6]

By 1959, I had become more aware of how Cleveland's racially seg-regated neighborhoods had blanketed schools like Glenville with a malign form of neglect. But it was still slow going for a young white teacher who gradually learned from his mostly middle- and working-class students and black colleagues what was happening outside of school.

Trying Out New Lessons

In 1958, I decided to experiment with different content to break out of those numbing instructional routines I'd been following.[7] For two of my five classes (the thought of doing this for all five overwhelmed me), I began to design lessons that differed from the assigned US history text (which had index entries for *slavery* but none for *Negro*).[8]

Drawing from my graduate courses at Western Reserve, I began to type up excerpts from primary sources and duplicate them on the department's one spirit duplicator (teachers of my generation will remember the "Ditto machine"—and the telltale purple fingers and the copies redolent with the aroma of alcohol). I based questions on the readings and assigned them to those two classes. For example, in conjunction with a textbook chapter on the thirteen colonies that dismissed the origins of slavery as unimportant, I would type up primary sources (including descriptions of slave auctions and bills of sale) and accounts from historians that spelled out the historical and moral issues surrounding the introduction of Africans into the colonies. The questions I added called for students to analyze the primary and secondary sources. In addition, I had the librarian gather the few books on "Negro history" that we had in our school and nearby libraries and put them in a special section.

By my third year at Glenville, I was using these materials in all five classes. Oliver Deex found a few dollars in the budget for me to buy the spirit duplicator masters and reams of paper that I needed.

But I had found that gaining students' interest in US history was only half the struggle. The innovation I had crafted energized me, but student response to the non-textbook materials was mixed. The novelty of studying Negro figures and broader issues of race triggered deep interest in maybe half of the students in the classes.[9] But many felt that such content was substandard because the textbooks didn't mention it. Moreover, they complained openly that other history teachers didn't have readings and used the textbook more than I did. Some students even asked me to return to the text. I was surprised at first that they wanted me to return to the deadening routine. Then I realized that using the textbook alone was all that they had ever experienced in school.[10]

Overall, however, I judged student response sufficiently positive for me to continue and, truth be told, I was excited about the new readings and ways of getting students to think about the past that I had developed. Sure, I was tired at the end of the day, but now I looked forward to the next day of teaching. Within four years of beginning as a novice history teacher in 1956, I had slowly introduced new content and the thinking skills of historians to my classes.

For each unit that I taught in US and world history (e.g., the causes of the Civil War, the Industrial Revolution, Ancient Greece and Rome) students had a "study guide" that included readings I had selected from historians, primary source documents, excerpts from *American Heritage* magazine (no longer published), textbook pages students should read, and study guide questions.[11] The study guide also included items that students had to identify, vocabulary words they had to define, and many questions I had formulated. Without knowing it, I was creating a new text.

The questions I developed included, for example, "Why did Latin America come to fear the Monroe Doctrine?" (for foreign policy) or "Why did unions wish to restrict immigration while employers favored unrestricted immigration?" (for a unit on industrialization of the United States). For the most part, they required students to get information from the text and sources I had available in the classroom. They also used history books set aside in the library and encyclopedias in the library or at home. Answering the questions formed part of homework and class discussions

At that time, I did not know about Bloom's Taxonomy or differences in the kind of questions I asked. So study guide and discussion questions often jumped from recalling textbook and lecture information I gave students to "Why?" questions that asked students to explain something not mentioned in the text.[12]

I also created an extra credit system for students who wanted higher grades for advanced work. To earn extra points, they could read articles and books and write up analyses supported by quotes and other evidence; they could also answer questions from a list of what I called "college questions"; for example:

- What civilization contributed more to modern life, Greek or Roman?
- What lessons about citizenship and democracy can Americans learn from the fall of the Roman Republic?

At the end of the unit, all students would turn in a notebook that contained items I had asked them to identify, defined vocabulary terms, and answers to the key questions in the study guide. Extra points were awarded if they drew maps, cartoons, or graphs of statistics, where appropriate. I would read each notebook, make comments, and give a letter grade.

I not only sought out different historical content but also different classroom tasks. I began using activities that increased student interactions with me and between themselves. In one class, for example, I had students create a history newspaper, for which they wrote articles for a specific time period—say, the assassination of Julius Caesar. In another class, the students would put Napoleon on trial after Waterloo. I also tried small group work on a few occasions for particular reading assignments, had students give reports and lead discussions, and used films and film strips followed by worksheets and discussion. But in retrospect, I must say I used these methods only sparingly.[13]

All these content-driven activities would turn up in short lectures I gave (students were expected to take notes and turn them in as part of the unit notebook) and whole group discussions I led. While the former grew shorter and the latter grew longer, anyone coming into my classroom—let's say a "back to the future" educator or scholar—would characterize what I did as clearly teacher-centered. That was still the norm in those times. But I was trying out different ways of getting content across and slowly experimenting with developing students' inquiry skills that gradually changed the mix of activities I included in lessons.

Current Events on Fridays

One thing I tried in either the first or second year of teaching was to set aside a full period once a week for current events.[14]

Why? At that time, the prevailing belief among teachers, including myself, was that history courses needed to connect the past to the present to make history both engaging and meaningful to students in ways that slogging through a textbook—from European explorers discovering North America to the thirteen colonies to the American Revolution to the Civil War, industrialization, World Wars I and II, and finally, the Korean War—could not. From my university education courses and my peers at Glenville, who included current events in their social studies classes, I had developed a strong belief in connecting present-day news to the past. Although the word *relevance* was seldom used in the 1950s, the progressive education notion of making past events real to students by identifying contemporary connections prevailed—in theory, that is.

So, on Monday through Thursday, I would teach lessons on the "golden age of Athens" or Andrew Jackson's Indian Removal Act. But I set aside Fridays for current events. I began posting *Time* magazine covers showing national leaders such as Kwame Nkrumah of Ghana, Nikita Khrushchev of the Soviet Union, Richard Nixon and Lyndon Johnson of the United States, and Mao Tse Tung of the People's Republic of China on the ledge above the blackboards that ran along the front wall and one side of my classroom. I would change these portraits and photos as leaders came and went in Africa, Europe, Asia, Latin America, and North America.

In those forty-five-minute periods on Fridays, I taught teacher-directed lessons on newspaper articles or international events that I found connected to something I had taught recently in US or world history classes, such as a coup d'état in a nation, a presidential election, an event that occurred in Cleveland, or something that happened in school. For example, I introduced articles on the Montgomery, Alabama, bus boycott (1956) and the Suez Canal crisis (1956).

Students would receive extra credit for bringing in newspaper and magazine articles that they could connect to what we were studying in class. They would summarize their articles and then, standing at the front of the room, take questions from peers. I recall that students in the late 1950s brought in articles about Little Rock, Arkansas, when the governor refused to protect nine black students who desegregated Central High School following a federal court order directing school officials to admit them.

I did make efforts to tie together the various history topics I taught during the week, but on Friday, chronological history usually went out of the window.

Did it work for me? Yes, because I could draw links between the chosen articles, *Time* covers, and discussions with each class. Some students who would not ordinarily respond to history lectures, answer study guide questions, or participate in class discussions during the week would raise their hands to reply to my current events questions; some even brought in articles that they reported on to the rest of the class. Did it work for most students? It's hard to say, beyond comments I have received from former students decades later.[15]

As I picked up in my graduate courses the tools historians use, I also designed more lessons on analyzing evidence, determining which sources of information were more or less reliable, and assessing what makes one opinion more informed than another.

Working on Thinking Skills

I began experimenting with direct teaching of critical thinking skills. I believed that such skills were crucial to a deeper understanding of history and for life itself. I wanted my students to acquire and use these skills daily. So in the early 1960s, I launched my US history courses with a two-week unit on thinking skills. My theory was that the students learning these skills at the very beginning of the semester would then apply them when I began teaching units on the American Revolution, Immigration, Sectionalism and the Civil War, and the Industrial Revolution.

In the two-week unit, I selected skills historians used and I believed were important for understanding the past, such as figuring out the difference between a fact and opinion, making hunches about what happened, judging reliability of sources, sorting through evidence that would support or contradict each hunch, and distinguishing between relevant and irrelevant information in reaching a conclusion.

To teach these skills, I chose a contemporary event—a criminal case covered in the local newspaper (Cleveland's Dr. Sam Sheppard found guilty in 1954 of murdering his wife), a nationally televised story (a TV quiz show scandal), and occurrences in the school (a teacher hitting a student)—and created a one-page story about each event that would require students to apply the particular skill we were discussing.[16] I also gave the class additional sources they could use (they had to determine whether sources were biased or not) to select evidence to support their conclusion.

Each forty-five-minute period was filled with engaged students participating in flurries of discussion, debating evidence, questioning each other's conclusions, and similar excitement. I was elated by the apparent success of this unit.

After the two weeks of direct instruction in critical thinking skills, I plunged into the Coming of the American Revolution unit and subsequent history material. From time to time, over the course of the semester, I would ask questions that I believed would prompt use of those thinking skills we had studied earlier in the year. Blank stares greeted me, with occasional "Oh, yeah" from a few students. When I designed homework that explicitly called for use of these thinking skills, few students applied what they had presumably learned. I was thoroughly puzzled.

This brings me to the concept of *transfer*, which I had studied in undergraduate educational psychology courses. For example, learning to get along with an older brother or sister helps in figuring out how to get along with others later in life. Learning math in middle school helps one in high school physics. All of these are instances of *transfer of learning*.

My theory was that teaching these thinking skills directly at the very beginning of the semester would lead to students applying them when I began teaching subsequent history units. Yet that two-week unit on specific critical thinking skills useful to understand history and apply to daily life did not transfer to the rest of the history units. The skills I believed my students had absorbed weeks earlier were missing in action when we got into the class content. Root canal work was easier than getting students to distinguish between a biased source and one less so or explain why certain statements were opinions, not facts. Where had I erred?[17]

In time, through reading psychologists' writings on the complexities of transfer, I discovered that teaching specific critical thinking skills and expecting students to apply what they learned to different situations depended on many conditions that were absent from my lessons. Even the concept of teaching these skills isolated from the historical content—as I had done—undermined the very goal I wanted to achieve.[18]

Nonetheless, puzzled as I was by most students' failure to apply what they had learned in the later history units, I still taught that two-week unit on critical thinking at the beginning of the semester for the next few years, marching through the lessons, one skill after another. I repeated this unit again and again because the students were so involved and loved to apply what they learned to their daily lives—and I felt good at the end of the school day, an uncommon experience for a veteran teacher.

Even had a colleague I trusted grabbed me by the shoulders then and told me how foolish I was in thinking that my students would transfer skills they learned in this unit to subsequent history units, I would not have believed it. I would have continued with what I considered a "best practice" that, in reality, had become a bad habit, one that continued into my years in Washington, DC, when I taught at Cardozo High School (that is another story, which will be told in chapter 2).

A subsequent generation of scholars and practitioners might have labeled my uncertain baby steps in changing the content of lessons and experimenting with a two-week skills unit at beginning of each semester as "teaching historical thinking," a concept that informs much of today's teaching. I will discuss this in chapter 3.

Using Technology in the Classroom.

That later generation of scholars and practitioners might also have been astonished and then amused by the low-tech approaches and electronic hardware and software I used then to motivate students to absorb, digest, and understand the knowledge and skills I was teaching.[19] Between 1956 and 1963, I used the low-tech blackboard, the textbook, and the Ditto machine daily. To make diagrams and draw pictures on the blackboard, I used different-colored chalk.

Every few weeks, I would use a "high-tech" film-strip projector—about thirty to fifty still images on a strip of film inserted into a machine. Once a month or so, I would borrow a film from the downtown Cleveland library or the district's collection and use the 16mm projector located in the social studies storeroom at Glenville.

Using a film projector, however, was a hassle and time-eater. I had to sign up for it because there was only one for the entire social studies department, get it from the departmental storeroom, and then wheel the cart and projector into my classroom. Then I had to thread the film onto the projector reel, preview it so I could prepare questions for students—both time-consuming—and then show it, keeping my fingers crossed that the machine would not clatter and break down.

No instructional television. No computers. No tape recorders. No VCR or DVD players. No TV monitors mounted on the wall or ceiling. No software for efficiently keeping track of absences or student grades. Looking back from 2015 to the late-1950s and early 1960s surely makes teaching then seem, well, Paleolithic—like comparing rotary dial phones to today's smartphones.[20]

Did those "old" technologies change my teaching? Hardly. For the first few years, as I've noted, my history lessons were predominately teacher-directed (lectures, reliance on the blackboard and textbook, Ditto-machine produced study guides, the occasional film or film strip), but slowly I began to include a mix of student- and teacher-centered activities (small group work, projects, debates, students' independent research) and fitting those lessons and activities to the few high-tech devices then available.

Student Responses to Changes

None of the above changes I introduced into my classes in the late-1950s—black history materials, current events, thinking skills, and classroom tech—went smoothly. Sometimes I had orchestrated the activity sloppily, gave fuzzy directions to students, or lacked key materials—sometimes all three in a disastrous, unfolding trifecta of failure. Many students dug in their heels when I asked them to participate in class discussions and perform tasks. Student interest would ebb and flow. Some students transferred to other classes. Others objected to some activities—"Mr. Cuban, why don't you teach like the other social studies teachers?"—but stayed in the class.

What really puzzled me was that some lessons and activities would die before my eyes in one class and yet would soar in another one the very same day. To be sure, in teaching five classes, errors that I made in one class, if I recognized them quickly, could be corrected in a subsequent one. Still, at the end of the day, I was mystified as to why students were engaged for most of the period in one class, while in another, it was like digging a ditch with a teaspoon.

I learned over time that rapport with a group of students—what some teachers call *chemistry*—would range from strong to just so-so or, in some instances, be lacking altogether. So chemistry was one answer to the puzzle. I would also attribute such lesson failures and successes to the time a class met—whether it was first period in the morning or the one right after lunch seemed to affect the mood of a class. Events in school—from a previous class, say, or something that happened in the corridors—would spill over into my classroom. Even the weather, it seemed, affected student mood. Still, all of this was guesswork about why lessons that fell flat in one class would energize another on the same day.

Learning from Students

Teaching could be spine-tingling on those occasions when students asked uncommon questions, and challenged me after class or school to pursue issues raised in class. What also moved me were those occasions when my students taught me. In my first few years, I was a learning machine, taking in knowledge about the community, students, school norms, and what worked and what flopped in my classes. My students taught me how long I could sustain an activity—lecture, discussion, small group work, a film—regardless of their initial interest. They taught me that sarcasm might get a laugh initially but corrode their sense of being part of a small community during their time in room 235. They taught me that there was far more to their lives and mine than learning history. I learned that lessons worked best when I entwined their life experiences and real-world events into studying the past and combining both into stories of individuals. I learned that student questions revealed how much they understood and how much had sailed far above their heads.

I also learned from individual students. Consider Carol Schneider (now Carstensen). She was a sixteen-year-old junior in my US history class at Glenville High School in 1959. I was twenty-five, just beginning my fourth year of teaching at Glenville. I had already begun to prepare classroom lessons in what was then called Negro history. I created readings to supplement the history textbook, which distorted the experiences of slaves, slipped over Reconstruction, and hardly mentioned Jim Crow life. Of my six classes, three responded very well to the readings. The other three classes—well, they were much less enthused. Carol was in one of those responsive classes.

Carol, who came from a working class family steeped in left-wing political ideology, was keen about history and had read widely. Within a few weeks, she and a cadre of friends were the stars of the class. They would come in during my thirty-five-minute lunch period and after school to continue talking about ideas raised in class and about school issues. For a young teacher, this was heady stuff.

One afternoon, Carol brought in John Wexley's book *The Judgment of Julius and Ethel Rosenberg*. She wanted to know what I thought of it. The Rosenbergs had been accused of being Soviet spies, and indicted and convicted of treason in 1951 for passing secret information about the atom bomb to the Soviet Union during World War II. They were executed in 1953.

I read the book within a week. I had known of the case through newspapers and magazines. Wexley's book argued that the Rosenbergs had been innocent of the charges; they were not spies and had been wrongly convicted and executed. I was stunned by the amount of evidence that Wexley had compiled from court records and independent sources. Moreover, he had arrayed the evidence into a persuasive argument that the Rosenbergs had been framed. I totally accepted this portrayal of the case, remembering the outrage I felt at the miscarriage of justice.

Carol and I met during lunches and after school to discuss the case itself and the material that Wexley had compiled. Whenever I would raise concerns about Wexley's sources or portions of his argument—some parts sounded too pat for me—Carol would rebut my points and counter the concerns. She would then ask me questions about Wexley's statements that she doubted. We had an intellectual give-and-take that, up to that time, I had never experienced with a student. I remember speaking to my wife and friends about the Rosenberg case and the Wexley book. For the first time as a teacher, discussions, even debates, with a student rippled through my life.[21]

What did I learn from Carol? I admired her intellectual and political engagement, her feistiness as a high school junior who questioned mainstream beliefs. We had rousing discussions about ideas in a book that, at the time, went against the grain. What I came to see in retrospect was that I, at age twenty-five, was ready to challenge conventional wisdom. She helped me do so.[22]

I also learned about failure in teaching. There were some students who I could not reach for any number of reasons. Two such students stick in my mind, decades removed from when they were in my classroom.

Lanky, always stylishly dressed and so clever, Harold drove me up one of my four walls. He was eighteen and in the eleventh grade. He had failed all of his subjects the year before he entered my US history class. Yet he scored in the top quartile on standardized tests.

Harold was never—and I mean *never*—on time to class; that is, when he chose to come to class. About five minutes after the bell, he would bang through the door of the room and waltz over to his seat. Passing a friend, he would lean over, hand cupped to his mouth, and whisper something. Anyone in earshot would laugh uproariously. Harold had arrived. Another lesson interrupted.

Whenever the class got into meaty discussions where students interacted over ideas raised in the lesson, Harold's insights and argumentation skills were superb. He used evidence to back up his words without any encouragement from me. He revealed a sharp, inquiring mind. But this did not happen often. Most of the time, he would wisecrack, twist what people said, or simply beat a point to death. When that occurred, class discussion swirled around him. He loved that. He was frequently funny and delivered marvelous, impromptu gag lines. In short, within the first few weeks of this class, he had settled into a comfortable role of "wise buffoon." He knew precisely how to psych teachers and how far he could go with each one.

I'm unsure how the class perceived Harold. When students worked in groups, no one chose to work with him. When I divided the class into groups, the one he was in quickly fragmented, and he would ask to work independently. On a number of occasions during class discussions, other students would tell him to shut up. I suspect that his fellow students liked him as a clown as much as he needed to act as one.

I grew to dislike Harold's behavior intensely, while trying hard not to dislike him. It was tough. I tried to deal with his wise buffoon act through after-class conferences and short phone conversations with his parent. After these conferences and phone calls, his intelligence would shine in class discussions. Time after time, however, he would back-slide. He would keep up with assignments for a week or two then do nothing for a month. He would cut class, and when we would see one another in the hallway the same day, we would wave and say hello to one another.

The truth is, I chose not to devote time and energy to Harold, con-sidering the 150 other students I had. In the last three weeks of the semester, when his class-busting behavior crossed a threshold, I told him that every time he was late, he would spend the period in the library working independently. It was a solution that satisfied him—he would make a dramatic tardy entrance, I would give him the thumb, he would turn, salute me, and exit. It quickly became a ritual. And that is how the semester ended.

Because of his sporadic attendance, missed tests and assignments—and I searched my conscience to separate pique from fairness—I gave Harold a failing grade. But I failed also. I could not reach Harold. He continued to stereotype me as the Teacher and I slipped into perceiv-ing him as a stereotype Pain-in-the-Ass Student. Did he learn anything from me as a person or from the content and skills I taught? I doubt it but, in truth, I simply don't know.

Now consider William. He was quiet in class. Kept back twice in ele-mentary school, the school psychologist diagnosed him as "below-aver-age" in tested intelligence but did not find any intellectual or emotional disabilities. Now eighteen years old, he was in the eleventh grade and earning As and Bs in his courses, including mine. In class, he would participate often in discussions, do his assignments and perform well on tests. Whenever the class worked independently on short research papers or contracts, he did especially well. And he was looking forward to graduating from high school.

After school one day—he would occasionally stop by to talk with me and also come in to talk while I was eating lunch—we had a long conversation about his future. I asked about college and he shook his head, saying "No." He had once wanted to be an engineer but now he had given up that idea. His father had encouraged him to go to college as well, but now, according to William, it was out of the question.

Why? I asked.

It turned out that William was a member of a religious group that believed Armageddon would occur soon and that God would save only those who accepted Jesus Christ as the Savior. He was a recent convert and a true believer in the imminent end of the world.

Before school, during lunch, and after school, we would discuss our religious beliefs. He brought in pamphlets from his group. We would discuss them, often returning to the question of his continuing his schooling. When our conversation would go that way, William would smile and, as if he were dealing with a very slow learner, politely explain once again that he believed life as we know it would end in a holocaust of earthquakes, fires, and hailstorms. The Bible foretold it, and it could occur as soon as the end of the decade. Since there would be few survivors, he had to prepare himself for the event. To attend college would be foolish. Given his beliefs, he was right.

I admired William for his staunch beliefs even when, without a blink of his eye, he said my family and I would die in the fire to come because we were unbelievers. I took him as seriously as he took himself.

In a high school of over one thousand students, he identified only one person as a friend. More than once, he told me, his beliefs had become the butt of jokes in classes and among other students. Much of his time outside of school was spent in studying, attending church meetings, and doing street ministry work on weekends.

By conventional criteria, I was effective with William; that is, he did his assignments, got high scores on tests, participated in class discussions, and developed a relationship with his teacher. He seemed to have learned history content and skills. The question I have, however, is: What did William learn from me as a person in the many hours we conversed over the semester? The answer evades me even to this day.

I can say that in one sense, I failed William. Why I failed, I am unsure. If part of a teacher's job is to get students to examine their values and clarify them while they are being examined, then I was unsuccessful. My job, as I saw it, was not to dismantle his beliefs but to get him to reflect on them. He surely got me to do so by throwing my questions back at me. But I had gone through that process—and still do. He hurled my questions back at me to defend himself. I sensed this and chose not to continue that line of questioning. So I believe that I failed William.

Given all that I have described about students who, for me, were unreachable, I can still say that teaching was exhilarating. When students willingly participated in discussions, asked questions that I did not know the answers to, and sought me out after class or during lunchtime to pursue issues raised in class, I soared.

But teaching was also draining. I cannot forget how tired I was by 3 p.m. I would see students before school at 7 a.m.; at midday, when I began eating bag lunches in my classroom; and after school. When I became faculty adviser for student activities, even more students would poke their heads in and ask to stay and chat. (Tiring as they were, I truly enjoyed these exchanges a great deal and developed close connections with individual students.) Also I was continually locating materials, filmstrips, films, and scrounging paper for the ravenous Ditto machine. Teaching was also exhausting because of the logistics involved before and after class and the need to be alert and quick in dealing with the many moving parts of teaching a lesson. Afterschool talks with students, grading of homework, and reading essays simply tired me out.

Added to these responsibilities were the demands of the night classes I was taking at a nearby university. Many days in those first two years, I would come home after school and take a nap. Imagine—a twenty-something taking an afternoon nap after work!

Eventually, I got a little help. My principal contacted a district social studies supervisor and told him about what I was doing in the classroom and the pressures I was under. That supervisor quietly allocated a small sum of money to the social studies department so that I could purchase books, paper, and—miracle of miracles—a Ditto machine.

GLENVILLE COLLEAGUES TEACHING HISTORY

After nearly five years, I had created in fits and starts, with many stumbles, a home-grown history course than I had neither anticipated when I arrived at Glenville in 1956, nor had heard about in other social studies classes in the school.

I recall colleagues who also taught a full array of social studies courses during the years I taught at Glenville—Jim O'Meara, Charles Kellogg, Lonnie Smith, Art Smith, and Richard Crampton. But my knowledge of how they taught history was indirect, scattered, and insufficient to describe in any detail. They probably introduced new ideas and activities into their daily routines, as I did. Had I observed my fellow teachers, located records, recorded interviews, or unearthed sources from archives, former students' recollections, and the Internet, I might have documented their instruction. But none of these sources are available. Too much time has passed. And the age-graded, departmental, and structural organization of high schools then—the grammar of schooling—both isolated and insulated us from one another, as they do with teachers now.

The little knowledge I do have about how colleagues taught came from what students had to say about their classes—a common source of information for high school teachers—and conversations with peers in the corridors and the teacher lounge about their students and their various classroom activities. There was no time in the daily schedule to watch other teachers in action; certainly, taking my one preparation period of forty-five minutes a day—my so-called "free period"—to observe a colleague was the furthest thing from my mind.

What I did discover through these indirect sources was that my colleagues, both white and black (myself included, in my first two years at Glenville), followed the dominant patterns of teaching that characterized social studies across the nation in the 1950s and early 1960s. While national data are sparse about teaching practices in social studies subjects, what is available shows that prevailing practices included lecturing to the whole group, covering history content chronologically, relying on the textbook, supervising homework, and administering teacher-developed quizzes and tests.[23]

When I first met him, Jim O'Meara was department head, a charter member of the Cleveland Teachers Union, a lawyer, and twenty-year-plus veteran of teaching in the district. (He eventually became head of the teachers union and presided over two strikes in the late 1970s and early 1980s.[24]) A large man who could be intimidating to young teachers, I found his Irish charm and occasional bluster arresting but, over time, off-putting. As department chair, he answered most of my questions, which were of the "How-do-I get-this?" and "Where-do-I get-that?" variety. From time to time, especially after I began using the Ditto machine to crank out study guides and readings, he would comment about my using a lot of paper. Occasionally, when just the two of us were in the teacher lounge, he would wonder out loud: "Why are you doing all of these extras, Cuban?" By and large, we stayed out of each other's way.

As I remember him, he was constantly on the move, leaving school early for meetings with teachers and district officials. As for his teaching style, according to recollections from students, he lectured—there was a podium in his classroom—most of the time.

Charles Kellogg taught world history next door to me, and I could hear him lecture. He laughed a lot, and I could see that he enjoyed good relations with many students, who came to see him during lunchtime and after school. He was also faculty sponsor of the World Affairs Council.

We would chat outside our open doors as classes were changing and students moved in and out of our rooms. We would exchange gossip about students, the principal, and bemoan particular school rules. Other than glances into his classroom as I passed by, I never sat in on one of his classes. My impression is that, like me, he lectured, led discussions, and leaned heavily on the text in his five classes.

Art Smith, Lonnie Smith, and Richard Crampton were other members of the department whom I came to know personally, but as with Charles Kellogg, I knew very little of what they did in their classrooms other than what students would say in passing—most of which was positive.

The structure of the age-graded and schedule-driven high school puts teachers into separate classrooms, places them in academic departments, and schedules time for adults in such ways as to prevent teachers and students from working together in the same subject area. Thus, it comes as no surprise that most teachers, like myself, knew very little about colleagues only a few steps away in another room. That was certainly the case at Glenville high school (and at every high school I subsequently taught in).

SLOW EVOLUTION IN ROOM 235

So I cannot say with any confidence how my colleagues taught or whether they made any changes in their own teaching as the years passed. But I did slowly change my lessons—in their content, activities, and organization. How come?

I wanted to be a better teacher than I was in my first year at Glenville. When I saw students doing homework for other classes while I was talking or watched their eyes glaze over when I asked questions, or when the brightest in the class passed notes to one another (or all three), I grew increasingly dissatisfied with my performance.

For me, teaching was in part a performance not only for my students—playing to the gallery, so to speak—but also for satisfying myself. Did I feign anger at times with the class when they were missing the central point of the lesson? Yes, I did. Did I try to provoke students by arguing against earlier things that I (or they) had said? Yes, I did.

Here I offer a lesson I taught that captures, in part, the notion of my teaching evolving over the years and my view of teaching-as-performance.

A Journalist Describes a Class I Taught

The year is 1961. Martin Mayer, a journalist commissioned to write a book on the social studies as practiced in US schools, searched for the teachers and ideas that could transform social studies as academics and practitioners had changed the sciences and math after the launch of the Soviet satellite *Sputnik* in 1957. I was among the hundreds of teachers he interviewed and observed. In that same period, the civil rights movement—sit-ins in the South to end segregation in restaurants, buses, and other public facilities—had begun, and stirrings were being felt in Cleveland.

I was twenty-six, in my sixth year of teaching at Glenville. I had just returned from Yale University on a John Hay Whitney Fellowship, an opportunity then given only to high school teachers. The director of the fellowship had given Mayer my name. I had read his recent book, *The Schools*, and found it a fluent, rich description of classes he had visited and, overall, a worthwhile analysis. But I was nervous that he was coming to watch me teach. No journalist had ever observed me.

The following is his account of Glenville and one lesson I taught:

> At Cleveland's Glenville High School, a small, crowded building set quite unpretentiously (for an American high school), in a neighborhood once almost entirely Jewish, now almost entirely Negro (as a Negro teacher put it, not without bitterness, "We had our ten years of integration, while the Jews were moving out and the Negroes were moving in.") This is not, however, a slum school. No place in America is positively good for a black, but Cleveland seems to be about the least bad. The parents of many of these students make a lower-middle-class income or better, the atmosphere in Glenville's halls is as free as it is in Scarsdale's, and the attitude toward education seems to have no more than the usual degree of suspicion. Still, these children are black, part of an actively repressed minority group. As seen on a very brief visit, Glenville would seem to be considerable of an accomplishment. One history class provided evidence that students here are learning more than just social studies: when the teacher made reference to "The Mar-see-yay," a mutter of "Mar-say-yez" rose from around the borders of the room.
>
> The teacher in this American History class is a hawk-nosed, lean crew-cut young man named Larry Cuban, A John Hay Fellow with a personal devotion to history. He balances American History around the Civil War for teaching purposes, but he does so out of respect,

not contempt, for his black students. He begins the class by handing out "a very short reading list—on which there will be no comments." Then he writes four names on the board:

> J.G. Randall
> Charles Beard
> [Kenneth Stampp]
> James Ford Rhodes

"We'll take these names to represent historians' views [on the causes of the Civil War]. You'll remember Beard's thesis—'the clash between the Lords of the Lash and the Lords of the Loom.' There were only 347,000 slave owners in the South, 3,500,000 who didn't own slaves. Now, how many of you would say slavery was the cause of the Civil War. Let's divide it three ways here—Beardians, Stampps, and Fanatics [Rhodes believed that pro- and antislavery fanatics caused the war]. The class shows five Beardians, thirteen Stampps, and three Fanatics, with nine keeping their hands down.

"I know," Cuban says, "there are some of you who say, 'There's a little bit of each.' That's fine. My opinion is that it was slavery. You've got to remember, though, that the facts don't change—historians' opinions change. You have a glass of water; you can say it's half full or half empty, it's up to you."

A boy contributes, "I've read Olmstead, and I think he's right. It was a clash of nations. It wasn't economic, it was social."

"All right," Cuban says, "Now, I say I could have prevented the Civil War. With Lincoln's ideas—what was that?"

A girl says, "Compensated emancipation."

"What does that mean?"

"Buy the slaves from the southerners and set them free."

"Would it have worked? Would it have prevented the Civil War? The class groans, "No."

"Why not?"

A number of ideas are thrown forth—the Northerners didn't want to spend the money, you couldn't set a price, the whole system was based on slaves. A girl says, "The Southerners wouldn't do it because it would make the blacks equal to them."

"Let's get back to Beard," Cuban says. "Here. Less than ten percent of the Southerners owned slaves, but they all fought for slavery. How could they persuade the ninety percent to fight? You try it."

He addresses two Negro girls and a Negro boy seated at his extreme left. "You're the slave owners. The rest of the class doesn't own slaves. You persuade them to fight for you."

One girl, giggling, tries, "Those Yankees, they want to come down and take everything away from you."

"Oh, no, they don't," Cuban says. "Just from you. I don't have anything they want."

"Our whole economy is based on slaves," says the boy.

"No, sir," says a boy in the non-slaveholding section, falling into the spirit of the situation. "My economy isn't. I got to do my own work."

The debate rages for a while, Cuban grinning over it, objecting where the 90 percent can't find a reply. "Come on, now, " he says. "Why will these four million fight for four years? If you can't come up with this, class, the whole thing is completely unreal, just something in a textbook."

Finally, in the heat of the argument, one of the Negro girls in the slaveholding section comes up with, "Remember those slave rebellions? Remember what happened on those plantations? The Yankees will come down here and raise up those Negroes to be your equals, and there will be no controlling them." The class roars with laughter at her, and she bends her head.

"Let's give it a name," Cuban says. He writes on the board," WHITE SUPREMACY."

He asks, "Any of you ever hear of U.B. Phillip?"

One boy has read it, and says, "He thinks that's the whole theme of Southern history."

The one white boy in the class, a West Virginia redneck, now makes his contribution: "You can find reasons all you like," he says. "I think they fought because they were told to fight."

Cuban says, "Maybe. Now when we discuss Reconstruction, we'll find this same argument of White Supremacy used to justify . . . what? Anybody know?"

And a Negro boy says, "Segregation."[25]

In this lesson, Mayer describes my performance, provoking and perhaps angering students to dig deeper for understanding how historians have disagreed among themselves about the causes of the Civil War and that their interpretations, anchored in evidence, also matter.

Mayer makes the lesson sound like a success. Perhaps it was. But many lessons I taught were mediocre. And there were many times when some—even most—students' reactions and inattentiveness told me clearly that I was performing poorly. Some lessons I designed were deadly dull. Dissatisfied with my performance and growing boredom with doing the same things every day help account for why I sought better ways of engaging students to learn history. I wanted to change what I was doing. And I did.[26]

I learned by trial and error what seemed to work with my students (Did they ask questions about the content I taught? Did they make explicit connections to their lives or previous lessons? Did they use evidence to support their opinions?). I changed my teaching slowly and incrementally because I trusted what I learned from students about what worked and what failed, I listened to certain Glenville colleagues who told me of their small victories with students I also had in my classes, and colleagues elsewhere who told me what succeeded in their classrooms and how they did it. And my performance improved as more (but by no means all) students responded well to the changes I made; interactions with students encouraged me,

Why did changes in my teaching occur so slowly? In part, my days were too full for time to reflect. Maybe driving to school in the morning or returning home or late at night, or in a quick exchange with a colleague during the thirty-five-minute lunch break.

But I've come to think it was mostly those persisting organizational regularities of the age-graded school in which I worked that shaped to a large degree what I did daily in room 235 at Glenville High School. Had I known about the grammar of schooling and its direct influence on how teachers teach, I might have made the connection then. However, as a young teacher struggling to do well in in this structured environment, I lacked the concepts and vocabulary to understand the context in which I worked.

The organizational context remained the same throughout my tenure at Glenville, but my beliefs in what I could do slowly changed as I experimented with new content, different classroom tasks, observed student responses, and used the varied technologies of the day. Those beliefs led to classroom changes as many students responded well to different activities, content, and lessons I presented.

THE ACCIDENTAL ENCOUNTER WITH THE NEW SOCIAL STUDIES AND CARDOZO HIGH SCHOOL

I was not alone in making these changes in teaching history. By the early 1960s, I had learned about other teachers across the country who independently had done much of what I had done in my classes; I discovered others who sought to teach history differently.

In 1962, I was invited to give a talk at the National Council of Social Studies conference in Philadelphia about my work in creating classroom readings at Glenville. I was part of a panel of teachers from Detroit and Cleveland who had ventured into the world of creating alternative materials to the standard history textbook. The title of the panel was "Experiments in Teaching Social Studies in Culturally Deprived Areas."[27]

After I gave my talk and panel members dispersed, a member of the small audience approached me and introduced himself as a professor at Carnegie Institute of Technology (soon to become Carnegie-Mellon University) and asked, "Do you want to write a book on Negro history?" That is how I met Edwin Fenton, who became one of the leaders in the New Social Studies movement, part of the larger academic-led movement of the 1960s that produced the New Math, New Biology, Chemistry, and Physics. (I take up the New Social Studies in detail in chapter 3.[28])

Fenton and his colleague David Fowler were editing a series of short paperbacks called Problems in American History for Scott, Foresman publishers. I accepted his offer eagerly. So in 1963, I began my first book and unknowingly enlisted in the New Social Studies.

I continued teaching a full load at Glenville while I was writing the book. Moreover, after finishing my master's degree in 1958, I had entered a doctoral program in history at Western Reserve University.

I had completed my coursework (in night classes), and my oral exams were approaching in the spring of 1963. Yet in that year I left Glenville to become a master teacher of history at Cardozo High School in Washington, DC. How come?

Even with the fulfillments of teaching, writing a book, collaborating with kindred teachers, a principal who supported me, and strong bonds with students, I became frustrated by what I later defined as the limits of classroom teaching. Although I enjoyed working with Glenville students and teachers, the intellectual growth I had experienced both at the school and in graduate work, produced a gnawing sense that teaching five classes a day was not enough intellectually for me. The bureaucratic reluctance of the Cleveland schools to reshape the social studies curriculum or recognize the needs of minority students annoyed me, and I can only guess that I must have irritated my superiors at the district office who often heard from me.

I also had other pressures to consider. In 1958 I married Barbara Smith. Evenings that I had used for reading and grading homework and weekends for preparing lessons for the upcoming week were no longer as available as when I was single. Marriage also meant that summers I had spent as a counselor and head counselor at a camp in the Pocono Mountains of Pennsylvania would come to an end, since I had to find a summer job to increase our income, especially after Barbara became pregnant with our first child, Sondra. Fatigue and the growing awareness that I needed to have a life outside of Glenville brought me face-to-face with choosing how to combine the demands of work and being with my family.

These events, plus the year spent at Yale University, and Sondra's birth in 1962 got me thinking of my future in teaching. I did find enormous satisfaction in working with students, developing a homegrown course where students applied historical concepts and skills in daily lessons. But earning $5,000 a year, combined with a panicky scramble each summer to earn more money for my family left me uneasy.[29]

To be sure, the discontent that I felt with "just" teaching and the growing confidence that I experienced after seven years in classrooms happens to many teachers, who begin to ask themselves: What will we do for the rest of our working lives? What kind of legacy do we want to leave others?

As the years went by, I had found that high school teaching was less and less of a challenge for me. Sure, I had experienced the excitement of creating lessons that worked with students; I also had trained five student teachers. Through my graduate courses in history and with the gentle but firm touch of Oliver Deex, I became deeply tied to ideas and their consequences in people's lives, although at the time I doubt whether I could have expressed it as I do now. Also, the emerging civil rights movement had engaged me. Sit-ins, demonstrations, and especially the Birmingham church bombings triggered strong feelings and responses from Glenville students and me. I wanted to do more in and out of class with my students.

In 1963, I was torn between staying in public school teaching and finding another outlet for the agitated energy and a growing ambition for a larger stage. The insistent impulse to learn, grow, and serve a larger purpose in a setting consistent with the values that I had come to embrace as a result of teaching at Glenville stirred lots of emotions. Only as I think now about those entangled impulses can I see that I was approaching a fork in the road.

After passing my doctoral exams in history in 1963, I applied for a number of college teaching positions. A small liberal arts college in Connecticut offered me a three-year appointment as an assistant professor of history contingent on finishing my dissertation, "Negro Leadership in Cleveland, 1880–1940." After much discussion with Barbara and friends, I considered what it would mean to leave public school teaching, the years of work in developing history lessons, and my growing convictions about the inadequate schooling that low-income minorities received. Yes, ambition and restlessness with teaching influenced greatly by years in the classroom remained, but I wasn't ready to give up what I had achieved. I turned down the offer.

As luck would have it, during the summer of 1963, as I prepared to return to Glenville, I was invited to apply for a position of master

teacher of history in a federally funded project that would take returning Peace Corps volunteers and train them to teach at Cardozo High
School in Washington, DC. The previous seven years had convinced me
that the core problem of urban schools and disengaged students was
pedestrian teaching locked into mindlessly using fact-filled textbooks.
The solution was better teachers who created can't-miss lessons that
would hook students into learning. This chance seemed just right, mix-
ing unfulfilled ambitions and idealism in preparing the next generation of teachers.

I applied for the position, was interviewed, and was hired. The day
before the March on Washington, driving a faded purple Rambler pull-
ing a U-Haul trailer, I arrived in Washington to set up a home for Barbara and eighteen-month-old Sondra.

CHAPTER 2

Teaching at
Cardozo High School,
1963–1967

The headline for the *Washington Post* article was eye-catching: "Slum Children a New Challenge to Peace Corps Group." Two weeks after I had started working at Cardozo High School, teaching two classes a day and supervising four recently returned Peace Corps volunteers, the article caused an uproar among the largely black faculty and students, who complained bitterly about how the article stigmatized students and the school. Not a great start for a "dramatic experiment in American urban education."[1]

I spent four years at Cardozo, initially as a master teacher of history and in the last two years as director of the Cardozo Project in Urban Teaching (CPUT), while still teaching tenth- and eleventh-grade history classes. Teaching high school students history twice a day and supervising the Peace Corps returnees who also taught two classes a day, as well as developing new materials for our classrooms was a dream job. Here I was, teaching both youth and adults on how to "do" history in classrooms by creating and using engaging instructional materials.

That dream had evolved out of my Glenville High School experiences, where I saw the core problem of black and mostly poor high school students' unresponsiveness to traditional schooling being solved by sharp teachers—like myself—creating lessons that hooked students into learning.

That dream and my perception of the core problem in urban schools, however, changed in the four years I worked at Cardozo and the subsequent five I worked in the DC schools. I had tempered (but not lost) my enthusiasm for the idea that knowledgeable and skilled teachers using strong and powerful lessons could reconnect disengaged students. Over the nine years I spent in DC, I came to see that the problem of the urban high school was far more complex than I had thought and my "solution" was only one factor among many that had to be dealt with in a large bureaucratic system coming to grips with a century-long legacy of racially segregated public schools.

I learned that teaching well was far more than delivering content and skills to students. It was far more than expressing idealism or having good intentions. It involved getting to know students in and out of school; it meant building relationships with fellow teachers; it meant learning more about the neighborhood and larger community; it meant acquiring skills in negotiating school and district rules while being constantly aware of how race played a part in teaching and schooling. I had learned some of these lessons in bits and pieces at Glenville but they coalesced during my time at Cardozo High School. As a result of these experiences, my perspective on school reform stretched well beyond what idealistic, strong, and imaginative teachers can do in their classrooms within one urban high school in a large district.

THE CITY OF WASHINGTON AND ITS SCHOOLS

In 1963, John F. Kennedy had been president of the United States for two years.[2] A nuclear showdown in Cuba had been narrowly averted. James Meredith, a black man, had been finally admitted to the University of Mississippi. The largest civil rights march ever had convened at the Lincoln Memorial. One out of five Americans was poor. A handful of American advisers were assisting the South Vietnamese to stave off Vietcong advances. Unemployment figures had dipped, and wages were rising. So were prices. And a new federally funded small pilot project at Cardozo High School recruited ten returned Peace Corps volunteers as teaching interns. These were exciting and difficult times.

By 1967, President Kennedy had been murdered and his successor, Lyndon B. Johnson, had launched the War on Poverty. James Meredith had left Mississippi, returned to run for political office, and lost. Race riots in Los Angeles, Cleveland, Detroit, Newark, and other cities shocked the nation. A half-million US soldiers fighting an unpopular war in Vietnam, while frequent antiwar demonstrations split the country. Wages continued to rise, but prices outdistanced them, and, to the surprise of economists, unemployment figures climbed upward. For many, these years were the worst of times.

But in one small part of a low-income section of Washington, DC, the pilot project that had begun in 1963 had spread to nearby junior high and elementary schools with such success that the superintendent and board of education incorporated the project into the District's program to recruit and train new teachers. By 1967, that project had also become the model of a federal effort, called the National Teacher Corps, to recruit and train young, bright college graduates to become certified teachers.[3]

CONSERVATIVE REFORM IN DISTRICT OF COLUMBIA SCHOOLS, 1958–1967

Future DC superintendent Carl Hansen came to Washington in 1947 from Omaha, Nebraska, to serve as special assistant to then-superintendent Hobart Corning. He entered a segregated city and school system hardly different from Atlanta or Birmingham. For over eighty years, the DC schools had been split into two divisions—white and black (*colored* was the preferred word then), each with it own chain of command and teaching staff. Acutely tuned racial etiquette, refined over decades, was expected on both sides of the color line in this dual system.

Like most white administrators of city agencies, Hansen wrestled with the effects of racial segregation, race relations within a dual system, the impact of poverty on children and youth, and how best to improve schools. Race and poverty formed a tangled knot that frustrated well-intentioned reformers in those years (and still do today).

Within a few years, Hansen moved quickly up the career ladder in directing white elementary and then white secondary schools. After the 1954 US Supreme Court decisions *Brown v. Board of Education* and *Bolling v. Sharpe* (the latter applied to segregated DC schools), Hansen presided over the end of the dual system and the beginning of a desegregated (albeit a majority black one), earning applause from local and national liberals of the day. Rancor from Southern Democratic chairmen of the DC appropriations committees, however, trailed him like a bad odor. In 1958, when Corning retired, the federally appointed board of education named Hansen as superintendent.[4]

By 1960, the District of Columbia was a city of nearly 800,000, with a majority black (55 percent) population. The school system enrolled over 136,000 students, of whom 80 percent were black (as were 68 percent of staff). To understand Washington, DC, and its schools then (and now as well), one must grasp two enduring facts:

- Desegregation had softened but did not end racial differences between whites and blacks arising from poverty.
- Split and overlapping external authorities governed the schools, undermining school board and superintendent management.[5]

Race and social class mattered deeply. When I say, "race and class mattered," I mean that remnants of the social caste system (and poverty) enshrined in segregated schools and facilities spilled over to face-to-face interactions between whites and blacks in schools years after desegregation. The first black teachers and students were desegregating previously all white schools in the northwest section of the city. DC officials were shuffling black faculties and administrators into different schools and posts. White teachers were entering all-black schools with all-black faculties. And there were ongoing conflicts about who made decisions for schools and in schools. Black officials staffed offices that once white administrators held. Black board of education members and top officials gained power in both the city and school district. And both white and black adults directly confronted the effects of poverty on students and the legacy of nearly a century of segregation before the *Bolling v. Sharpe* decision. But although Hansen left in 1967, it was not until 1970 that the majority black board of education appointed the first black superintendent.[6]

The second enduring fact is divided governance of the city and its schools. For nearly a century, Congress had governed the District of Columbia, including the schools. For example, the House and Senate District of Columbia committees, led by Southern white Democrats since the 1940s, which was responsible for allocating funds, scoured the city and school budgets, annually questioning city and school officials about their requests. Those congressional chairs also approved appointments of the three commissioners (one of whom came from the US Army Corps of Engineers) who governed District agencies; These commissioners also appointed a panel of federal district judges who, in turn, appointed a nine-member, white school board of education, which appointed the school chief for the dual system.[7]

Then, as now, congressional authority over the DC public schools made Congress a "super board of education." The schools often became a local laboratory for introducing favorite reforms. The convoluted Rube Goldberg design of overlapping authorities made the District of Columbia unique among US cities and school districts.[8]

The two facts of persistent racial issues after the demise of de jure segregation and the context of congressional authority and oversight colored the actions taken by the majority white school board in approving Carl Hansen's Amidon Plan and the four-track system for all secondary schools. The plan, in Hansen's words, was a "return to the sanity of order and logic in curriculum organization and to the wisdom of teaching subject matter to children in a direct and effective manner, using with judgment what is known about how we learn." In an obvious reaction to what was then called "progressive" education, these planned changes in curriculum, school organization, and instruction stressed subject matter, phonics, direct instruction, order, and discipline in tightly prescribed periods. It moved teachers to center stage, where they orchestrated what content and skills children learned and how they learned them.[9]

The four-track system, in which administrators assigned students to Honors, College Preparatory, General, or Basic tracks on the basis of their tested ability and past academic performance, had been installed in 1956 for high schools. In 1958, Hansen extended it to junior high schools. The system was far from perfect. If a student showed marked improvement or decline in one track, then theoretically he or she could move upward or downward. This theoretical "mobility," however, was seldom seen in practice. And if tests masked a student's ability, administrators ended up assigning that student to the wrong track. This form of ability grouping became a lightning rod in the 1960s for local civil rights and community activists, who claimed that the poorest black students were regularly condemned to the lower tracks and ended up dropping out of school.

Both Amidon and the four-track system were reforms to school and instructional organization reflecting an educationally conservative view of how teaching, content, and learning ought to occur in desegregated schools.[10] By 1962, Carl Hansen's conservative educational ideas and program dominated the system. The superintendent and his staff defined the policy issues, produced alternatives and research to support options, and then recommended policy choices to the board of education. The board complied.

LIBERAL SCHOOL REFORM COMES TO WASHINGTON, 1962–1967

The political climate shifted when the Kennedy administration came to DC. Liberal newcomers to Washington in both the Congress and White House believed urban problems could be solved with energy, resources, and commitment. Poor housing, unemployment, and crime could be reduced and failing schools could improve, particularly high schools with large numbers of dropouts. These problems became targets of the new administration. And the bull's-eye of that target was the Cardozo neighborhood.

The city was a laboratory ripe for experimentation. The federally funded Washington Action for Youth (WAY) organization and its director, a "dynamic and abrasive" New York City social worker named Jack Goldberg, arrived in 1962 and quickly locked horns with Hansen over how best to improve the DC schools. Hansen had already installed the Amidon Plan and tracking in secondary schools, and here was a director of a new community-based antipoverty organization with different views of school reform poaching on his territory.[11]

WAY chose the Cardozo neighborhood, including the high school and its feeder schools, as a target area on which to focus its resources and programs. Goldberg and the Cardozo High School principal, Bennetta Washington, became political and social friends within a few months. Pilot reform efforts in employment, delinquency prevention, and schools began in mid-1963. Through funding from the President's Committee on Juvenile Delinquency and Youth Crime, the Cardozo Project in Urban Teaching (CPUT) welcomed teachers and interns at the same time.

Goldberg recalled some early meetings with Hansen: "We had a few face-to-face confrontations. We talked about the track system. He had the attitude of who the hell are you guys to tell me what to do. You know the professional educator idea. What also bothered him was the Cardozo-WAY alliance [Principal Benetta Washington was an ally of Goldberg's]. Bennetta was strictly on his shit list."[12]

And Hansen perceived equal antagonism from Goldberg, claiming that, "Goldberg openly was after the Track system."[13]

What occurred over the next four years was a struggle between professionals lined up on opposite sides of the reform divide, with Cardozo High School in the middle.[14]

And here is where I enter the saga of reforming the DC schools. As a master teacher of history working under the supervision of Bennetta Washington in the Cardozo Peace Corps Project in Urban Teaching—a pilot effort overseen by WAY—the project, the high school, and I were peripheral players in the ensuing reform battles over the district school system's direction for the next four years.

THE CARDOZO PROJECT IN URBAN TEACHING, 1963–1967

The Peace Corps Project in Urban Teaching (CPUT) was conceived in the heady days of the early 1960s, when John F. Kennedy was president and his brother, Robert, was attorney general. The call that President Kennedy made in his 1961 inauguration speech, "Ask not what your country can do for you—ask what you can for your country," inspired young men and women across the country. The Peace Corps, led by Sargent Shriver, was one of many efforts, including CPUT, drawing smart, idealistic college graduates to government service.[15]

So how did ten Peace Corps veterans end up teaching at Cardozo High School? English teacher Joan Wofford designed the project with Bennetta Washington. They sought to solve two major problems identified by federal school reformers: reduce dropouts from "slum" schools and meet the dire need to staff these schools with certified teachers who offered more than a college degree and a pulse.

Wofford believed that returned Peace Corps volunteers (PCVs) could apply the knowledge and skills gained from teaching English and doing community work overseas to largely minority and poor urban high schools in the United States through developing new curriculum and working with students and their families in their neighborhoods. In the process, these PCVs would become certified teachers within one year. The result would be fewer dropouts, increased student academic performance, heightened expectations for college and employment, and a new crop of teachers for urban schools.[16]

Theory and Goals of the CPUT Pilot Project

Like many federally funded one-year projects the application for CPUT stated the primary goals but left the theory driving the goals implicit. The stated goals were:

- "[D]evelop new curriculum for reaching students in an urban school." Such lessons would be "more directly related to the life experiences of the child."
- "Motivate student who appear to be apathetic toward school activities."
- "Increase teacher's understanding of the home, community, and other environmental forces which affect the child's ability to learn."[17]

But as Bennetta Washington put it when she invited returning PCVs to apply for teaching positions:

> The idea, in brief, is to place 10 Volunteers who have spent two years teaching, directly into the urban high school classroom to see whether they, together with a special staff of Master Teachers and consultants, can emerge after a year with some conclusions about what should be taught in the urban classroom, how it should be taught, and how best to go about training teachers for their gigantic task . . . This task . . . is to make the urban classroom a catalyst for those economic, social, and intellectual changes which are required if the public school is to become the way up and out for kids desperately caught in that vicious cycle of slum living in which the cultural and economic deprivation of so many families is passed on, inevitably, to so many children.

Washington ended the letter by saying:

> Did we say inevitably? We did not really mean that. Indeed, this pilot project is based on the premise—the hope—that returning Volunteers can help demonstrate that the circle can be broken and that the school is the place to begin.[18]

The idealism embedded in the pilot program of recruiting people who had already worked in a foreign country and asking them to break the persistent cycle of poverty afflicting big city high schools is obvious. Equally obvious is the bold assumption that these teacher-interns (seven white and three black Peace Corps veterans, guided by two white master teachers) could develop curriculum materials anchored in knowledge of students and the community that would engage students sufficiently to reverse low academic performance, high dropout rates, and juvenile delinquency.

In short, the theory driving CPUT was that minority youth dropped out of school because the teaching was unimaginative, the content they studied was irrelevant, and their teachers were unconnected to the realities of the neighborhood within which they lived.

Those goals and theory were put to the test at Cardozo in 1963. School opened a week after the March on Washington. I met my two classes and four CPUT history interns. The principal assigned the project to room 101, where the fourteen desks for the interns, master teachers, and secretaries were crowded together with paper and Ditto machines. The room was a constant beehive of activity. No partitions separated interns from master teachers and secretaries; it was an open space workroom where teachers, student teachers, and administrators flowed back and forth in an egalitarian fashion not easily replicable in most schools.

I was now part of the DC schools. Over the next nine years as a teacher and administrator in the district, I learned far more than I ever expected about teaching, curriculum, school organization, teacher education, and how school systems adopt and adapt reforms.[19]

TEACHING HISTORY TO HIGH SCHOOL STUDENTS WHILE TRAINING INTERNS TO TEACH

All of the classes that master teachers and interns taught covered the four tracks. But the principal made sure that the US history classes that were hardest to teach—General and Basic—were distributed evenly among interns and master teachers. Many of the students in these tracks had limited reading skills and had repeated grades in elementary and junior high schools. Except for a handful who tried to succeed academically, most of these students' experiences had been negative, and they were clearly disengaged from academic subjects. Motivation,

FIGURE 2.1   CPUT project office.

then, was a constant issue facing all of us. Here is one entry from the journal of history intern Dirk Ballendorf, describing his experience in a Basic class two months after the school year began:[20]

> Most all of the teacher's time is spent on motivating his students. Methods and technics [sic] are experimented with in an attempt to arouse student interest. This work is time-consuming, exhausting, and very often discourage [sic]. Motivation is a personal and varied thing which changes from day to day and from student to student. Students who wish to learn need little or no motivation, and so then more time can be spent in teaching them. Here at Cardozo the opposite is the case.[21]

An entry of about three weeks later read:

I presented a highly structured lesson in geography class today. It was concerned with the "effects of the tropics on human activity." I had a self-contained type of lesson prepared. A mimeographed sheet of source material which the class read. The activity was virtually spelled out for the student. Although there was room for sound reasoning and questioning on the students' part, there was never any question as to where the next step in the lesson would be because it was there for them to see and they had but to do it. This was very successful. I will use this technic [sic] again. It seems that a structure is very helpful and important to them.[22]

Issues of motivation and lesson structure in teaching history across different tracks came up time and again in my own teaching, the frequent post-observation conferences I held with the interns, and our weekly after-school seminars on curriculum and instruction.

The Cardozo Environment

While my teaching experiences at Glenville and work with student teachers from Cleveland universities helped me considerably at Cardozo, I had neither experienced the organizational disarray nor the extent of student disengagement, the low percentage of students preparing for college, and spillover of neighborhood poverty at Glenville. The socioeconomic differences between Cardozo and Glenville students became evident to me during the first semester. While color surely mattered, socioeconomic class had a profound impact on the high numbers of students in General and Basic classes and low numbers of students in the Honors track.

In 1963–1964, Cardozo had just over two thousand students, of whom 99 percent were black and mostly poor. The faculty was 90 percent black. As for the distribution of students across the four tracks, 35 percent were in the General track and 28 percent were in Basic classes, 32 percent were College Preparatory, and just over 5 percent were in Honors track.[23]

Cardozo was an age-graded high school covering ninth through twelfth grades. Like most US high schools, it was organized into academic departments, with self-contained classrooms where individual teachers taught. A daily schedule divided the school day into forty-five-minute segments, and groups of students moved from one classroom to another when the bell rang. In each class, the teacher was expected to manage the group, cover prescribed textbook content, and then determine whether each student had learned the material. The school year was divided into nine-week segments in which teachers evaluated student progress toward completion of the course that would, in time, permit those who passed courses to receive a diploma at the end of four years. These regularities— the *grammar of schooling*—were taken for granted and, like wallpaper, went largely unnoticed by master teachers, interns, parents, and visitors. They governed the high school throughout the school year, except in the early weeks of the fall semester.

Within the first month, the interns and I realized that the school was in complete disarray. Class size ran to forty-five or more and changed daily as counselors shifted students from one teacher to another. Not until mid-October did class enrollments settle down. Daily announcements on the public address system—including administrative requests, dates for upcoming events, and names of students released for athletic games—continually interrupted lessons.[24] Moreover, there were never enough US history, geography, and government textbooks, so students had to share. The library contained only seventy-five books for all US history and about the same number for ancient, medieval, and modern European history.

Within the school, students roamed the halls at will. Administrators would shoo wandering students into classrooms or herd them into a detention room. Neighborhood fights would often spill over into angry outbursts in hallways and classrooms—years before gangs and drugs afflicted the city and schools. Reports of stabbings in the cafeteria or hallways put all of us on alert. City officials assigned DC police officers to the school during the year.

Despite the general unpredictability, the Cardozo faculty, including CPUT teachers and interns, met their classes daily and taught, experiencing some small victories and many defeats to engage students in learning.

Teaching History Classes

In my initial years at Cardozo, I taught US history to one General and one Basic track class. I used lessons I had developed and taught at Glenville mixed in with black history materials. I no longer did current events Fridays as I had at Glenville, since being in DC opened up so many opportunities for in- and out-of-school activities. Some interns and I took our classes to see Congress at work—students learned about filibusters, as the Civil Rights Bill was being debated in both chambers—and the Supreme Court when it was in session. I took a few classes to the Frederick Douglass House and its newly established African Art Museum. We would have federal and local legislators and executives visit classes. I also started an after-school History Club for students in 1963 that lasted through 1966.

That was the good news. Unfortunately, there was also plenty of bad news. It became increasingly clear to me and the interns that teaching Basic and General classes (the few College Preparatory and Honors classes in social studies usually went to veteran Cardozo faculty) was incredibly difficult, given student disengagement from academic learning and the enormous spread in students' reading skills. Intern Dirk Ballendorf was not the only one to have trouble motivating his basic classes. So did I—my journal entry for January 30, 1964, reads:

> My basic class is perplexing. How do you teach kids at the tail end of their education when all of the mistakes in their education have been compounded and neglected? What can be done? What approaches work? I do know that warmth is *not* enough." (emphasis in original text)

Here I was, a veteran of seven years teaching at Glenville, yet four months after I began teaching at Cardozo, I was flummoxed about how to motivate my Basic history classes. And my interns saw that groping when they observed me also. What we learned together was that hooking a critical mass of students into a lesson in the first two to three minutes of the forty-five minute period was essential for there to be a reasonable chance that the lesson would engage students in the content and skills being taught.

Borrowing from my experience at Glenville, the interns and I produced readings drawn from primary and secondary sources—poetry, fiction, newspaper articles—that we felt could capture student interest. Some examples were a lesson on the Boston Massacre in 1770 from the points of view of a British soldier, a local patriot opposed to the British, and Crispus Attucks, a black sailor killed by the British. One intern created a lesson on the six-shooter taken from Walter Webb's *Great Plains* to show the inventiveness of frontiersmen. We used excerpts from the book of Genesis in the Bible and Babylonian myths to demonstrate cultural diffusion in world history classes. One lesson devised by an intern used Thucydides' description of the plague during the Peloponnesian War to capture the flavor of fifth-century Athens.[25]

We worked on these readings, always looking to see what happened in the classes when they soared or sank, sharing ones that worked in room 101 and in quickie, five-minute conferences before and after each of us taught. These lessons also came up often in our after-school weekly seminars.

Teaching Interns

The interns' weekly schedule was packed from 7 a.m. to 3 p.m. Every day, they prepared for and taught two classes. They were also expected to work at the nearby community action agency during the week, usually in the evenings. In addition, they took after-school seminars at Cardozo (Humanities, Sociology, Psychology, and Supervised Internship among them). Not only were they to apply the concepts were drawn from these seminars to their daily teaching, but also they would get credit from Howard University toward a master's degree and teacher certification from the DC schools. CPUT, in effect, became an uncommon experiment: a school-based teacher education program rather than the familiar university-based programs.

In the first year of the project, the interns felt torn between competing obligations of curriculum development, community project work, and these after-school seminars. Given their limited time, they had to make choices between these duties, knowing full well that even the best manager of time would seldom finish all the required tasks. The resulting tensions pinched interns sharply during the life of the project.

As master teacher in history, I was responsible for observing interns' classes, conferencing afterward, and teaching the weekly Supervised Internship seminar (what universities called Curriculum and Instruction). I would observe one or two interns daily and then confer with them later in the day or the next morning.

Issues of race—among interns, master teachers, faculty, and students—were ever-present in classes, community work, interactions between regular Cardozo faculty and interns, and the after-school seminars. For example, here is one observation from my journal:

> Observed Rosalie's class yesterday. Today she tells me that Bernard, a student, asked her what the white man was doing in class. She explained to Bernard the project in which she was an intern teacher but the kid, she said, was resentful of a white man supervising his black teacher. (September 24, 1964)

Neither ignored nor focused on, discussions of race in seminars and between interns and master teachers were common but often unplanned. They touched on the experiences of black students having white teachers for the first time, relations between black teachers and black students, and similar issues.

In the first year of these weekly seminars, the interns and I worked on how-to topics (e.g., different ways of motivating students, putting together daily lessons, classroom management, grading practices) and historical content (e.g., slavery in the United States, the causes of the American Revolution, the impact of African geography on different economies and societies). In classroom observations, follow-up conferences, and weekly seminars, the experiences I brought from Glenville in developing materials on black history, using primary and secondary historical sources, and focusing on thinking skills coalesced in the initial two years of the project.

Materials from the New Social Studies (discussed in detail in chapter 3), flourishing by 1965, made their way into our weekly efforts in creating lessons. The work of psychologist Jerome Bruner informed how we approached teaching; we applied Benjamin Bloom's taxonomy in our work on cognitive skills. What grew from this mélange of cognitive psychologists, historians, and veteran teachers was an approach to lesson planning that leaned heavily on developing students' thinking skills through history content. We variously named these kind of lessons using terms circulating among advocates of the New Social Studies: "classroom inquiry," "the inductive method," "Bloom's Taxonomy," and "discovery." These catchphrases described our daily classes involving students in content- and skill-driven lessons, units, and projects.[26] We asked application and interpretative questions (e.g., "Why did John D. Rockefeller, the wealthiest man in America in the 1890s, give away most of the fortune he earned from the oil industry?") that required students to use sources beyond the textbook, work individually and in small groups to come up with evidenced-backed answers, and then defend publicly what they said.

From my journal for November 21, 1964:

> Funny, how inductive method firmed up as way of teaching over the past summer. Last year the seeds were there in the seminar readings, group discussions—the direction was laid down. But summer reading of Bruner et al. firmed it up and we have pushed it [with interns].

Because students had experienced at Cardozo and feeder schools traditional teaching approaches (e.g., lecture, textbook, worksheets), as had interns when they attended public school, weekly Supervised Internship seminars covered not only creating inquiry lessons but also delivering short lectures, classroom management techniques, smart ways to use out-of-date textbooks, preparing worksheets and quizzes, and other teacher-centered approaches so that interns would have a broad repertoire of tools when they entered their classrooms. Our repertoire expanded and shrank as the interns and I learned from our daily teaching practices, as lessons would fly or flop in front of our eyes.[27]

THE KENNEDY UNIT

By the third year of CPUT, the interns and I began to go beyond individual lessons and develop multiweek units for our classes that, once drafted, we would use jointly across the different grades in order to judge their strengths and weaknesses. In 1965–1966, we collaboratively developed one such unit on the assassination of President John F. Kennedy.

We planned the unit to be taught the first two weeks of the semester to develop and strengthen thinking and writing skills. This unit resembled one I had developed at Glenville to teach historical thinking by initially grabbing students' interest and then applying the skills to subsequent history lessons (see chapter 1).

Using the 1964 Warren Commission report on the Kennedy assassination as our starting point, intern Jay Mundstuk, Ike Jamison (a regular faculty member who joined the project), and I worked over the summer to develop the eight-lesson unit. The events were still fresh in our students' minds, and the question of whether Lee Harvey Oswald was the lone assassin or part of a conspiracy that planned the president's murder was a topic that students debated constantly whenever it arose in different classes.

The unit was aimed at General track students. While a few students were reading at or above grade level. the majority were two or more years below grade level. It was these students, we felt, who had been ignored by recent curriculum materials (the "New Social Studies") and for whom the usual social studies fare was tedious. We wanted to teach them the reasoning skills that would be needed in all social studies courses as well as on the street and at home. We wanted a subject that would seize our students' minds in figuring out answers to tough questions.

Material in the popular media was abundant. Besides the Warren Commission report, there was the deluge of attacks heaped on the Commission (e.g., Oswald was the shooter and acted alone). Moreover, in 1965, the memory of President Kennedy was very dear to many of our teenage students, who named Kennedy as the best president ever. Mystery still surrounded Lee Harvey Oswald. His role in the assassination piqued our students' curiosity. We named the unit "Who Killed Kennedy?"

The unit was organized into a series of lessons, the first of which raised the question, "How do we know who the assassin was?" We used this question to get students to state their beliefs initially and then, as the unit unfolded, to cast doubt on their beliefs when we presented evidence from the Warren Commission and some of the conspiracy-driven articles and books that had appeared within months of the assassination.

As the students sorted through the evidence, we had them use the thinking skills that were built into the unit's lessons—these were the same skills that I had taught at Glenville. The overall purpose of the unit was not to "prove" Oswald innocent or guilty. We wanted students to read carefully and judge the credibility of available sources, come up with hunches about who killed Kennedy, use evidence to reach a conclusion, and be able to defend their conclusions both orally and in writing. We were more concerned with *how* students reached a conclusion and created an explanation for what happened—a process embodied in the above skills—than the conclusion itself.

The Lessons

On the first day of the unit, we presented newspaper articles, photos, and personal accounts of how events in Dallas on November 22, 1963, affected people. We got students to recount what had they experienced and to answer the central question: *Was Oswald the assassin?* Students were asked to write an essay answering the question. From this assignment, we would get a sense of the level of our students' writing skills and the positions that they staked out. We planned to return to this initial essay at the end of the unit.

In the second lesson, we presented students with accounts from *Time* and *Newsweek* magazines detailing the "facts" of the assassination and evidence against Oswald. We asked students to build a time line of events. In doing so, they began to see that the journalists' accounts were imperfect sources because they contained discrepancies and contradictions.

The third and fourth lessons directed students to build a lawyer's case against Oswald. The sources we gave them included eyewitness accounts, rebuttals of those accounts, Warren Commission excerpts, and conflicting statements about Oswald the person. For example, we wanted students to wrestle with the fact that Oswald was a good enough shot to have killed the president, a moving target, with rapid-fire shots at a distance of over two hundred yards. Students saw how conflicting statements made it very difficult to draw a conflict-free conclusion that satisfied the available evidence.

In the fifth lesson, we shifted to an investigation of Oswald himself. Previous lessons had established his presence at the scene of the murder and evaluated his marksmanship. What about motive? Did he have a reason to kill the president? We gave students excerpts from Oswald's diary and firsthand accounts of people who knew him. We asked students to share their hunches, and, through back-and-forth discussion, the class discovered that it was nearly impossible to ascertain Oswald's motives.

The sixth lesson was structured as a game: "How Good a Lawyer Are You?" We pushed students to develop categories for all the information they had read, digested, discussed, and written about. We divided the class into groups to see which could most accurately categorize statements concerning the assassination and defend their choices satisfactorily. A panel of students and the teacher judged the competition.

The seventh lesson was a review of the material. In this period, the groups created in the previous lesson either prosecuted or defended Oswald, making use of all the sources and information they had gathered.

The last lesson tested students on the knowledge and skills they had gained from the unit. The test comprised multiple-choice questions and a final essay question that asked students to answer the same question posed in the first lesson of the unit: *Was Oswald the assassin?* We wanted to see whether the final essay reflected any growth in knowledge and use of the thinking and writing skills on which the unit was grounded.

Problems with the Unit

One purpose in teaching the unit was to raise doubts in our students' minds about the reliability of information. We asked them to question sources and to be skeptical of "facts." We succeeded in that respect, but overshot the mark: By the end of the unit, there were far fewer believers in the conclusions of the Warren Commission. Some students continued to believe in Oswald's guilt, others were confused about whether he was guilty at all. A small number even supported a conspiracy theory, with Vice President Lyndon Johnson at the center of the cabal. Most of the class did see how ambiguous supposedly conclusive evidence is when carefully scrutinized and how difficult it was to establish incontrovertible facts in this case. But as a result, many students swung to the extreme of believing nothing. By the end of the unit, we had a group of students ready to throw out both the conclusions of the Warren Commission report and historical knowledge on the grounds of insufficient evidence. In retrospect, we might have placed more emphasis on what *can* be reasonably accepted from conflicting evidence.

Evaluation of the Unit

Overall, most students got As, Bs, and Cs on the factual recall test we gave. This was a promising result, given that many of these General track students ordinarily received Ds and Fs on unit tests.

Also encouraging were the results of a survey of student opinion, answered anonymously. We found that students enjoyed the unit, two-thirds giving it an A, with no Ds or Fs. They overwhelmingly agreed that the unit should be taught to other classes, even though many said they were now confused about Oswald's guilt and said they did not like the difficulty they had in coming to a conclusion.

In the fall of 1966, this thinking skills unit on the Kennedy assassination was taught to fifteen social studies classes. Thirty-eight years later, Bill Plitt, who as an intern teacher had used the Kennedy unit in 1966, used it again. He was teaching US history at Falls Church (Virginia) High School, and asked his "reluctant" learners the same question that drove the unit in 1966—*Did Lee Harvey Oswald assassinate JFK?* Plitt recalls the experience of teaching the unit to a different generation of students in 2004:

> Initially, I wondered whether my current students would know anything about the assassination or whether they would care. What I found was surprising. Unlike my first class of students, my current students were not alive when J.F.K. was assassinated but their parents were . . .
>
> For youngsters who did not have a history of participating in discussions, attending classes regularly, completing homework, feeling confident in writing complex essays, or performing well on traditional tests, my students performed exceptionally well on this unit. They completed more assignments than usual and joined in class discussions without pressure from me. They were engaged intellectually. Indeed, my students proved that they were able to perform at a higher level of thinking. They brought in additional resources, gathered first-hand accounts, and watched commentaries and documentaries on their own. They created persuasive essays justifying their opinions . . . [28]

Plitt used the Kennedy unit to introduce the first semester in 2004 for the same reasons I had used a thinking skills unit both at Glenville and Cardozo High Schools. I thought then that generic thinking skills can be taught directly through high-relevance content that would engage and energize students to learn crucial skills not only to be applied later in the semester across all social studies classes but in life as well. However, I did not use the Kennedy unit after I left Cardozo in 1967. I had changed my mind about this approach, largely because my hope that students would transfer the thinking skills they learned to subsequent units in the US history course was not realized.[29] So after at least three years of teaching such a unit in the first semester of the school year at Glenville and now Cardozo, I concluded that I would

FIGURE 2.2   Bill Plitt teaching (1966).

drop this exercise and work toward integrating different cognitive skills applicable to history within each unit of the US history course.

Although the Kennedy unit largely failed, insofar as students did not continue to apply those thinking skills after it was over, it was a success in engaging students in spirited discussions, debates, and learning to work in small groups. The unit helped create a community within many, but not all, of the fifteen classes. That was a significant plus.

CPUT AND REGULAR CARDOZO FACULTY

Also a plus was that two of the six veteran teachers in the Cardozo history department asked for copies of the unit to use in their own courses. That was a small victory, since relationships in the first year between CPUT and regular faculty who taught a full load of five classes a day were, at best, fair and, at worst, hostile.

The regular faculty was 90 percent black and highly experienced in the DC schools. Of the ten Peace Corps returnees, seven were white. It would be naive to say that race had no part to play in the initial hostile relations between faculty and CPUT. However, the relationship warmed up noticeably as the pilot project turned to Cardozo's experienced social studies, English, and math teachers—called "affiliates"—to help supervise interns in subsequent years.

There were solid reasons for the ill feeling between CPUT and regular faculty. Hype surrounding the project overpromised and underdelivered on curriculum products and other materials that would help the faculty. With the hullabaloo surrounding the launch of CPUT, Cardozo regular faculty expected new interns and staff in room 101 to develop curriculum materials that would turn around hard-to-teach classes by engaging students far better than traditional textbooks and worksheets. But early on, veteran faculty saw that the Peace Corps interns were novices in curriculum development who had multiple responsibilities outside of the classroom. They also saw (more likely heard from their students) that interns designing new materials, even with two experienced master teachers, struggled in teaching Basic and General classes. Thus faculty expectation for access to new materials and ways of teaching soon curdled into disappointment and even cynicism. That disappointment surfaced repeatedly in the form of disparaging comments made in these teachers' classrooms, particularly in those with students who had no classes with CPUT teachers.

Moreover, there were stellar teachers on the regular faculty whom project designers ignored. That CPUT was separately located in one large room on the first floor of a three-story building both insulated and isolated interns and master teachers from the rest of the school. CPUT teachers taught only two classes a day (every regular faculty member taught five). Master teachers and interns had plenty of typewriters, paper, and machines to produce new materials. What appeared to be a cornucopia of resources stung regular faculty who had to scrounge for these same things. All of these factors negatively influenced early relationships between faculty and the project.

FIGURE 2.3   Team teaching at Cardozo.

Consider the following incident. Like the interns, I taught two classes in other teachers' rooms. Within a month, Principal Bennetta Washington and Joan Wofford, the master teacher of English who had designed the project and was a close friend of Washington's, received a note from the head of the social studies department. In it, he complained that I had not erased the board or picked up paper before leaving the room of a regular social studies teacher I used during first period of the day. He did not bother to talk to me about the issue. At the first social studies department meeting of the school year, he had no interest in staying to discuss any issues—he wore his hat and coat, ready to depart in less than fifteen minutes. I did try to schedule another meeting so that the four interns could meet with the other department members, but the suggestion was dismissed. Had I been more sensitive to relations with regular faculty, there might have been some improvements. But I was not. The note and the rejection of a meeting with interns were only the tip of an iceberg of initial hostility to the project.

That hostility and separation melted over time as the project involved English, math, and history faculty as affiliates supervising interns, and as these former Peace Corps volunteers relieved some of the burdens on regular faculty by directing plays, producing the *Purple Wave* (the school yearbook), and working with different members of the regular faculty. However, those Cardozo faculty not involved with the project held on tightly to their initial and negative perceptions of CPUT over the years.

REFLECTIONS ON TEACHING STUDENTS AND INTERNS

From my four years of teaching my own classes as master teacher of history and supervising history interns, I learned a great deal about teaching and supervising young teachers.

I brought from Glenville High School the study guides and readings I had created, and a traditional chronological development in US history. My mode of teaching was largely teacher-centered, though tilting increasingly toward student involvement in classroom lessons to grasp historical ideas and thinking. The flowering of the New Social Studies movement infused new materials and ideas about "inductive learning" and "inquiry" lessons into intern decisions as we developed our own classes. For me, these discussions and decisions fueled further movement down the path of student participation in lessons. Teaching only two classes while watching interns teach gave me time to try out new student-centered techniques in the crucible of actual classrooms.

One experiment that we tried in the pilot project was to have English and social studies interns and master teachers team-teach a unit. English intern Roberta Rabinoff (now Kaplan) and I taught a unit on the American Revolution by using Howard Fast's novel *April Morning*. Roberta and I tried to get at different kinds of truths, such as literary truth of what a novelist had imagined happening at Lexington and what historical sources from British soldiers, Boston patriots, and bystanders said occurred on that April morning in 1775. We taught small groups and constructed activities that individuals worked on as we met with them.

Changes in my teaching did occur. From my journal for October 18, 1965:

> A thought occurred to me how my teaching has changed since 1963. Study guides, rigid chronological framework had altered. I've come to practice what I've been preaching and, best of all, given the time to innovate.

What that journal entry meant was that my lessons were combining both teacher- and student-centered activities drawn from readings in the New Social Studies and activities that interns and I had created. Traditional structured lessons that included lectures, textbook assignments, worksheets to fill out, and guided whole group discussions slowly merged with newly developed activities such as small group work, projects, and simulations. I was creating a hybrid approach that fit my experiences at Glenville and Cardozo.

Teaching teenagers and supervising interns at the same time as working in a large school district undergoing reforms also influenced my thinking about what urban school problems needed to be solved and which solutions might best solve those problems. In short, my teaching and my ideas about school reform had evolved as a result of working four years at Cardozo High School.

I had arrived in DC with the dream of creating new curriculum materials and training new teachers to engage low-income black students sufficiently to finish high school and go to college. Working at ground level of daily teaching, supervising interns, and later directing the entire project, I entered the fractured universe of federal and local governance of the DC schools, a rule-driven track system of ability grouping, and racial tensions bubbling in both city and schools. I learned about the racial politics that dominated one urban school system.

While how I taught history at Cardozo evolved from what I did at Glenville, my experiences in the DC schools as a teacher and administrator changed my views considerably about the fundamental problems facing urban schools. I came to Cardozo thinking that the core problem of urban schools miseducating children and youth was the absence of enough knowledgeable and skilled teachers who developed their own curriculum materials. What I learned was that while effective teaching and engaging lessons were very important, organizational pathologies at the policymaking level and within the bureaucracy mattered greatly to how and what teachers taught daily. I learned that schools are not independent entities floating over neighborhoods and social networks. The history of race and the enduring poverty that children experienced within families and in a city mattered greatly to what happened in schools and classrooms. I learned that reform ideas, talk, and organizational changes directed at improving how and what teachers teach may affect what happens in schools but may not reach inside classrooms once teachers close their doors and begin teaching.

All these lessons meant the solutions to these problems were both different and more complex than I had thought. Later generations of reformers who arrived in DC to do good learned similar lessons.

CHAPTER 3

The New Social Studies and the New, New History

THE NEW SOCIAL STUDIES, 1960s

It's not a "man bites dog" media story, but a university professor who willingly chooses to teach at a high school for a semester is still uncommon. According to his account, this history professor learned a great deal by teaching at Taylor Allderdice High School in Pittsburgh, Pennsylvania:

> I have now been at Allderdice for five months, long enough to see sharp differences between high school and university teaching situations. From the very beginning the sharpest contrast has been in the physical environment and pace. Allderdice crowds into one building 3,200 students while [my university] has about 1,400 spread over 80 acres. The only room available at Allderdice for quiet study is a chemistry storeroom. At [my university] I share an office the size of the men teachers' room at Allderdice, with one colleague.
>
> Moreover, nothing is leisurely at Allderdice. Clerical chores, opening exercises, and hurried conferences with students and colleagues crowd the hour between 8:00 and 9:00 a.m. The five-minute break between classes is far too short to reinvigorate a teacher. Lunch half-hour is a race upstairs in the midst of a throng of students, a contest for a place at the head of the line, a few minutes respite in a crowded cafeteria where masses of students sit within eyesight, and another dash to open the classroom before chaos erupts in the hallway.

Since January, I have been teaching six classes a day on Monday, Wednesday, and Friday in order to be free to teach and observe at other schools on Tuesday and Thursday while my three Allderdice colleagues take my classes. By seventh period on these crowded days, I teach poorly, my energy dissipated, and my nerves worn thin. How my colleagues stand a similar pace year after year I do not understand.

My schedule—and the schedule of regular high school teachers—gives me far too little time to see students individually. Sixth period is usually crowded with appointments. I can never talk to students over coffee, a happy pursuit which probably occupies far too much of my time at [the university]. Like many of my colleagues at Allderdice, I am unable to give students the individual attention they deserve, except by writing lengthy comments on their essay examinations and other papers . . .

If it were not for the excitement of the AP [Advanced Placement] program, the constant stimulation from five colleagues who are teaching AP history in three high schools, and the sharp analytical minds of the 160 students I see one to three times a week, there would be very little intellectual stimulation in my high school job. Except during hectic lunch periods, there is no time to chat with colleagues from other departments.

Historians at [my university] will be surprised to learn that I miss department meetings where we frequently become involved in long discussions of history and teaching techniques. I find a half-hour to write and do research only late at night after preparations are ready for the next and I miss conversation with colleagues who are carrying on similar research. High school, therefore, seems much less the free market place in ideas I had come to know at [my university], and opportunities for creative growth and development are not as great, except as one grows as a teacher.

Nor are teachers in high school accorded the considerations as professional people which we know in universities. They are required to be clerks, truant officers, and policemen. Books are chosen for them, and courses of study are usually planned by others, although, of course, every teacher has numerous opportunities to develop original methods of presentation if he wishes to do so . . .

High school teachers pay far more attention to their students as developing human beings than we do in the universities. One teacher after another has been able to supply me with details about a student's personal problems and family background which have been most helpful. The counselors, principal, and vice principal, at least at Allderdice, seem to know every child in the school personally and to help them over innumerable hurdles. In college, we are more likely to let a student sink or swim unless he is in really serious trouble . . .

My students at Allderdice are more fun to teach than their counterparts at [university]. Of course, I have only very able history students at Allderdice while many of our mathematical wizards [in the university] have somewhat more limited verbal skills. Ability differences, however, are not the heart of the matter. The more significant difference is that most of my high school students are hungry for intellectual stimulation. They are anxious to examine historical issues in the light of evidence, and they respond eagerly when challenged with a knotty problem of historical interpretation. Moreover, they seem more willing to express personal opinions and to put their opinions to the test of evidence than many college students. The false sophistication which marks many college freshmen and sophomores seems entirely—and happily—absent . . .[1]

The year is 1960. The professor is Edwin (Ted) Fenton, then an assistant professor at Carnegie Institute of Technology (now Carnegie Mellon University). Teaching AP courses at a high school for the first time, Fenton, a Harvard-trained historian, went on to become one of the major figures in what he, other academics, teachers, and policy makers came to call the *New Social Studies* (NSS).[2]

Turn now to the story of how one high school teacher got involved in the curricular reform and stayed with it for decades.

In the spring of 1965, the superintendent in the township where I taught . . . called me, a fifth-year social studies teacher, to his office. I was told there was a need for an "expert" to coordinate the adoption of an innovative social studies program, "just like the new math." A few weeks later, I was appointed the district's first coordinator (K–12) of social studies, with teaching responsibilities in the high school. My mind flashed back to October of 1957 when *Sputnik* intruded on the academic tranquility of my liberal arts college, producing an unprecedented interest in reforming pre-collegiate education. I also remembered when, two years later, I had begun teaching high school and had discovered what had not been reformed: social studies teaching, which was still organized around fat textbooks with "checkup" questions. I was anxious for something new.

The timing was fortuitous. My concerns were mirrored in the pages of *Social Education*, which featured article after article on social studies reform or even "revolution." We were on the brink of a "renaissance of education in America," announced Harvard psychologist Jerome Bruner as he promoted an engaging instructional theory associated with the structure of the disciplines and inductive learning . . . Everything seemed to be coming together. In my first report, I boldly recommended that the township adopt a K–12 social studies curriculum "drawing on history and the social sciences" and "taught by induction and a conceptual approach as much as possible." It would be supported by NSS materials then in preparation. The board—whose president was familiar with Bruner—readily approved my proposal and offered support in terms of summer employment and materials; after all, this project was a new math for social studies . . .

Implementation initially proved to be a chilling experience. I soon learned that the jargon of revolution—"structures" and "concepts"—was not the stuff of teacher-talk. A committee of teachers under my direction finally compiled a report in the summer of 1967. The report proposed a program that included the social sciences—history, economics, political science, geography, and sociology/anthropology . . .

This was hardly the revolution that I had in mind. Still, it produced the first organized social studies program—with related supporting materials—in that township's elementary schools since its post-World War II expansion . . .

Most of my time, however, was given to promoting NSS in my high school department . . . Copies of Fenton's *The New Social Studies* (1967) were purchased and duly distributed to members of the department, who also viewed his in-service films. Again, it was not an easy sell; there were uncomfortable lapses of silence during department meetings when NSS was discussed . . .

We did not, however, use any of the other materials in the Fenton series. *A New History of the United States: An Inquiry Approach* (1967) struck the department and me as too restrictive in both content and process for a mandated course . . .

> By late 1969, 1 began to sense from my experiences both in the
> schools and at professional meetings that the steam was already run-
> ning out of NSS . . . I faulted the abstruse terminology, the disjointed
> projects, and grandiose expectations but concluded it was a revolu-
> tion "worth fighting for" . . .[3]

William Goetz's experiences with the New Social Studies and
Edwin Fenton's teaching of high school AP courses—courses aimed at
what were then called "able" students—mirror the strong academic presence of discipline-based professors creating new texts for high-achieving students and piloting materials in schools where like-minded
teachers would try out the experimental materials in their classrooms.
Those features had been embedded in the previous decade's movement
to transform the content and teaching of math and sciences in public
schools. The New Social Studies was a latecomer to the movement. But
in the early 1960s, it made up for lost time.

The movement to revitalize history and social studies in the 1960s was
the latest in a series of efforts to inject zest into studying the past and
present social issues in public schools.

The movement stretches back to the early twentieth-century. When
Columbia University historians James Harvey Robinson and Charles
Beard called for teachers to teach history as part of the social sciences,
making it relevant to students' interests, and to use historians' skills
to find answers to present-day questions, these academics kick-started
the New History. Robinson and Beard's political influence as progressive historians extended to the various national committees meeting to
revise the social studies during and after World War I.[4]

This progressive academic elite left their thumbprints all over the
key documents of the day, including the highly influential National
Education Association's Committee on Social Studies report issued in
1916. Calling for four years of history to be taught in public high schools,
the Committee proposed major changes: modern European history to
replace ancient and English history; a new ninth-grade Community

Civics class where students got involved in solving urban housing, congestion, and recreation problems; and a Problems of Democracy class in the twelfth grade, where the social sciences could be brought to bear on high-profile social and political issues students identified.[5]

Between the 1920s and 1940s, New History advocates, including social scientists and practicing historians, pushed for curricular changes in public schools that addressed problems of interest to children and youth. These progressive reformers influenced both the language educators used and the content of state and local curriculum guides. However, only a fraction of teachers converted the progressive vocabulary and curriculum guides into daily lessons. In subsequent decades, the New History's language and content nearly disappeared from curricular documents, textbooks, and classroom practice.[6]

By the early 1950s, spurred by Cold War rivalries and the launch of the Russian satellite *Sputnik*, another generation of academics—expressing faith in the role of public schools in foiling foreign threats and curing domestic ills—sought to reshape the content students learned in K–12 classrooms. This view was quickly taken up in the political arena. Reform-drenched rhetoric, laws, policies, and regulations manifested strong social beliefs about how US schools had to change to meet the Soviet threat during the Cold War by having the next generation of Americans better educated than their rivals. New Math, New Physics, and New Social Studies signaled the nation and world that the United States would be second to none. Faith in education as the panacea to cure national ills was restored by these curricular reforms.

As leaders of the New Social Studies, historians Edwin Fenton and Richard Brown, along with cognitive psychologist Jerome Bruner, sociologist Robert Angell, economist Lawrence Senesh, and other academics, received federal, state, and private funding to develop new courses, textbooks, instructional materials, audiovisual activities, and summer institutes and other ways of introducing experienced and novice teachers to the discipline.

Advocates proliferated.[7] By 1966, there were over fifty social studies projects (history, economics, political science, geography, sociology, and psychology) aimed at K–12 public school "able" students. These projects were funded from a wide variety of sources—the US Office of Education, the National Science Foundation, corporations, professional associations, and private donors. Creating new instructional materials, training teachers, piloting lessons in classrooms, and entering agreements with publishers, these projects sought to transform traditional fact-after-fact history teaching into new courses filled with engaging materials where teachers moved beyond reliance on textbooks, instead using methods of inquiry to get students thinking, seeing, and writing about the past. They wanted to get at the very structure of history and teach it in ways consistent with how historians study the past.[8]

Fenton, for example, describes a lesson in the tenth-grade European History course that he and colleagues developed in Pittsburgh in the mid-1960s:

> For the third lesson, students read two accounts of the Hungarian Revolution. One is from Radio Moscow; the other from *TIME*. We tell them to pretend that these two pieces of evidence are all that remain after a nuclear holocaust and that they have just landed from a spaceship with the ability to read both Russian and English. What happened in Hungary?
>
> We make two points with this lesson. First, we ask students to try to agree on three pieces of data from the two accounts which they will accept as facts. They quickly isolate three on which both accounts agree. This procedure leads to a discussion of the criteria which historians use to test the credibility of data ... We then list three facts about Russian and American society which we gleaned from the documents. This enables teachers to return to the point previous[ly] made [in previous lessons] about the way in which a person's frame of reference determines how he classifies data.[9]

Richard Brown, a University of Massachusetts historian in charge of the Amherst Project in American History, was also caught up in the national sense of so many academics that their time had arrived. Brown pointed out the distinction that the project made about what students need to learn from history:

> We were committed to the idea that "history" is primarily a way of learning and secondarily a body of knowledge ... To be sure, we agreed that history as a body of knowledge is also important—the more that one knows of the past the better one's ability to ask good questions of it—but nonetheless, we viewed the body of knowledge as essentially a treasure trove to be used rather than "mastered" as an end in itself ...
>
> And what students had to master was how to make sense of different sources, the use of evidence, and the asking of questions. Those questions would come out of their experiences.
>
> The polestar of the Amherst Project was the idea that student learn best when they are acting as inquirers, pursuing into evidence questions that grow out of their own lives ... We thus viewed history in the classroom as essentially utilitarian, not something to be "learned" as an end in itself but as a body of experience to be delved into by students learning how to learn while growing in the process ... The focus of [our work] was on critical inquiry ... The teacher's role was to pique the curiosity, to aid, abet, and guide, and to be a role model of inquiry rather than the answer-giver.

Brown gave an example of the Amherst approach to history in a unit that I and hundreds of social studies teachers at the time used in classrooms: "What Happened on Lexington Green: An Inquiry into the Nature and Methods of History":

> [T]he student is faced with conflicting eyewitness accounts of a dramatic modern confrontation [e.g., an urban riot] and [then is] asked how one knows what happened about anything in the past. Using the Battle of Lexington as a case study, he or she confronts eyewitness accounts of what happened, moves on to conflicting historical interpretations of the same evidence, analyzes several examples of how modern textbook writers recount what happened, and ends up with Plato in the cave reflecting on the nature of truth and reality.[10]

Those working on the Amherst project completed seventy units for eleventh-grade US history, most of which were aimed at college-bound students, with a few slated for "slow learners." They conducted workshops for hundreds of teachers in writing and teaching these units, and worked closely with teachers using the units in various school districts across the country. Unlike Fenton, however, they did not create new textbooks. Federal funding for the Amherst Project ended in 1972.

By that year, the New Social Studies was in decline. It didn't go out quietly, though. One of the last projects, led by Jerome Bruner and a team of academics and specialists, called "Man: A Course of Study" (MACOS), caused considerable public uproar. The turmoil was stirred by MACOS's inclusion of anthropological material about the life and death of Netsilik Eskimos and triggered another social studies war thirty years after the one involving the content of social studies textbooks. The flaming end of the New Social Studies was spectacular, but it was the end nonetheless. The curtain fell on the last act of this drama, and the movement slipped off the radar.[11]

THE HISTORY OF A REFORM: A PLAY IN THREE ACTS

Stories in novels, films, television series, and theater often follow an arc—a beginning, middle, and end, or problem, conflict, and resolution—a familiar sequence that stretches back to ancient Greek drama. In the New Social Studies of the 1960s, a similar three-act play unfolded in the policy-to-practice journey of so many curricular innovations in US schools as they were adopted and then traveled a pothole-riddled road into classrooms.

The metaphor of the traditional three-act play can also be used to illustrate the way school reform becomes a theater of political expression. This is a point that educational policy historian David K. Cohen made nearly four decades ago:

[S]chools might be seen as a great social proscenium, a stage on which terrific struggles over the content and character of the culture were played out. The creation or adoption of a progressive curriculum [in the 1920s and 1930s] was in some respects a declaration about culture, childhood, and society. These wars were of course serious; powerful forces were arranged in the struggles, they could be won or lost, and the consequences were often far from trivial.[12]

Cyclical math, science, and history wars are dramas of popular beliefs and societal traditions about which knowledge is most important for students to study in those subjects, as is the legislation behind education reform. Consider No Child Left Behind as an instance of reform and political drama. Why, for example, was the phrase "scientifically based research" mentioned 111 times in the law? Why did student test scores have to be displayed by ethnicity, race, and special needs? Why was the target of the law that every single student test proficient in reading and math by 2014? Answers to these questions are not in the motives of President George W. Bush or legislators; these central features of the law express Americans' deepest social beliefs—a faith in science and scientifically constructed tests as meritocratic instruments for achieving equal opportunity. Science is the symbol of modernity, progress, and social justice. These social beliefs get played out as reforms on the stage of schools. [13]

Looking at ambitious reforms embedded in laws, state policies, and school district regulations as political expression of deep social beliefs is an explanation of the motives that underlie reform that goes beyond the familiar writings that concentrate myopically on analysis of goals, objectives, and benchmarks ending in an evaluation of outcomes.

While I do engage in the rational analysis of curricular reforms, I also offer this alternative way of looking at the New Social Studies in the 1960s and the resurgence of history curriculum and instruction since the early 1990s—as dramas that play out deep public beliefs that most explanations of school reforms miss.

Act I—The Problem

For the New Social Studies, Act I begins during the 1950s. Fears that Soviet scientists had outdistanced their US counterparts led to the National Defense Education Act (1958), a burst of new curricula in math and science, and the pouring of federal dollars into universities and public schools to turn out scientists, mathematicians, and engineers.

Social studies, the stepchild of academic subjects, awoke to the changes that had occurred in sister disciplines, including cognitive psychology, when Jerome Bruner's *The Process of Education* appeared. With the federal government and private donors funding the first wave of New Social Studies curriculum projects, an academic crowd entered stage right, starry-eyed with promises that children and youth would discover concepts in history, economics, geography, and other social studies, becoming critical thinkers just like scientists. Academics and funders, of course, made mistakes, and the internal and external conflicts began to gather on the stage as Act I ended.[14]

Act II—The Conflict

In Act II, conflicts between academics over the place that history should have in the social studies curriculum split both social scientists and the practitioners who were having trouble implementing the new materials. Squabbles between funders and grantees over resources drew media attention as new lessons and textbooks entered classrooms. Not only did the new materials prove hard to put into classroom practice, but their use also gave rise to conflict as parents and critics questioned the content; for instance, the example I mentioned above where religious groups in Southern and rural districts proved antagonistic to the idea that their children should learn customs practiced by Netsilik Eskimos.[15]

These Act II conflicts are anchored in the different ways social studies reformers believed students could become "good" citizens.[16] These ideas go back to the 1920s, when New History courses entered the curriculum. From the various strategies for achieving the political purpose of transmitting citizenship, three traditions of teaching and content selection have competed with one another in how experts and practitioners view teaching the social studies in general and history in particular, then and now.[17]

First, there is the sturdiest tradition—of transmitting knowledge directly to teach citizenship. For example, teaching history as a chronological story providing both knowledge of founding documents and transmitting values including a reasoned pride in country will get students to become "good citizens." Direct teaching of citizenship guides content selection and can be achieved pedagogically through time-honored lectures and worksheets or analytic skills of parsing primary sources and interpreting documents or combinations of approaches. Whichever way teaching occurs, conveying to students love of country and the ideals and daily practices of good citizenship is central to this strategy.

Another way of achieving good citizenship was through teaching students how historians and social scientists create knowledge. Reformers in this camp believed that students learn to think clearly in daily life when they learn the ways social scientists use varied sources, ask different questions, and frame problems. As Edwin Fenton put it decades later, "How can we teach students to think like historians?" The tradition can be traced back to the efforts of James Harvey Robinson, Charles Beard, and other historians at the turn of the twentieth century. Implicit in this tradition is that as students learn how historians deal with sources and interpret the past, children and youth will develop strong feelings for the nation and its ideals.[18]

Advocates of citizenship transmission point out that students mimicking social scientists and historians miss the all-important content of America's founding documents and the lives of the individuals whose efforts created and sustained the nation over the centuries. In other words, in the press toward teaching students how academics create knowledge, the ideals of the nation and patriotism—the all-important content of what happened and who did what—get short shrift.

The third strategy for turning children and youth into good citizens is reflective inquiry. Barr, Barth, and Shermis defined reflective inquiry as a way of teaching citizenship as follows:

> Inquiry as a method means that a teacher and his students will identify a problem that is of considerable concern to them—and to our society—and that relevant facts and values will be examined in light of criteria.[19]

The heart of the definition is the notion that as both teacher and students inquire about relevant student-framed problems, students will acquire decision-making skills. Content selection crosses disciplinary boundaries in as educators look for problems that are "personally sensed" by students and "socially shared" (e.g., racial discrimination, pollution, crime, climate change, poverty, urban congestion). Teachers within this tradition draw from varied materials and multiple pedagogies ranging from lectures and guided discussions to individual and group projects. Champions of this approach assume that as students acquire decision-making and problem-solving skills, they will be learning the practical skills that make good citizens.

Here again, advocates of citizenship transmission argue that student-framed problems may miss the essential facts of how the nation was founded, grew, and became a world power in just over a century. In the same way they disparage the tradition of students learning how social scientists and historians practice their craft, critics point to the inquiry process of learning as pushing aside the fundamental knowledge about their past that all Americans must know and take pride in.

Among historians and advocates for social studies, these traditions of conveying content and skills shared the same purpose—that students would become good citizens—but the pedagogical strategies for achieving that purpose diverged and competed with one another over the decades, and continue to produce conflict to this day.[20]

All three social studies traditions of teaching have attracted professional attention over the century. Although sometimes merging into one another, they have also been the grounds for disagreements over how best to teach history to achieve citizenship. The various approaches flowered into the New History movements in the opening decades of the twentieth century and the New Social Studies in the 1960s. In each instance, these contending ideas triggered discord among social studies advocates and discipline-bound academics. By the end of Act II, the conflicts are in full bloom and resolution seems distant.[21]

Act III—Resolution?

Act III traditionally resolves the conflicts and ends with a restoration of order. In the NSS story, though, there is no coming together, no reconciliation between contending factions over which purpose-embedded tradition for teaching history and social studies should be primary. Act III ends badly—the "resolution" of this play is the end of conflict brought about by the ultimate downfall of NSS (a "tragic hero," if you will) but not the end of the wars.

Continued friction between historians, social studies experts, and social scientists over the proper place of history in the curriculum, evident since the introduction of the subject in the 1920s, persisted into the 1970s. Persistent criticism of teachers as not being fully prepared in social science disciplines, especially history, was yet another chorus heard repeatedly during these years. These tensions went unresolved. Testy exchanges between academics, policymakers, and practitioners worsened as disappointing data on classroom use of project materials emerged.[22]

According to national surveys, case studies, and reviews of the research literature covering the years 1955–1975, only 10–20 percent of social studies teachers used NSS materials in their classrooms. And when it came to inquiry teaching this national report concluded:

> Teachers believe that inquiry teaching is too demanding of students and an unproductive use of instructional time. Transmission of knowledge is important to teachers, with content to be used to socialize students as good citizens. Socialization to do well in succeeding years of school is also viewed as important. Parents and teachers

share these views, so teachers rarely teach about issues controversial in the community.[23]

By the late 1970s, the downward trajectory of their use in classrooms led to NSS materials being dumped into closets. Hardbound, three-pound textbooks that were the norm for most social studies teachers even at the height of enthusiasm for the New Social Studies replaced lighter, softbound NSS materials. By the end of the 1970s, researchers and practitioners had relegated the New Social Studies to the dustbin of school reforms as new ones gained the political spotlight.[24]

Altogether, the unyielding rhetorical tensions between competing traditions went unresolved while classroom practice, as the available evidence showed, crowned the political tradition of direct transmission of citizenship the winner. The swift exit of the New Social Studies from classrooms within a decade ends Act III, leaving the stage empty and the audience ready for the next uneasy conflict.

WHY DID THE NEW SOCIAL STUDIES END SO BADLY?

A number of highly visible participants in the movement have reflected on what happened in that glorious decade of sheer energy, ample funds, and ceaseless efforts by academics, curriculum experts, policymakers, and teachers to alter history and social studies curriculum and classroom lessons. In reading these retrospectives on the demise of the New Social Studies, I have found, in light of earlier curricular reforms, the following reasons to be persuasive.[25]

- Top-down development of curricula and materials aimed at high-performing students left most classroom teachers and their students in the lurch. The concepts, sophisticated language, and high reading levels had typical elementary and secondary school teachers scrambling, since they often lacked in-depth preparation in the discipline they taught and worked with students who had a checkered range of reading, thinking, and writing skills.

- Curriculum developers ignored students' needs and context. Concentrating on curriculum goals stressing the structure of a discipline and deep inquiry into topics ignored two staples that curriculum developers historically have used to generate new materials: attention to students' psychological and emotional needs and their social interests; content mirroring the economic, social, and political context in which students lived.
- Classroom teachers were neglected by those developing and piloting curriculum materials and preparing teachers to use these lessons. Instead, materials were created "for" teachers, went largely unpiloted, and did not include sustained teacher training.
- Finally, the New Social Studies was overwhelmed by a cascade of political and social changes as the 1960s unfolded: the ever-expanding war in Vietnam, urban riots triggered by clashes between blacks and police, the assassinations of John F. Kennedy and Martin Luther King Jr., and cultural shifts prompted by youth experimentation in lifestyles that challenged mainstream US values. Because schools are thoroughly embedded in the larger society, these dramatic events spilled over into urban and suburban schools throughout the decade making NSS efforts to reform social studies content and instruction seem irrelevant in comparison.[26]

Even with the expiration date stamped clearly on the New Social Studies at Act III, remnants of the movement persisted across scattered classrooms. A small minority of teachers initially trained in NSS materials continued to teach the history units and lessons for decades, although course titles may have changed.[27]

Traces existed not only in tattered NSS textbooks and well-thumbed materials a half-century old but also in commitments some teachers, curriculum specialists, and academics had made to the social science and reflective inquiry traditions, especially in how historians and social scientists questioned sources, sorted out reliable from unreliable accounts, and interpreted the past. These adherents, however, were only a tiny fraction of those engaged daily in teaching history and social studies as reforms swept across US schools in the following decades. But of course, the end of these reforms did not halt the next generation of reformers to summon public schools to solve other domestic and foreign troubles.[28]

THE WAR OVER NATIONAL HISTORY STANDARDS, 1990S–PRESENT

Older readers will remember the Back-to-Basics movement in the 1970s; the raising of graduation requirements in the 1980s; and the standards, testing, and accountability movement, incubated in the late-1980s, that has flourished since the mid-1990s. In those latter decades, threats to economic vitality and market share in global competition, according to policy elites, posed mortal threats to the livelihoods of all Americans. These school reforms, decade after decade—a fine display of political theater—included repeated calls for curriculum changes in academic subjects.[29]

Thus, in the 1980s and 1990s, responding to these global economic threats, another generation of reform-minded civic and business leaders, professional associations and foundation-funded groups pushing math- and science-laden curriculum signaled the nation that major upgrades in academic subjects were under way. Solving the current serious economic problems, reformers claimed, required establishing higher curriculum standards, expanding standardized tests, and holding schools, teachers, and students responsible for grasping new academic content and skills.[30]

Again, history and its sister subjects were largely ignored in the initial national reform movements. As in earlier decades, history teaching was Cinderella awaiting her prince. And the prince arrived in the early 1990s, national history standards in hand. Lo and behold!—historians and social studies educators launched another effort to revive the teaching of history in K–12 schools. As before, academic historians pronounced the subject to be in a sorry state, hardly visible in the curriculum and receding even more in classrooms.

As before, renewed interest in history and the social sciences burst into a war enacted in the political theater over content and skills in the mid-1990s. Within a few years, interest in the traditions of social science and reflective inquiry experienced a renaissance, mirroring in many respects the NSS of two generations earlier.[31]

Unlike the New Social Studies researchers, however, academics two decades later received federal and state grants not to run projects or develop classroom materials but for creating national (and voluntary) history standards. The debut of national standards, however, became a disastrous smashup that buried the idea of even voluntary history standards. In the backwash of that failure, a small movement, again led by academics, to develop history materials and lessons for teachers began and has thrived since.

If this sounds like political theater again, or yet another three-act play, that would be correct. Act I describes the years after the New Social Studies exited the stage and the gradual renewal of attention to history as a subject in the late 1980s and early 1990s, and the budding of another effort to transform the teaching of history. Act II becomes the high-profile confrontation over the national history standards and their wreckage; at the beginning of Act III the New, New History starts to grow on the blasted earth. Act III, however, is only beginning. Whether the slow formation of the New, New History will persist, and whether it will resolve the tensions so evident in the previous act, I do not know.

Act I begins with the withering of the New Social Studies in the 1970s. Events pick up with the publication of the *Nation at Risk* report in 1983 and its Chicken Little pronouncement ("The sky is falling!") that US public schools were damaging the economy. That message led to a national movement for raising graduation standards, introducing better tests, and holding schools responsible for making improvements. In response to that message, another new (maybe "new" should be in quotation marks at this point) round of national and state math, science, and history standards appeared throughout the 1980s causing near-panic among academics, curriculum specialists, policymakers, and, of course, teachers over both the content and pedagogies recommended within each subject's standards.[32]

By the end of the 1980s, historians and social scientists had said "me, too" and joined the growing movement to raise the low profile of history in the social studies, stressing that these subjects would produce the next generation of critical thinkers, problem solvers, and engaged citizens.

To establish publicly how mediocre history had become as an academic subject, advocates of reforming history standards pointed to students' low performance on national and international tests and the low history requirements for high school graduation. The establishment of the Bradley Commission on History in the Schools in 1987 stirred great interest among historians and K–12 educators in transforming both content and the direction of history instruction for the next decade. Familiar questions about the central purpose of citizenship and contentious pedagogical debates over traditions in the social studies arose again. Predictably, all-too-familiar struggles erupted over a well-funded effort to create national history standards in the early 1990s, which culminated in another "culture war" over what historical content is appropriate for students to study.[33]

Both participants and researchers have told the story behind the Senate voting 99-1 in favor of a resolution condemning new history standards produced by historians, curriculum specialists, and teachers.[34] Senator Slade Gorton (R-WA) summed up the essence of the conflict over what content from the past should students learn by asking his colleagues:

> Is it a more important part of our Nation's history for our children to study—George Washington or Bart Simpson?... With this set of standards, our students will not be expected to know George Washington

from the man in the Moon. According to this set of standards, American democracy rests on the same moral footing as the Soviet Union's totalitarian dictatorship.[35]

Popular radio show host Rush Limbaugh chimed in with his rebuke of the standards' focus on historical thinking and interpreting the past by telling his listeners: "History is real simple. You know what history is? It's what happened." The authors of the standards, he went on, "try to skew history" by saying "Well, let's interpret what happened because we can't find the truth in facts ... So let's change the interpretation a little bit so that it will be the way we wished it were."[36]

What Gorton and Limbaugh wanted students to learn was a commemorative version of the past—the familiar *heritage* view—rather than one where students apply historical thinking. Different traditions of teaching history conflicted on a national stage.

Historian Gary Nash, who with his colleagues had drafted the standards, stated the issue this way:

> Should classrooms emphasize the continuing story of America's struggle to form a "more perfect union," a narrative that involved a good deal of jostling, elbowing, and bargaining among contending groups? A story that included political tumult, labor strife, racial conflict, and civil war? Or should the curriculum focus on successes, achievements, and ideals, on stories designed to infuse young Americans with patriotism and sentiments of loyalty toward prevailing institutions, traditions, and values?[37]

Nash and his colleagues wanted content invested with historical thinking skills (grasp of chronology, differentiating between facts and interpretations, analyzing sources, considering multiple perspectives, and so on) and students who could craft meaning from the past. Or as a sympathetic congressman noted: "History isn't like math where two plus two equals four. It's a lot more than facts, and they don't always add up to the same sum."[38]

Those who created the new history standards also wanted students to be patriotic, but not in the traditional sense of unquestioned loyalty to the United States. They wanted a "democratic patriotism" that saw the past as a struggle to put constitutional and Judeo-Christian ideals into practice.[39] As teacher union leader Al Shanker, a member of one group that advised Nash and his colleagues, put it:

> The struggle to define our democracy still continues and it will as long as our country does. It has helped turn abstract principles like equity, justice, individual rights and equality of opportunity into political movements, laws, programs, and institutions—concrete things. And if our children walk away from an American history course without understanding this, the history they have studied is a travesty.[40]

The conflict over what students need to know and how they should study the past and its political purpose—continuing a tradition of good citizenship—is, of course, the same battle fought by earlier generations of historians, teachers, and voters.

Another way to frame those conflicting views of teaching, struggles revived by the New Social Studies of the 1960s and again in the 1990s, is to consolidate the contending ways of teaching into the *heritage* and *historical* approaches to creating a usable past for students to learn.

The *heritage* approach uses the past to recreate the present to "tell ourselves who we are, where we are from, and to what we belong."[41] Obvious examples of the *heritage* purpose at work in schools are the US flag in every classroom and daily recital of the Pledge of Allegiance. Beyond these are lessons that focus on the Founding Fathers of the Revolutionary period and heroes such as Davy Crockett, Abraham Lincoln, Frederick Douglass, and Susan B. Anthony to gather from the past a legacy that all American students should know. In the hands of some legislators (recall Slade Gorton), pundits (recall Rush Limbaugh), textbook authors, and teachers, the *heritage* purpose can be simplified to an official story encased in state standards and content aimed at inspiring pride in the United States, loyalty toward country, and the overall purpose of inculcating "good" citizenship.

In mapping out their strategies for teaching history, champions of the *heritage* approach sought to transmit their version of citizenship.

The key word is *transmit*, which is often translated to mean teacher lectures, student note-taking, and teacher-directed lessons. The fact, however, is that such transmitting can be done through different pedagogical approaches. That diversity in pedagogies became clear with a decade of federally funded Teaching American History grants.[42]

The *heritage* strategy became official federal policy in 2001 with the passage of Teaching American History (TAH) legislation sponsored by Senator Robert Byrd (D-WV). The law made available over $120 million dollars a year to universities and school districts. The monies were to be used to teach US history and improve student achievement. As the Federal Register put it:

> Students who know and appreciate the great ideas of American history are more likely to understand and exercise their civic rights and responsibilities. Their understanding of traditional American history will be enhanced if teachers make the study of history more exciting, interesting, and engaging. Students need teachers who have a thorough understanding of American history as a separate subject within the core curriculum, and incorporate into their teaching effective strategies to help students learn.[43]

With over a thousand TAH grants made in nearly a decade, amounting to almost $900 million, many universities and school districts worked with thousands of veteran and novice teachers across the country. Anecdotally, teachers appreciated the opportunities and gave positive marks to university professors for increasing their historical knowledge and opportunities to develop lessons in summer and year-long TAH programs. While committed to the heritage approach, TAH programs across the country differed in combining different social studies traditions (e.g., citizenship transmission and how social scientists and historians practice their discipline).

When it comes to evaluating these efforts over a decade, however, the verdict was damning. The external evaluators who examined sixteen TAH programs found no evidence that they raised student achievement or that teachers used the class-friendly lessons developed by TAH after they returned to their schools or that project directors created district networks of teachers to implement lessons.[44]

The *heritage* approach has—then and now—contended with the *historical* approach. This approach is based on the idea that history is not a single account of the past but many accounts. The goal is to equip students with the intellectual and academic skills that historians and citizens use daily. Historians seek verifiable truth as they sift evidence to answer questions and interpret what happened in the past; they reduce bias in their accounts by closely examining their own values as they read and analyze sources.

In history classrooms, it means that students investigate the past through different sources and produce stories and analyses from many accounts consistent with the evidence they have before them. In doing so, they gain the skills of sniffing out biased sources, evaluating documents, and providing multiple perspectives on an event or person. They think, write, and discuss different views of what happened. Students learn that history is an interpretation of the past, not a telegram that yesteryear has wired to the present. In short, they become historically literate.[45] In other words, unlike the heritage purpose of transmitting a national story that heightens students' appreciation of country, the historical approach combines the purposes of working as historians do and engaging in reflective inquiry. Champions of the historical approach claimed that they helped students become "good" citizens this way.

Of course, these competing aims in teaching history are an incarnation of that paradox facing public schools of having both to conserve community beliefs, values, and traditions and simultaneously prepare student with the knowledge and skills to change those very same traditions, values, and beliefs.[46]

This *historical* approach was integrated into those standards denounced by the Senate and eventually junked in the mid-1990s. But the resounding defeat of the new history standards in 1995 was hardly the end of the tensions between the *heritage* and *historical* approaches to teaching children and youth. An echo of that media-hyped conflict was heard in 2014 after the Educational Testing Service (ETS) announced that it had revised the "Framework and Examination" for the Advanced Placement US History course. AP courses in history exemplify the *historical* approach to teaching the subject with students handling primary sources ("document-based questions"), interpreting facts and writing accounts that interpret the past. ETS continued this emphasis by offering in the framework more flexibility in choice of content and more focus on analyzing the Declaration of Independence, the Constitution, and other "founding" documents than in the previous course. There were other content changes that reflected local history. Overall, the new framework and test remained a testament to the historical approach.[47]

In Jefferson County, Colorado's second-largest school district, school board members Julie Williams and her colleagues, part of a politically conservative majority elected to the school board in 2013, objected to the new ETS Framework; the school board voted to have their own homegrown AP course for tenth-graders. The Williams-led majority on the five-member board said that the AP Framework

> ... rejects the history that has been taught in the country for generations. It has an emphasis on race, gender, class, ethnicity, grievance and American-bashing while simultaneously omitting the most basic structural and philosophical elements considered essential to the understanding of American History for generations.

Instead, an AP US history course needs to "present positive aspects of the United States and its heritage" and "promote citizenship, patriotism, essentials and benefits of the free enterprise system." Here was a reprise of the conflict over the new history standards that the US Senate had rejected nearly twenty years earlier.[48]

The board action triggered protests from over a thousand students, who staged various walk-outs and student protests over a ten-day period, protesting what they and supportive parents called censorship of content taught in schools. Throughout the county, there were heated school board meetings where parents on different sides of the issue tangled and raw feelings erupted about the proper content for the course in US history.[49]

Eventually, the Jefferson County protests died down. No war erupted. The conservative majority on the school board backed away from dumping the revised AP course and substituting their own. But the incident reveals anew that the *heritage* approach to history content remains alive among voters, taxpayers, parents, teachers, and students.[50]

THE NEW, NEW HISTORY

But as in many dramas confrontation and conflict are far from over. Even before the demise of the new history standards in 1995 and while protests erupted over the revised AP US history course twenty years later, efforts to have teachers and students use the *historical* approach had been incubating in university offices and classrooms across the United States. These efforts have emerged in what I call the *New, New History*.[51]

As with the New Social Studies, academics took the lead in stumping for the New, New History. This slow-growing movement, scattered as it is across the country, has thus far avoided the volatile struggles over which content to teach while keeping a low political profile in securing federal and private grants. Proponents of this approach—professors, social studies curriculum specialists, and classroom history teachers—have centered their attention on educating beginning teachers in the *historical* approach. They have as well created usable lessons that introduce students to historical thinking and writing textbooks that support this approach for novice and career teachers. Although groups offer instructional units similar to those created by the New Social Studies during the 1960s, the New, New History, goes well beyond those materials in using teacher-friendly digital lessons and assessments tailored to the age-graded school conditions that teachers face daily, a factor missing in the earlier movement.[52]

One of the leaders of this New, New History movement is Professor Sam Wineburg at Stanford University. Trained as an educational psychologist at Stanford in the late 1980s, Wineburg worked under the tutelage of Professor Lee Shulman, who, after receiving Carnegie Foundation grants to assess teaching and learning across subject areas, recruited able graduate students. Wineburg's peers included Suzanne Wilson and Pam Grossman, both of whom have also gone on to illustrious academic careers.[53]

Appointed assistant professor of educational psychology in 1989 at the University of Washington's school of education, Wineburg launched a career that garnered teaching awards and research grants. He worked with teachers in the Seattle public schools in various projects, including the initial materials used for getting students to read and think like historians. He published articles in both psychological and historical journals that generated even more grants. In 2002, he joined the faculty of Stanford's Graduate School of Education, working with doctoral students, beginning social studies teachers, historians, and psychologists. Wineburg's previous work with Roy Rosenzweig at George Mason University moved him toward incorporating digital historical sources into units and lessons for teachers to use.[54]

Wineburg expanded his agenda by starting the Stanford History Education Group (SHEG). His doctoral students designed lessons that dipped into primary and secondary sources, showing teachers and students how to read and think like historians. One doctoral student developed document-based lessons on the Civil War for middle school teachers in San Francisco and in her dissertation designed an intervention for history teachers in five high schools. These ideas and practices of historians also found a home in the Curriculum and Instruction courses that he and doctoral students taught for entry-level social studies teachers in the Graduate School of Education. Finally, Wineburg created a network of partners and resources—including the Library of Congress, American Historical Association, Organization of American Historians, National Council for the Social Studies—that covered both the discipline and teachers across the country.[55]

From the collaborative work with doctoral students and teachers, SHEG increased production of teacher-friendly lessons in US history and world history demonstrating how historians read documents, evaluate sources, and interpret historical events ranging from the role Pocahontas played in seventeenth-century colonial America to Japan's taking of Nanking, China, in 1937. Posted on the Internet, these lessons could be downloaded for free. In early 2015, SHEG topped 2 million downloads. And it has added coaching services and professional development workshops for social studies teachers in San Francisco, Los Angeles city schools, and Lincoln, Nebraska.[56]

With recognized standing in psychology and history, Wineburg bridges the worlds of research and classroom practice. Moreover, he is familiar with the earlier movements in the social studies—the New History and the New Social Studies—as well as the contemporary New, New History. Rarely, indeed, can scholars bridge disciplines and practice while retaining a deep familiarity with past and present social studies reform efforts.

Wineburg's comparisons and contrasts to the New, New History with the New Social Studies of a half-century earlier offers glimpses of how he sees the past and present moments in history education:

> As for the relation between Reading like a Historian and the New Social Studies, obviously there's a great deal of overlap. I cut my teeth on the Amherst history project materials and Charles Seller's *As It Happened*, a textbook made up of almost exclusively primary sources. The whole issue of inquiry comes from the movement. So, in a sense, we owe a tremendous debt to our predecessors.

Wineburg has also pointed out the differences between NSS and his current efforts:

> First, all of our materials come with extensive scaffolding. We "tamper" with history . . . by actually changing primary sources (and still calling them "primary"). We built this approach in high schools in San Francisco's Mission [district] where 99% of the kids are native Spanish speakers and reading at 4th or 5th grade levels in the eleventh grade but often *thinking* [original italics] at college levels . . . So our approach from the start had to deal with the reality of teachers in urban schools. Our lessons don't go for a week either; each is tailored

to a fifty-minute class. And we recognize that teachers simply don't have the time to surf the net in search of documents or the appropriate graphic organizers to accompany a lesson. We provide everything.

Second, the New Social Studies did little in terms of testing their ideas in any kind of formal research setting. Lots of great stories; not much by way of rigorous evaluation. We field tested this work in San Francisco using a quasi-experimental design. And we continue in on-going field testing.

Third, we focus on explicit teaching of cognitive skills in a way that would have been foreign to the "discovery" ethos of the 60s. I am a Vygotskian [a Russian psychologist and researcher who believed that children learn through social interaction] by heart and temperament.[57] We provide teachers with guidance in how to explicitly model the cognitive skills they use when they interpret a document. We don't want classrooms to [be] guessing games. If students don't know how to "source" a document, their teachers need to *model* [original italics] it for them . . . making their own thoughts and hunches audible so that kids can have an explicit model of what a skilled reader does with a difficult text before trying to decode it themselves.

Fourth, we have taken up the issue of . . . formative assessment. When I codirected the DOE's [US Department of Education] National History Education Clearinghouse, I got into a lot of *hot water* [original italics] when I basically blew the whistle on Teaching American History grants that were dedicated to "critical document analysis" but then were testing kids with multiple choice items on battles of the Revolutionary War. It seemed like their two only options in the social studies testing world [were] multiple choice tests or 10–12 DBQs [document-based questions]. Neither was a useful tool for quick on-going formative assessment that gave teachers insight into what their kids were thinking and the processes they used. So with Rich [Shavelson] and Ed [Haertel]'s help, I took up the assessment mantle . . . That, too, is different from the New Social Studies.[58]

In citing the similarities and differences between SHEG and the the New Social Studies, Wineburg made certain critical decisions in developing coaching and materials in order to extend their use in classrooms longer than NSS materials lasted.

The first strategic decision Wineburg mentioned is shaping SHEG materials to the urban teacher's work conditions within age-graded schools, the students they face daily, and the overwhelming demands of meeting standards, accountability, and testing requirements. He and his colleagues adapted lessons to workplace conditions. In effect, he acknowledged the deep grammar of schooling shaping teacher behavior and worked within its boundaries.[59]

As he points out, designing well-scaffolded fifty-minute lessons for teachers to use with students reading on different levels diverged from NSS leaders decades earlier who, more often than not, pitched their secondary school materials to "able" students (with the exception of Edwin Fenton, who realized that error in 1965 and launched his inaptly named "slow learner" project). In addition, Wineburg built in formative assessments and highly interactive digital materials within SHEG lessons, adding further appeal to teachers.[60]

Another strategic decision was to align the lessons to the Common Core state standards in literacy. Wineburg realized that if SHEG lessons—containing cognitive skills embedded in how historians analyze sources, detect bias, and interpret facts—were to last longer than the NSS materials had, they had to be tightly coupled to the Common Core standards' focus on literacy skills. Literacy improvement was built into most of the skills (e.g., how to source a document, how to corroborate the accuracy of a source) contained in SHEG-produced lessons. By fastening these materials to the standards' literacy requirements and their accompanying tests, chances of a longer life span for this *historical* approach to teaching increased.[61]

Beyond strategic decisions, Wineburg made a personal decision in teaching, writing, and scholarship. Over the past few years, he has decided to reach beyond the specialized (and small) audiences he had written for in psychology and history journals to the larger audience of social studies teachers. In speeches and articles, Wineburg talked about his "crisis of faith" in academic research, making clear that he no longer believed published research in peer-reviewed journals with readership in the low thousands would improve teaching practices. Working more directly with schools and teachers was a new direction he charted for himself and SHEG.[62]

Whether all of these strategic and tactical decisions will sustain SHEG lessons for more than a few years, I cannot say. Nor can I say anything about the effects of these lessons on students, since no studies have yet been done to determine their effectiveness. I can say that Wineburg and his colleagues have digested the lessons from the earlier generation of NSS reformers and have made adaptations that have a reasonable chance of continued use by history teachers. The curtain has fallen on Act II, and Act III has begun. Resolution of the conflicts appear in the New, New History. Whether it will persist and end the play or shatter in the years to come is too early to say. If the past has roots in the present, count on another play on the teaching of history being staged.

After tracing the unfolding of the content and teaching of history and the social studies and efforts to reform both in the past century, I return to history classrooms at Glenville and Cardozo High Schools in 2013–2014. In chapters 4 and 5, I describe and analyze how much continuity and change in the content and pedagogy of history had occurred in these schools and classrooms over the past half-century.

In chapter 6, I assess the degree to which the *historical* approach has taken hold in history and social studies classrooms in US schools. Then, after comparing what has occurred in both high schools during the past five decades, I answer the central question of this book: *What has changed and what has remained the same in the content and pedagogy of high school history over the past half-century?*

History Teaching Now— Glenville High School

IN THE CLASSROOM AT GLENVILLE, PART 1

World History with Gary Hart

It is 8:00 a.m., and the bell has rung for first class of a ten-period school day. Ninth-graders trickle into their world history classroom in ones and twos. They wait to sign in on a sheet located on a desk near the door. The teacher who is standing at the door asks one student to remove his hat. He does. By the time the tardy chimes ring, there are twelve students in the class. In the next ten minutes, seven more students wander in. One student is using his mobile phone. The teacher says, "We can do this the easy way or the hard way. Put it away now, or I will take it and return it to you at 2:30." The student pockets the phone.[1]

On the front whiteboard, veteran history teacher Gary Hart[2] has written the following:

- History standard 9.1.C: Analyze the reasons that countries gained control of territory through imperialism and the impact on people living in the territory that was controlled.[3]
- Read pp. 345–350.

Underneath the history standard are three questions:

1. What is racism?
2. What is social Darwinism?
3. Who is Shaka?

On a bulletin board fixed to the back wall, Hart has posted student papers with perfect scores on a quiz of multiple-choice questions. Near the teacher's desk is a small room, almost a closet, with a placard over the door saying "Fitting Room"—a holdover from the days when Glenville had a full array of vocational courses and this had been the Home Economics Clothing room. Desks are arranged in clusters of four so that students face one another. As students come in, they sit with friends or alone. The teacher's desk is in the center rear of the room, facing the whiteboards. Except for the laptop on the teacher's desk, there are no other computers in the room.

At 8:10, Hart, a stocky six-foot-tall man in his early fifties, wearing a brown suit with a brown tie and a beige shirt, sits on a stool in the center of room and says, "Ladies and gentlemen, please copy down the three sentences on the board. They will be on the test Wednesday." About half of the class takes notebooks from their backpacks or from the metal racks underneath their desks. Three students ask classmates for sheets of paper and pens. After waiting a few minutes for students to write down the questions, Hart asks: "Now, ladies and gentlemen, what is the answer to the first question?"

No one answers. He says, "We talked about this on Friday. Look at your notes." Two students are resting their heads on the desks. On one side of the room, four are talking to one another as the teacher waits for a response. Hart turns to the four chatting students and asks, "Are we working or talking?" No response from any of the four; they continue to talk.

Hart then asks students to turn to pages 345–350 of the textbook, copies of which are stored on the metal racks below the seat of each desk chair.[4] He directs them to answer the three questions on the board and complete a one-page worksheet that he has copied from the teachers' manual for the text. At this point in the lesson, nearly fifteen minutes after the tardy chime has rung, and with twenty-five minutes left to the period, there are nineteen students.

Hart passes out the worksheets, and three-quarters of the students retrieve their books, open them to the assigned pages, and begin working on either the three questions on the whiteboard or filling in answers to the six questions on the worksheet, "Imperialism Case Study: Nigeria." In a genial manner, Hart walks around, helping individual students. At one point, he turns again to the four students chattering to one another and says, "I'm hearing a hen party." They stop talking and begin writing, but resume their conversation after two minutes. Hart then moves one of the four students—who offers no opposition—to a desk next to me at the rear of the classroom.

Within five minutes, all the students, except for the three still talking to one another, are answering questions on the whiteboard and filling in the worksheet. The quiet is shattered by an announcement from the principal's office about end-of-school day sport activities.[5] After the interruption, Hart threads his way among the clustered desks to see how individual students are doing and if they have questions. Three do. He responds quietly and directly to each of their questions.

It is now 8:35, and Hart tells the class: "OK, the bell is about to ring in a few minutes. Put your books under the desks." He repeats this three times. When the chimes ring, Hart stands at the door collecting completed worksheets and answers to the whiteboard questions.

Hart teaches three classes of world history to ninth-graders and one US history course for tenth-graders between 8:00 and 11:00 a.m.[6] He takes a lunch period, then teaches two more world history classes in the afternoon. He has taught in the Cleveland schools for sixteen years, the last eight at Glenville, from which he graduated in the mid-1970s. Between classes, Hart told me about his students and the school:

> The biggest problem I have is the tardies. There are no consequences for them. They just show up with a pass from the office. Just a few days ago, I called a mom about her daughter, who was often late to

class and was acting out in class. She told me that her daughter was my responsibility between 8 and 2:30. She then hung up on me.

Hart complained about the pressure he feels from the administration on turning in reports—"more paperwork now than ever before"—and the pressure of being evaluated by the principal when he has to teach a lesson and meet with the principal afterward, adding that 50 percent of his evaluated performance is based on student test scores on the Ohio Graduation Test.[7]

He also told me about his four-times-a-year pizza and root beer parties for students who earned As and Bs. It is an "invitation only" after-school party, open only to students who receive printed invitations. His wife takes care of the pizza and he handles security at the door.

African American History with Mike Allison

Down the corridor from Hart is Mike Allison, who teaches African American History and US Government. The lesson I will be observing today is part of the unit he teaches on the civil rights movement.[8]

Standing in the hallway outside of his classroom—a school policy as students move from one class to another—the 5'11"<<COMP: Use foot and inch marks, not quotation marks>>Allison sports a gray-flecked goatee, mustache, and a ponytail of braided dreadlocks. He is wearing a lavender tie on a patterned light-purple shirt with dark-gray cargo pants. A lean man in his mid-fifties, he has taught in the district for thirty-six years, twenty-eight of which have been at Glenville. He is friendly with students as they pass by, calling many by name or "sister" and "brother." Many students say "hi" back, wave, bump fists, or shake hands.

As the tardy chimes sound, Allison closes the door and enters a bright, large classroom (once the Commercial Art room). On the wall behind the teacher's desk in one corner of the room is a large bulletin board filled with photos of students. As in Hart's classroom, the only computer device in the room is the laptop on Allison's desk. On the opposite wall is a glass-enclosed case displaying photos of famous individuals and events in the civil rights movement in the 1960s. Student desks are arranged in a horseshoe. Allison sits at a student desk in the center of the horseshoe with a slide carousel projector cued up for the day's lesson.

According to Allison's records, twenty students are enrolled in the course. When the tardy chimes ring, there are three students in the class. Within ten minutes, there are four more. Five minutes before the end of the period, an eighth student enters.

He begins with a game he invented. To each of the three students present, he passes out four cards with questions and answers on events during the 1950s and 1960s. Then one student asks a question and another student has to figure out which of the answers on the four cards he or she has is the correct one. As a tardy student enters, Allison pauses and asks, "Are you ready to learn, brother?" He then gives the latecomer the four cards and explains the game quickly. The students are immediately involved, and the group expands to eight as latecomers arrive. All eight use the Q & A on their cards as they trade questions and answers.

Allison sits close to the students, listening and from time to time coaching those who are having difficulty in either providing an answer or matching the right one to the question asked. For example, one question on affirmative action has the students stumped. Allison gives an example of one of his students who applied to Clark University in Atlanta, a historically black institution, and Akron University (about forty miles from Cleveland), a largely white institution. Akron had encouraged black students to apply and, in the past decade, had selected more and more black applicants. One student grasps the example and chooses "affirmative action"—the answer on one of his four cards. In the midst of the game, a PA announcement interrupts the lesson, telling teachers that they must turn in a letter of commitment that day if they want to reapply for their position next year (I'll come back to this issue below). After the interruption, the game continues.[9]

Allison turns to the slide carousel. The first slide he projects on a pull-down screen is labeled: "You Can't Kill an Idea." In rapid-fire questions, he asks: "What does that mean?" After a few scattered responses, he tries another question: "What one word captures the civil rights movement?" Students yell out answers such as: "Marches." "Protests." "Freedom." "Riots." "Equality." "Rights." "Prejudice." Allison picks "freedom" and "equality," and says these are what the movement was about.

He then advances the slides, and a photo of a mostly empty bus with one black woman sitting in it appears on the screen. He asks: "What is this picture about?" Students offer different details about the black woman (age, color, tired look on her face, etc.), the white bus driver (age, color, facial features, etc.), and the fact that no one else is on bus. Allison then asks one student, "Sister, what is this picture depicting?" Before she answers, he admonishes the others: "No one else help her." She answers, "Bus boycott," and he smiles.

He then goes to next slide, which shows a photo of angry white women, men, and students yelling at and spitting on fifteen-year-old Elizabeth Eckford, one of the Little Rock Nine black students who entered Little Rock (Arkansas) High School after in 1957. By this time, a eighth student has entered the classroom. Allison asks the students what the photo depicts. Students call out: "She looks calm," "White people are sure angry at her," "Except for her, there are no other black people around." Allison points out that Eckford was their age. He keeps students' attention focused on photo as they supply additional details. He then asks, "What would you do if there were hundreds of people screaming and spitting at you?" The students' chorus of responses ranges from running away from crowd to fighting back to crying to doing what Eckford did—not responding to crowd and walking silently toward the school entrance.

The teacher runs through more slides. One shows James Meredith, the first black student entering the University of Mississippi. None of the students recognizes Meredith; another shows a white child in a small crowd holding a sign that says, "Who Needs Niggers?" along with a painted swastika and Confederate flag. One of the students asks Allison about the swastika. He explains the symbol. Then he asks about the flag. No one in the room can identify the flag.

A slide comes up showing a black woman being arrested for entering a "whites only" library. Allison says to the class: "Listen, I can't get you to go to the city library, which is free and open to everybody." Another slide features two black athletes at the 1968 Olympics in Mexico City, with raised fists in a black power salute. Most of the students recognize the photo. A photo of Rosa Parks, all students identify. Ditto for the police photo—mug shot—of Malcolm X. When the photo of a 1963 crowd appears on the screen, students yell out in chorus "the March on Washington!" As a follow-up, Allison asks the eight students what the obelisk behind the marchers is. Some students shrug; others say, "I don't know." No one identifies the Washington Monument.

For each slide, Allison pokes, prods, and pushes students to offer details, and then segues to questions that seek the meaning of these different events during the civil rights movement. Effortlessly, he gave present-day examples that tied his students' experiences and knowledge to events a half-century ago.

By the end of the forty-minute period, all of the students, including latecomers, are thoroughly engaged with the Q&A over the slides. After the bell rings, two students move over to see the photos in Allison's glass case.[10]

The prevailing teacher-centeredness in the lessons and the variation in student response mirrored the teaching and student reactions I saw in my own teaching and that of colleagues at Glenville High School a half-century ago.[11] But despite the strong similarities in the way both teachers directed their lessons—what scholars have called teacher-centered instruction—there are marked differences in the degree of student engagement, teacher use of different activities and materials, and level of student-teacher rapport in these classes.

IN THE SCHOOL—THEN AND NOW

Hart's and Allison's classrooms offer a glimpse of teaching history in a contemporary big city high school. Any observer, however, would be foolish to generalize to the entire school from watching just two teachers teach only a half-dozen lessons. A smart observer would want to know more about the school setting itself (e.g., enrollments, organization, curriculum, extracurricular activities) and what events and factors in the school district (e.g., school board reforms, available resources) unfolded in the city, state, and nation that might also influence what teachers do or do not do in their lessons. A few of my observations, entering Glenville High School and walking the corridors, noting the daily routine, and attending a sports assembly offer an expanded view of what happened in school beyond lessons taught during the ten-period school day.

Security upon Entering and in the Halls

Security practices differed greatly from when I taught in the late 1950s and early 1960s. Now uniformed security aides monitor students and adults as they enter school, using a walk-through metal detector and an X-ray machine for backpacks, purses, and briefcases. Every visitor goes to the main office and signs an entry log, recording who is being seen, the time entered, and time exited. The visitor receives a stick-on badge and wears it for the entire day. Uniformed security aides with walkie-talkies patrol the hallways, telling students to get into classes, shepherding a few directly to the classroom, and asking for passes (signed either by an office aide or a teacher). The clear objective is insuring that students are in their classes. During lunchtime, non-uniformed aides monitor each of the three floors of the building, breaking up clumps of students and shooing them into their classrooms or sending them to the first-floor lunchroom, where they are supposed to stay until the end of the period.

School Routines

A half-century ago, when I taught at Glenville, the senior high school covered tenth through twelfth grades. Today, like other Cleveland high schools, Glenville is an age-graded ninth- through twelfth-grade school organized by departments where individual teachers have their own classrooms for daily lessons. The routine—the grammar of schooling—has not changed much in the fifty years since I taught at Glenville.[12] A bell schedule divides the school day into forty-minute segments and groups of students move from one classroom to another. Teachers and security aides constantly monitor hallways to keep order. In each class, the teacher is expected to manage the group of students and cover pre-scribed textbook content, then determine whether each student had learned the material. The school year is divided into nine-week seg-ments in which teachers evaluate student progress toward completion of the course that will count toward the award of a diploma at the end of four years.

Pervasiveness of Posters and Slogans

An observer walking the corridors would soon notice that the walls are covered with motivational posters. I do not recall any such post-ers a half-century ago. I trace the use of posters in urban high schools such as Glenville to the early 1980s, borrowing from the then prevalent corporate restructuring and reculturing movement aimed at making US companies more efficient and profitable.[13] In these years, civic and business leaders realized that minority youth would eventually become the majority in the labor market. These leaders saw in urban districts a direct analog of companies, where low-performing urban schools could be "restructured" and "recultured" to raise academic benchmarks and student achievement. Such improvements, these leaders believed, would help produce knowledgeable and skilled graduates who would contribute to the economy.

The Effective Schools movement in public schools arising in the late 1970s mirrored corporate efforts to improve profits—their bot-tom line. For schools, the "bottom line" was standardized test scores, high school graduation rates, and percentage of graduates attend-ing college. Research evidence on Effective Schools focused attention on the *correlates* of successful schools (as measured by student test scores). Researchers found common features in largely minority and poor schools where scores exceeded the predicted performance of such schools. They included:

- "The leadership of the principal who gave substantial attention to the quality of instruction;
- A pervasive and broadly understood instructional focus;
- An orderly, safe climate conducive to teaching and learning;
- Teacher behaviors that convey the expectation that all students are expected to obtain at least minimum mastery;
- The use of measures of pupil achievement as the basis for program evaluation."[14]

Eventually, the correlates of Effective Schools expanded to include "Climate of High Expectations" and "Clear and Focused Mission." Building a school culture for student achievement not only in classrooms but for the entire school gained increased attention. With growing dedication to higher test scores for low-performing students, efforts to make schools "effective" by following five, six, or more factors associated with high-achieving schools in low-income neighborhoods prompted many school leaders and teachers to display motivational posters in school hallways and classrooms.[15]

Sports and Academic Achievement

Posted slogans and posters aimed at spurring students to achieve academically may well enhance credibility if they accompany a winning high school sports program. Glenville has glittered in that arena, especially in interscholastic football. In November 2013, after I observed four history classes, I walked down the hallway and watched an assembly of a few hundred juniors and seniors sitting quietly and respectfully honoring the entire team, three of whom had through hard work, self-discipline, and proven skills, become national high school all-stars. Other members of the football team were on the stage. Many also had in hand university football scholarships. They were part of a team that had consistently beaten rivals, won the state championship, and was on the cusp of becoming state champions again. Coach Ted Ginn, a former high school aide, had slowly built a football powerhouse that had also become a pipeline to university.[16]

The disconnect between what values and habits I saw in Hart's ninth-grade world history classes and the values and habits displayed by members of the football team—who practiced daily, played in interscholastic competition, and had to pass academic classes to stay eligible for football—got me thinking: Does a school's athletic achievements and media attention lift school spirit and pride sufficiently to flow over non-athletes to work hard, stay academically focused, and persevere in school?

As one would expect of research on such a question, results are mixed. The record clearly shows that Glenville is a school that attracts aspiring footballers. But because I did not spend sufficient time in the school or visit a larger sample of classrooms, whether the hard work it takes to build winning teams—young men and women/basketball, baseball, football—spills over the rest of the school, particularly in kindling student engagement in classroom lessons, I do not know.

The brief and fragmented description of the current school setting sheds only partial light on the larger question of how Glenville today compares and contrasts to Glenville a half-century ago. To help fill in that larger picture, I offer table 4.1.

CHANGES IN THE CITY AND DISTRICT SCHOOLS: THE CONTEXT SHIFTS OVER A HALF-CENTURY

My observations of 2013–2014 and table 4.1 may help in portraying the immediate setting of Glenville High School, but ultimately fail to capture the larger contexts in which the school has been embedded for decades. These larger contexts have altered dramatically over the past half-century.

Principal, teachers, and the rest of the staff as well as students in 2013–2014, like an earlier generation of their peers, were responding to demographic, political, economic, and societal changes that had

TABLE 4.1   Summary of then and now at Glenville High School*

	1956–1963	2012–2013
School grades	10–12	9–12
Number of students	1,247 (1961)	719 (down from 1,663 in 2003)
▪ Minority (%)	99 (1963)	99
▪ Poor (%)	No measure of poverty used	85 (free and reduced-price lunch)
▪ Special education (%)	No category	30
Number of faculty	46 (1961)	24 (excluding counselors and special education teachers)
▪ Minority (%)	70 (1963)	67 (2003)
Graduation rate (%)	65 (author estimate)	53
College enrollment (%)	35–50 (author estimate)	40 (2011)
Curriculum offerings	Honors, College Prep, General, Vocational Tracks	Career and College Readiness Academy; Health and Sports Academy
Advanced Placement courses	NA	Biology, Calculus
School schedule	8 periods of 45 minutes	10 periods of 40 minutes
Technology access for teachers and students	Classroom blackboards, films and projectors, filmstrips and projectors, audio recorders	2–3 computer labs in school; 2–3 desktop computers of different ages in most classrooms; each teacher has laptop
Testing	No state tests; teacher-designed classroom tests	Ohio Graduation Test in reading, writing, math, science, and social studies; teacher-designed classroom tests
Consequences for low academic performance	Students failed the grade or subject; no consequences for school's low academic performance	Has not met state standard for Adequate Yearly Progress since 2005; school put on Academic Watch and then Academic Emergency; restructured twice, becoming an Investment School in 2013
Extracurricular programs	Sports (male only), drill team (female only), choral groups, National Honor Society, band, student newspaper, yearbook, drama, student government	Sports (male and female), Junior Reserve Officers Training Program (ROTC), Chess Team, Drill Team, student government, newspaper, Yearbook Club
Roaming in hallways	Few students in halls when classes were in session	Depending on period of day, students in hallways fairly constant during school day
Discipline	Paddling; referral to administration, and suspensions	Referral to administration, suspensions
School security	Teachers and administrators	Metal detectors at only entrance to school; uniformed security guards; school aides with walkie-talkies

*Information gathered from school report cards and data collected by Ohio State Department of Education for years 2003–2013 (http://www.city-data.com/school/glenville-high-school-oh.html); journal of author, 1961–1963; school archives of student newspapers and yearbooks (1956–1964); current schedule and other school documents collected in visits in November 2013 and May 2014.

occurred in the nation, city, and district school system. These profound changes shaped Glenville's organization, curriculum, and instruction and to some degree, how history was taught.

Demographic and Political Change in Cleveland

Like many Midwestern and East Coast cities in what media came to call the "Rust Belt," Cleveland began losing jobs and population in the 1950s as manufacturing companies moved or closed down. Between 1950 and 1970, for example, Cleveland's population went from 915,000 residents to 751,000, a nearly 20 percent drop. Subsequent decades would see even more Clevelanders exit the city for the suburbs, so that in 2010, just below 400,000 residents remained within city limits.[17]

While the overall city population shrank, its black population soared. The migration of blacks from the South after World War I resulted in one out of six Clevelanders being black in 1950. With the subsequent departure of whites for suburbs and further in-migration from the South, the black presence had more than doubled by 1970; and by 2000, the majority of the city's population was black.[18]

As the overall population declined and became increasingly minority, poverty increased as well. In 1970, median income of a Cleveland family was 24 percent less than the Cleveland metropolitan area— i.e., the suburbs in surrounding counties. In 1980, that income gap had widened to 85 percent. In these years, signs of poverty such as drug violations, crime, teenage births, and youth delinquencies increased dramatically.[19] Unsurprisingly, beginning in the mid-1960s, Cleveland experienced increased racial friction and riots over police treatment, low-quality housing, and unemployment in the Glenville and Hough neighborhoods.[20]

Schools reflected these demographic and social changes. The proportion of Cleveland schools' enrollment that was white fell from 41 percent in 1970 to 15 percent in 2012. By the latter year, 85 percent of Cleveland students were minority and 99 percent were classified as poor.[21]

In these decades, the loss of manufacturing jobs, population shifts, racial turmoil, fiscal crises, and state and city government takeovers of the district schools created a toxic mix of ingredients with which schools struggled.

Consider 1978. In that year, the city defaulted on its debt—the first major city in the US to do so since the Great Depression—the teachers' union went on a monthlong strike to protest low pay, and a federal judge who two years earlier had found the school district guilty of intentionally segregating its black students ordered mandatory busing to desegregate schools.[22]

Over the next fifteen years, another teacher strike erupted, the state put the district into fiscal receivership, and busing was implemented, all of which created severe shortages of funds, leading to staff cutbacks. When the district school board went to voters to raise taxes, Clevelanders repeatedly said no, causing even more budget cuts in services and staff. Unsurprisingly, superintendent turnover was like a whirling revolving door.

Desperate to attract companies to invest in Cleveland, business and civic leaders saw a high-performing school system as essential to bringing new firms and their employees to the City by the Lake. But the downward spiral continued. All of these events accelerated the out-migration of both white and black students, resulting in a much smaller and trouble-wracked school system—from a high of 154,000 students in the mid-1960s to 41,000 in 2012—crippled by insufficient funds, socially isolated schools, low academic achievement, high drop-out rates, and violence.

As fiscal difficulties accumulated, struggles over busing, low scores on state and national tests, and declining high school graduation rates added fuel to a growing movement for a mayoral takeover of the district. In 1995, federal judge Robert Krupansky, calling the school system "a rudderless ship mired in mismanagement, indecision, and fiscal irresponsibility," ordered the state to take over the district.[23]

After the state takeover, community leaders renewed calls for city hall to run the schools. Mayor Michael White, who had been elected in 1989 (his campaign slogan was: "Cleveland Is Open for Business"), watched in dismay as district schools deteriorated. He and the Cleveland delegation in the Ohio legislature lobbied for a law permitting mayoral control of schools.

In 1997, the Ohio legislature authorized Mayor White to take over the schools. It also voted in a voucher plan for the district and that Cleveland voters would vote again in 2002 to determine whether mayoral control would continue (voters did approve city control over schools in 2002, and it continues in 2015 under Mayor Frank Jackson, who has served since 2006). White dumped the old school board, appointed a new one, and picked a superintendent (now called a CEO).[24]

As noted, those political and organizational changes in the district produced a turnstile superintendency. Between 1975 and 1998, there had been seven superintendents, six of whom served for less than four years. Since 1998, when the state superintendent relinquished district control to Cleveland's elected mayor, there have been four superintendents (CEOs), including an interim appointment. Such rapid superintendent turnover over a quarter-century had weakened staff morale, reduced chances for earlier reforms to be sustained, and led to cynicism among civic and business leaders as well as parents about comprehensive plans and innovations that each new superintendent brought to the district. In these decades, judicial decisions, state mandates, and mayoral initiatives produced a torrent of reforms seeking to overhaul a low-performing, financially strapped district with shrinking enrollments in which few voters and parents had faith.[25]

Effects on Glenville High School

Now I come to a basic question: *To what degree and in what ways did these contextual changes in Cleveland and its schools over the past half-century affect Glenville High School?*

The demographic and governance changes and the cascade of reforms described above naturally influenced what happened at Glenville High School. Since macro-contexts matter in shaping the micro-context of the school and individual teachers' classrooms, I give a few examples to show how federal, state, and district initiatives affected Glenville High School's funding, organization, curriculum, and instruction.

In 2001, the federal No Child Left Behind Act required all states to have students proficient (as measured by state tests) in reading and math by 2014. Incremental penalties for noncompliance would be imposed over a five-year period, ending with restructuring (as occurred at Glenville High School) or closing of the school.

In 2005, the Ohio legislature mandated the Ohio Graduation Test, covering five areas that matched the academic subjects students were required to be taught (see the description of Gary Hart's US history class above). Students had to pass the test to receive a diploma.

Glenville consistently performed near the bottom of Cleveland high schools, failing to meet Adequate Yearly Progress since 2003. In 2007, Glenville, like other selected high schools, escaped closure by restructuring into four schools-within-a-school.[26] Recently arrived superintendent Eugene Sanders picked Glenville to receive donor funding to create the Science, Leadership, Arts, and Bridge Academies, each with separate budgets and block scheduling of eighty-minute periods.

Then the district CEO switched to a portfolio strategy (parents could choose from among charter schools, magnets, and theme-based schools), creating new schools while closing many small neighborhood schools (for example, sixteen were closed in 2010 and seven more in 2011). Glenville survived.

The next CEO chose Glenville, still a low-performing school, to receive a three-year federal School Improvement Grant (SIG). Jacqueline Bell, the veteran principal who had been there for earlier district-driven initiatives, dropped the four small schools and created a new ninth-grade academy and Information Technology Academy. The school also threw out the block scheduling of eighty-minute periods and went back to a ten-period school day with forty-minute periods. These changes were consistent with state and federal requirements to restructure if state proficiency levels went unmet.[27]

Within two years, the Information Technology Academy was no more. As Bell told me, none of the grants provided the resources to hire new teachers for the academies and the professional development needed to develop teachers' knowledge and skills. Both the schools-within-schools and subsequent academies were, in her words, "window dressing."[28]

Then in 2012, the state legislature had approved Mayor Frank Jackson's initiative, called the Cleveland Plan for Transforming Schools. The Cleveland Plan gave the city autonomy to use funds differently than stipulated by the state and focus on its portfolio strategy by getting rid of persistently low-performing schools, helping midlevel performing ones, and increasing the number of high-performing schools. For the first time since 1996, voters ratified a tax increase that would provide resources to implement the Cleveland Plan. In 2013–2014, twenty-three low-performing schools that had to be restructured immediately were named Investment Schools and given extra resources.[29]

CEO Eric Gordon named Glenville High School as one of those Investment Schools. That meant that the entire staff, including the principal, would be replaced before the next school year. As an Investment School—with outside partners in the city and nation to help it—the school would again have three years (the same expiration date as the privately funded school-within-a school innovation of 2008 and a federally funded School Improvement Grant it received in 2011) to show improvement in students' academic performance.

Underfunded and top-down imposed reforms, each having a short shelf life, have shaped Glenville High School over the past decade. In each restructuring, skimpy funds provided inadequate help for teachers to develop their capacity to digest these reforms and enact them in their classrooms.

These "innovations" occurred in a district culture focused on raising test scores swiftly and holding teachers responsible for student performance (district policy required that teacher evaluations be determined, in part by principal observations and student test scores).

Thus far, the portfolio strategy and one-after-another district reforms have trickled down into one high school in ways that have yielded perverse and unanticipated outcomes: decreased student enrollment, high teacher turnover, and continued low academic performance.[30]

IN THE CLASSROOM AT GLENVILLE, PART 2

In examining Glenville classrooms, obvious questions arise. Did the changing macro-contexts, particularly the torrent of reforms that spilled over Glenville, touch history lessons of the four teachers I observed and interviewed? If so, how? And how did the similarities or differences in their teaching lead to their ultimate rehiring or dismissal under the Investment Schools initiative, which called for the replacement of the entire staff, including the principal, in 2014? To answer these questions, I have already described the lessons of Hart and Allison, now I describe the lessons of two other history teachers in the department: Barry Rabson and Lawrence Otter.

US History with Barry Rabson

Because Barry Rabson invited me in after the class had begun, I did not see the opening of the lesson.[31] The second-period class has twelve students who are sitting at small tables arranged in rows facing the front whiteboard. The teacher's desk is at the rear of the room. On the teacher's desk is a laptop computer—again, the only computer in the classroom. When I enter the room, Rabson is standing at a small table at the front of the room, his laptop projecting a slide on an LCD screen (the screen was his personal property, he told me later).

On the whiteboard, Rabson has listed the state standard for the day's lesson about the end of World War II. Pull-down wall maps of the United States and the world, a poster of the presidents of the United States, and student work dot the other walls. The clock on the rear wall does not work.

Barry Rabson, a short, thickset man in his late forties, sporting a luxuriant mustache, is wearing a dark sport coat, light-colored pants, and a shirt with a bright red tie. This is his second year at Glenville, although he has been in the Cleveland schools for nearly two decades. He strides back and forth in front of the room asking questions, often fidgeting with the clipboard listing student names in one hand and a remote device for the LCD projector in the other hand. He scans the room constantly.

Not only has Rabson been a social studies teacher for many years in other schools, but he also served as an assistant principal at another Cleveland high school. After four years, however, he was laid off when the district closed the school and reduced the number of assistant principals. He exerted his seniority rights in the collective bargaining contract and returned to the classroom. He taught at two other high schools before coming to Glenville last year.

As I sit down in the rear of the room, Rabson introduces me as a former teacher who taught at Glenville fifty years ago. He then asks the class whether I would be a primary or secondary source on teaching at the school a half-century ago. The student chorus, "Primary source!"

Rabson then tells the class to "get your brain ready and write down the objective for the day." Most students do. When he calls on individual students, he addresses them as "Mr." or "Ms." When he asks questions of the entire class or admonishes them, he calls them "Ladies and gentlemen."

The slide about the lesson "Healing the Wounds of War" lists "GI Bill, Cold War, and Baby Bomb" (a student later corrects Rabson, and he changes the phrase to "Baby Boom").

Rabson asks the class for a definition of the GI Bill. Students yell out different answers. He picks one, repeats it, and then says: "I hope you write it down and remember it." Most students do, some do not. He does the same Q&A for "Baby Boom." As this back-and-forth continues, there is a steady hum in the class from pairs and trios of students talking. One student is using his cell phone stealthily. The teacher says nothing to this student or to the class about the murmur that ebbs and flows.

An announcement from the main office interrupts the class.

When he moves to the phrase "Cold War," Rabson connects it to the current Civil Defense sirens that go off periodically in Cleveland

to alert people to floods and earthquakes. He explains that sirens—
he punches a button on a recorder and the wail of a siren startles the
class—were used in response to the fear of Soviet attacks on the US
during the Cold War. He asks students to take notes on this. Most do
not pick up their pens.

As the period winds down, Rabson directs the students' attention
to page 827 of the textbook, where the above three items from "Healing
of Wounds of War" are defined and described.[32] "I expect you to know
this for the test," he says. Then he asks students to write down their
answer to the final question—"Why was the GI Bill important to baby
boom generation?"—and turn it in as they leave the class. He calls this
exercise an "Exit Pass," and reminds the class how many points answering the question will get them.[33]

Most of the students turn to the page in the text and begin writing
their answer to the Exit Pass question. Some continue to talk quietly.
Rabson walks around the room, checking what students are writing
and jotting down points on the clipboard. The chimes sound and about
half of the students turn in their answers.

US History with Lawrence Otter

A floor above Barry Rabson's classroom, Lawrence Otter, a teacher in
the Cleveland schools for thirty-nine years, of which twenty-eight have
been at Glenville, teaches US history and government courses. Ten
sophomores enter the room on time—one tardy student enters a few minutes later and hands a note to the tall, middle-aged Otter, who is wearing
dark pants, a light blue shirt, and floral print tie. Each student goes to a
carton along the wall near the door and pulls out a folder holding his or
her final project. This final unit of the school year is a research project
where each student chooses a decade of the twentieth century and has to
produce a four-page newspaper from that time. Otter has worked with
the class over the course of the school year on distinguishing between
primary and secondary sources in history. Students are using primary
sources—newspaper articles, photos, cartoons, and ads taken off the
Internet—to create a newspaper for the decade they have chosen.

Last week, they worked on page 1, which has to have at least one headline story of the decade (for example, the 1940s headline of one student's newspaper was "US Goes to War After Pearl Harbor"; another student had the headline for the 1930s, "Prohibition Ends"). In addition to the headline story, page 1 has to include at least one other story pertinent to the decade. Today, they are working on page 2, for which each student has to write an editorial expressing the student/editor's opinion of a key event during the decade.

Students take their folders to their desks and begin working on mock-ups of pages 1 and 2. They easily converse with one another about their tasks, sharing materials (paste, scissors, etc.), and asking for classmates' opinions

After a few minutes, Otter takes the roll and then asks students for their attention. They get quiet. He directs their attention to the whiteboard in the front of the room, where the required parts of each newspaper are written:

- "Political cartoon
- Other news stories
- Letters to the Editor
- Advertisements
- Local news for Cleveland and Ohio"

Otter reviews the project details and asks for questions. There are a few about what an editorial is and what political cartoons look like. He points to a pile of newspapers on a desk at the front of the room: "Look at the editorial page of the *Plain Dealer* and other newspapers there. You will see editorials and how they express opinions. Also cartoons." He then asks students to resume work on page 1 if they have not finished it or to begin on page 2. Students go to their desks and spread out the photos and articles that they have collected for their decade. These materials came from the few hours that they had spent in one of the school's computer labs.

Desks are arranged in rows facing the front of the large classroom. There is one computer on a desk in the back of the room.[34] The walls are covered with posters and historical photos depicting different periods of US history and the three branches of US government (the other subject that Otter teaches). Classroom rules printed on placards hang from fluorescent lights (e.g., "Not in dress code, no points"; "Visible electronics and headphones, no points"). One wall is decorated with handwritten sheets of papers listing US government concepts and key vocabulary words. On the rear wall, a poster shows the pyramid of Bloom's Taxonomy of Cognitive Skills. On the front whiteboard are listed the Ohio social studies standard and objective for the day.[35]

As students work, they freely move about the room, taking turns at the computer. Otter moves from desk to desk to see each student's page 1 and where each student is on page 2. One student is engaged in a conversation unrelated to the project; he puts his hand on her braids and gently turns her back to the desk and the draft headline article she had been working on the previous day. She returns to the task. As Otter told me later, "One-half of the kids I now have in my classes, I had their parents as students."

As Otter moves around the classroom, he invites me to do the same. I ask each student what decade he or she had picked, what the headline story is, and what the editorial is going to be about. Students, both shy and outgoing, relate the details of the decade they are working on and what they have learned thus far. A few ask me questions about decades since the 1930s. I remind one student that in the 1940s I was in elementary school. She doesn't know what to say, and I move on.

When Otter needs to print out an article he has found for one of the students on the years before World War I, he leaves the room for about five minutes. After he leaves, four students pull out their cell phones and start texting; a few others chat about the previous weekend, and the rest continue working on the project. When Otter returns, cell phones have been put away and chatting ceases. During the forty-minute period, I see only one student who is not engaged in the task. Otter walks over and speaks with the student, listens to the student's reply, then moved on to another student. The disengaged student puts his head down on desk. There is both a relaxed and serious attitude among students as they work on their projects. Otter interacts simply and directly with them, and they with him.

A few minutes before the period ends, Otter asks students to finish up what they working on. When the chimes sound, students return their folders to the carton near the door. One student stays on, asking Otter about the editorial she is writing. They talk for about five minutes, and the student then leaves.

After the class ended, I asked Otter how he usually teaches US history when he is not doing an end-of-year project. He told me that he often begins a class with a lecture, moves to readings he has duplicated for students. He follows with a discussion, and then students work individually or in small groups on the next day's assignment based on the readings. What about the text? Otter has copies of *American Anthem* available on a cart in his room and uses it a few times a week for primary source material.[36]

Where did he get the idea of the project? I asked. He said that the College and Career Academy administrator on his floor, whom he worked with, described what she had done in one of her social studies class and suggested he try it out. She talked through the introduction to the unit, different tasks that had to be done by the teacher, monitoring the work daily, and other activities. In his twenty-eight years at Glenville, it was the first time he did a newspaper project in US history. Of course, he added, he had done other research projects using primary and secondary sources with his world history and government classes in past years.

I commented on the serious and relaxed climate of the class as students worked on their projects. He pointed out to me that these eleven students had been identified in the ninth grade as having college potential, so a counselor and the principal decided to keep the group together in the tenth grade as a college prep class. He was delighted with the group and said it was "the best class I ever had in US history."

Otter did say that, for the most part, administrators over the years, particularly the current one, have "left him alone." He prized the autonomy he had at Glenville but disliked the district and state "requiring all students to be on the same page." He was equally averse to the district's intervention in classroom teaching—"control freaks," in his words. Teachers now, he told me, "have no say."

Otter did tell me of one top-down reform he had embraced nearly a decade earlier because he thought it would benefit students and appealed to him: splitting Glenville into four small schools. Directives to the school promised that teachers would design schedules, team-teach, and collaborate on projects. He went to meeting after meeting—"up the wazoo." Teachers decided on dividing the small schools from one another in the three-story building with gates and barriers. But when the schools opened in September, "they [the district] told us to forget all that we planned and here is what you have to do. All that collaboration, all those decisions we made were gone." Since then, he told me, when subsequent reforms have come to the school, he has remained uninvolved.

He has also seen a big change in the culture of the school. He told me that when he began teaching at Glenville, students did not roam the halls, but now roaming was common.[37] Moreover, he said that since the 1980s, most vocational courses have disappeared from the school. The belief that everyone should go to college has replaced the idea that some students will do better if they work with their hands and heads on practical things, especially if they have part-time jobs during their high school career. "So many kids are taking college prep yet do not go to college," he told me. These changes were, in Otter's opinion, negative.

Because of principals' respect for his work with students over the decades, Otter has carved out a zone of autonomy that permits him to do research projects, try out experiments—all in the sunset of his career. He ended our interview by saying, "I have fun every single day."

As a restructured high school in 2014, Glenville staff would have to reapply for positions at Glenville, including the four history teachers in the department, when Glenville became an Investment School in 2014. Bell told me that she had been again named principal. It should come as no surprise that, of the four history teachers in the department, Bell rehired Allison and Otter; Rabson and Hart were not rehired.

DID MACRO-CONTEXTS INFLUENCE MICRO-CONTEXT OF CLASSROOM?

Did the changes in the city, district, and Glenville High School itself influence history teaching? Indeed they did. The introduction of standards, testing, and accountability even before NCLB and certainly in the decade following its enactment saw the growth of high-stakes consequences for students (e.g., high school graduation rates) teachers (e.g., student test scores as a basis for teacher evaluation), and schools (e.g., labeled as failures). These reforms—planned changes—led to intensified preparation of students for state tests, curriculum narrowed to courses tied to tests, and increased teacher resentment toward test-based evaluations. Taking place within the underlying regularities—the grammar of schooling—of the age-graded, departmentally organized high school, these massive efforts to transform academically failing schools like Glenville into high performers unintentionally reinforced, even strengthened, teacher-centered, content-driven instruction.[38]

The result has been that current macro- and micro-contextual influences on teaching still tilted toward the teacher-centered side of the pedagogical continuum. So even with very different macro-contexts that Glenville High School experienced then and now, even with repeated attempts to reshape history instruction in line with the "New Social Studies" in the 1960s and the "New, New History" since the 1990s, persistent regularities in instruction bonded one generation of teachers to another.

And that is puzzling.[39]

The classroom lessons taught by Mark Allison, Gary Hart, Lawrence Otter, and Barry Rabson revealed again how four teachers in the same high school department at a time when city, district, and school contexts had changed dramatically since the late-1950s and early 1960s, still taught history in a similar manner to Glenville teachers a half-century earlier; that is, there remained a remarkable stability in teaching, although there was variation in what these four chose to teach, the approaches they used, and how students responded. This puzzle of persistent patterns in instruction over a half-century at Glenville amid major shifts in the macro-contexts—including repeated efforts to alter that manner of instruction—remains. I take up this puzzle in chapter 6.

But before I turn to that question, I will take a look at Cardozo High School in Washington, DC, fifty years later.

CHAPTER 5

History Teaching Now— Cardozo High School

IN THE CLASSROOM AT CARDOZO, PART 1

World History with Mike Topper

On the front wall above the interactive whiteboard (IWB)[1] Mike Topper had posted classroom rules on the first day of the semester of his ninth-grade world history course:[2]

1. Be Respectful!
2. Work Hard!
3. Keep Head Up and Off Desk!
4. Raise Hand to Speak One at a Time, and Stay on Topic!

Just to the side and below the smart board, Topper has printed out in large black letters a list of rewards and penalties for behavior, which he calls the "Four Token System":

- Keep all of your tokens to receive daily rewards, weekly positive phone calls, and monthly prizes.
- Loosing [sic] tokens results in negative consequences as follows:
  □ 1st token lost—warning.
  □ 2nd token lost—no rewards. Written up in Discipline and Behavior Log.

☐ 3rd token lost—phone call home or home visit. Student completes Behavior Reflection.

☐ 4th token lost—Referral to administration.[3]

The IWB is in daily use. Right now, it shows the "warm-up" activity that the district expects its academic subject teachers to use in beginning a lesson—often a question, puzzle, or proverb.[4] As students enter the room, they know that they are supposed to take out paper and begin writing on what is posted on the IWB.

After the opening warm-up activity, Topper told me in our interview, he usually moves into a ten-minute lecture, during which he often flashes slides from his laptop onto the IWB to illustrate important points; he also displays text and worksheet assignments.

Today, however, there is no warm-up exercise. The IWB shows announcements and an agenda for the lesson in the textbook unit "Reunification of China":

- "Test tomorrow.
- Read 'Print Invention' on p. 249. Do 3-2-1.
- Read 'Young People in China' section and answer the three questions on the page.
- Read p. 266 and do 3-2-1."[5]

To the side of the IWB, a whiteboard lists the daily lesson objectives, the world history standard under which the lesson falls, and what students will be able to know and do as a result of the lesson.[6]

On a side wall toward the back of the room is a large poster showing a pyramid with levels of cognitive skills drawn from Bloom's Taxonomy.[7] Next to it is a bulletin board displaying student work that received a score of 100 percent. Across the room, there is a large box holding "interactive notebooks" for each of the students.[8] When students enter, they take their notebook from the carton; at the end of the period, they put it back. Five new desktop computers with chairs and desks line the rear wall.

Desks are arranged in rows facing the front of the room. The teacher's desk, with an open laptop, is in a corner at the front of the room near the IWB.

Twelve students arrive before tardy bell. Topper, a thin young man of medium height, is wearing a sport shirt with a multicolored tie and dark pants. He tells students in a slightly hoarse voice that he will lock the doors now because a "hall sweep" is in progress. In these sweeps—which are particularly common in the week before a holiday—security aides, uniformed and in civilian clothes, round up students who are still in the corridors after the tardy bell has rung. These students are taken to the cafeteria, where an administrator records their names and then issues a pass to class. Being caught in sweeps repeatedly can lead to suspension.

After pointing to the day's lesson on the IWB, Topper says, "Listen up! Still a little sick from yesterday and my throat is sore, so don't let me talk over you." He continues, "The questions in the textbook you will answering are level 1 questions, not application or evaluation."[9]

Topper then looks at one student and says, "Mr. Washington, help me out and take off your hat" (he addresses all students "Mr." and "Miss"). The student takes off his cap.[10]

Topper directs student attention to IWB and addresses each item on the lesson agenda, including the test tomorrow. He asks if there are any questions. There are none. He reminds students that they will write on clean pages in their interactive notebooks and at the end of the period will turn in answers to the questions and 3-2-1s.

Eight students rise and get textbooks from the shelf. The rest sit and chat. As students turn to textbook pages and begin writing in their notebooks, a few yell out questions about items they will have to work on. One student calls out, "Topper, I need help." The teacher walks over, listens to the student, and then answers questions. Another student walks to door, slips the wooden "bathroom pass" off the wall hook and exits. The hum from students talking to one another grows louder. Two of the chatting students have yet to retrieve a textbook. Topper tells them to begin the assignment. They grudgingly get the textbooks, still whispering to each other as they return to their desks and open the books. Another chatting ninth-grader defies him, saying, "Leave me alone," and Topper does. The student who took the bathroom pass earlier returns; another student takes it and leaves.

Thirty minutes after tardy bell has rung, all of the students seem to be working on reading the text and writing the 3-2-1s. In the next twenty-five minutes, Topper walks out of room into the hallway to take a cell phone call. When he is out of the room, seven students stop reading or writing and begin talking to one another. When Topper returns two minutes later, he walks around the room, checking to see if students are on task and writing in their notebooks, and to check if there are any questions.

The bell rings for the daily homeroom period that occurs during this period. This is a ten-minute intermission in the school day for the principal, other administrators, and students to pipe in announcements of the day's activities, upcoming events, and names of students who must report to the office. When the PA system comes on, Topper returns to his desk and works on his laptop. Few students pay attention to the announcements pouring out of the wall-mounted speaker.

After announcements end, Topper asks students to resume their work. He reminds the group that there will be a test tomorrow and that answering all of the questions will help them on the test. He tells them that their notebook pages will be collected before the bell rings ending the period—these are their Exit Passes.[11]

About five minutes before the bell, Topper asks the class to return the textbooks and interactive notebooks. Students then return to their desks to get their backpacks and belongings together as they await the bell. When it rings, eight of the twelve hand in pages torn out of their notebooks to Topper, who reminds them of the test the next day.

Since completing a semester of student teaching and graduating college in a nearby city, Mike Topper entered Cardozo as a first-year teacher of history. In the World History I syllabus, he wrote the following description of the course:

The purpose . . . is to view civilizations from the Fall of Rome to the Age of Revolutions and think historically about how such civilizations impacted the development of the world. We will continually wrestle with questions that cannot be easily answered. In order to do so, we will develop a toolbox of 'historical thinking skills" that will be useful for everything inside the classroom and for being a powerful citizen outside of the classroom.[12]

The three goals and objectives for the course would make any partisan of the New, New History beam:

1. Formulate (develop) historical questions and defend answers based on inquiry and interpretation.
2. Communicate findings orally in class and in written essays.
3. Develop skills in reading strategies, discussion, debate, and persuasive writing.

Topper specifies in the syllabus which historical thinking skills he seeks to develop in his ninth-graders such as: being able to explain "historical significance," finding and using evidence, analyzing primary sources, and figuring out the "cause and consequence" of a significant event.

These are ambitious goals for a first-year teacher anywhere, much less at Cardozo. He told me that he likes it at Cardozo "because expectations for academic work are higher than [the city where he did his student teaching]." "Here," he said, "administrators come into your classroom and observe what you are doing. Also, master educators [former teachers hired by the district to observe and evaluate other teachers] have already come by a few times. Here, you really need to work with kids."

US History with Kerry Faulkner

A floor below Topper, Kerry Faulkner teaches US history in a large, airy and light classroom with four tall windows looking out over the city. The Washington Monument punctuates the horizon. It is late May, and there is a lot of activity in Faulkner's second-period US history class as the date for the final research paper approaches. Having spent fifteen years at Cardozo following two years of working for the Franciscan Order of the Catholic Church in Papua New Guinea, Faulkner is not easily rattled by the unexpected over the course of a day or as he says: "My students never cease to surprise me in both positive and negative ways."[13]

Rap music plays quietly in the background (Notorious B.I.G. is artist for this week; last week it was Tupac Shakur) as eleven tenth- and eleventh-graders enter and sit at four of the six pods of desks clustered together. The teacher's desk is in the corner; on it is his laptop, lid open. Five new desktop computers sit at the rear of the room. Posters, student work, and large photos of civil rights movement figures line the wall along one side of the room. Below the light switches and thermostat is a poster of Bloom's Revised Taxonomy. On a whiteboard at the front of the room, Faulkner has itemized the DC standards and objectives that will be covered by today's lesson.[14]

On the interactive whiteboard, Faulkner has listed the tasks for the day:

1. "Warm Up
2. DCPS Survey
3. Using Citations . . . A Must
4. To Library . . . Research Paper"

Of medium build and height, wearing a white shirt with a blue flowered tie and blue slacks, Faulkner hands out a warm-up sheet to each student. The sheet contains a list of the items that he will evaluate in the research paper and what he will be looking for in each section of the paper. Students have to answer a question that Faulkner has designed, but can choose their research topics from a list he has provided. He reminds students to look at the original handout on doing a research paper. Assessing (or grading) their papers is the last item on the original handout. Faulkner tells the students that knowing what is expected in writing the paper will prevent surprises.

The following section on the research paper comes from Faulkner's syllabus for the course:

Students will complete a 4–5 page, college-level, MLA formatted, organized and analytical research paper. Students will explore and argue using primary sources as evidence of "foundational ideals of the United States have been followed in our modern history." Due to project's size and scope, it's completion largely affects 2nd semester grades and the course. Without it, course failure is nearly certain.[15]

Julio, José, and Nick are talking and doing nothing during the warm-up as the teacher talks, asks questions, and responds to students. Faulkner, who is bilingual, interrupts his Q&A and tells the three in Spanish to pay attention. They do for a few minutes, then resume chatting.

After going over each item on assessing the research project in the warm-up exercise, Faulkner turns off the rap music and takes out his guitar, strums chords, and begins singing "Eyes on the Prize," a song that students heard during the previous unit on the civil rights movement. Students join in with clapping, and a few add their voices since they know some of the words. Playing the guitar and singing songs a few times a week after the warm-up is a routine that Faulkner developed over the years to celebrate music and artists that he has found connects him to his students.

After the song ends, Faulkner again reviews the rubric on assessing the research paper and asks students if there are any questions before they go to the library to work on their final project. One student asks about the due date for the final paper. Faulkner points out that this coming Friday is due date—it was underlined twice on white board. After back-and-forth with a few students over the date, he moves the date to the following Tuesday, saying that if the project is late, points will be deducted. "If you turn in research paper on Friday [original date]," he says, " you will get extra points added to your score." A few students write down the new date.

There are no more questions, so Faulkner and I walk with class to the library/media center, a well-lit, spacious room with a row of twenty desktop computers below the windows.

About half of the students take out their notebooks, the guide for doing a research paper, printed sheets, photos, and other items that they have compiled. These students log on and get to work. Four students sit and face the screen without logging in. Faulkner patiently goes from one to the other to get them started. For the Latino students, the teacher speaks entirely in Spanish. He knows what each student is doing in his or her project because he uses Google docs and can tell easily where individual students are in their writing or whether they have even begun to write.

What became clear to me as I watch Faulkner interact with students is the easygoing yet firm relationship he has with them, even those who are off-task and whisper to one another. Using a blend of humor, friendliness, and seriousness, Faulkner cajoles students into working on the task. To one student, he says, "Don't give up or give in."

I look over the shoulder of each student to see what is on the screen, ask what the topic is, what he or she is working on today, and what he or she likes most about the project. Except for two students who appear to have completely lost their way—Faulkner works with each of them during the hour spent in the library—the others are forthcoming and show obvious interest in what they have chosen to study and write about. As I observe and listen to each student, the range of reading and writing skills becomes most obvious. Some students read at college-level, while others are stuck at fifth- and sixth-grade levels. One student asks me questions about writing the first paragraph of her report on the use of drugs at Cardozo. She shows me what she has written and we have a back-and-forth about what a topic sentence would look like.

Faulkner gives students a five-minute warning and tells them to keep working and then shut down and log out. In the remaining minutes, students raise their hands at their computer stations and

Faulkner moves from one to the other, answering their questions. The bell sounds, and students leave the library.

Faulkner enjoys teaching at Cardozo, and administrators recognize his strengths. During the 2008 and 2013 reconstituting of the high school, two different principals rehired him to continue teaching US and DC history. After fifteen years at Cardozo, he "continues to learn from students, challenging as they may be." What he doesn't care for is frequent district testing of students, the frequent changes in principals—he has worked under five different principals while at Cardozo—and persistent student tardiness and absences that goes unpunished by school officials. He believes that both absences and tardies undermine his work with students.

As for the new evaluation system established by former schools chancellor Michelle Rhee in 2009—where he is observed five times during the school year by school administrators and master educators—he understands the fear of being judged "ineffective." He says, "I'm constantly creating and storing lessons to engage my students to keep my job." He believes that the evaluation policy is unfair in that if you are graded "highly effective" and get a cash award, you have to sign away job protections that are in the union contract. Also because Cardozo students, not necessarily his, have low scores on the DC test and because those school scores get factored into the judgment about his effectiveness as a teacher, whatever conclusion his bosses make about his performance is "unfair."

As with Glenville history teachers in 2013–2014, the pattern of teacher-centered instruction with occasional mixes of student-centered activities prevailed among the profiled history teachers. How much of these persistent patterns in instruction, however, was due to the individual teacher's personality, time spent in teaching, background in the discipline of history, and knowledge of pedagogy and how much was due to the age-graded school setting, socioeconomic background of students, larger district norms and practices, and changes in the city itself—the macro-context influencing the micro context of the classroom—remains an open question.

To help readers answer the puzzling question about the persistence of teacher-directed history instruction at contemporary Glenville and now Cardozo, I provide a description of the DC high school over the past half-century of school district reforms that buffeted its schools first one way and then another. I also reflect on the revolving door for DC superintendents and Cardozo High School principals that was influenced by larger demographic and political changes in the city of Washington.

IN THE SCHOOL—THEN AND NOW

The School Setting

Central High School sat atop the 13th Street hill in northwest Washington, DC, overlooking the city. Erected in 1916 to serve eleven hundred white students, by 1950, only a few hundred white students attended the school. School district officials decided to give the building to the "colored division" of schools to become the new home of the all-black, business-oriented Cardozo High School.

With fewer resources than the segregated white schools, however, in time Cardozo soon became a once-again overcrowded and shabby neighborhood high school. In 1963, the year I arrived in the no longer *de jure* segregated school, there were already nearly two thousand black students in the deteriorating building.

Between the 1960s and the late 1990s, patchwork repairs kept the building in barely adequate condition. Many of the bathrooms were nonfunctioning. Windows were stuck. Rooms darkened by decades of dirt and narrow and dingy hallways characterized the school. It was in a word, dilapidated.

In 2014, however, the raggedness of a neglected building was gone. Between 2011 and 2013, Cardozo High School underwent a $130 million dollar renovation.[16] The new building is a beauty. Its original hardwood floors were refinished. Classrooms were rebuilt and computers installed. Each floor was provided with eco-friendly and spacious bathrooms. New rehearsal rooms for the band and choir and a modern swimming pool and basketball court enhanced extracurricular activities. New skylights made the interior airy and bright. Outdoor patios had been glassed over, allowing students and teachers to eat there in any weather. A new large metal sign in purple letters standing on a large block of handsome stone announces that the building is Cardozo High School, the Home of the Clerks.[17]

After the renovation, the school reopened in 2013 as the Cardozo Educational Campus, housing students in grades 6 to 12. But the changes were not only to the physical building. Because of persistently low test scores and graduation rates, DC Chancellor Kaya Henderson dumped the entire staff and "reconstituted" the school by appointing a new principal and inviting all teachers to reapply for their positions.[18] Thus, within two years, two structural makeovers, one bricks-and-mortar and the other organizational, occurred. (This was the second time in five years that Cardozo had been "reconstituted"; the first occurred when Chancellor Michelle Rhee had overhauled the school in 2008.)[19]

Now organized as a six-year secondary school, Cardozo has about seven hundred students, Nearly 30 percent are Latino and 68 percent are black; 1 percent are white. One-third of the student body is identified as special education and over one-quarter of the students are English Language Learners. Nearly 100 percent qualify for free and reduced-lunch, the measure of poverty the district uses. The renovated and reconstituted school is obviously under capacity.[20]

A brand-new neighborhood middle school-senior high school, district administrators hoped, would attract more students from both the increasingly gentrified immediate neighborhood and demographically changing city, reducing the outward flow of Cardozo youth to charter and magnet schools elsewhere in DC.

Rebuilding the physical structure typically does not alter deeply embedded organizational structures that dominated school routines and cultures for decades. Sorting out superficial changes from underlying shifts in organizational routines is challenging but necessary.

Security

This change hit me immediately when I entered the front door of Cardozo. In the 1960s, the only security in the school was provided by administrators and teachers cruising hallways to clear students during the school day. When there were fights—and the occasional stabbing occurred—the local police precinct would assign officers to the school before and after the school day. When weapons entered the building (assistant principal Herman Clifford was shot dead in the main hallway in 1969), however, police officers were assigned to the building for a while.[21]

In 2014, portals in the Cardozo's vestibule beep constantly and uniformed security guards pass wands over entering students and adults, asking those who set off alarms to reenter X-ray scanners and pick up backpacks, wallets, keys, and cell phones from the conveyor belt.

During the school day, hallways were largely clear of students, while highly visible uniformed aides carrying walkie-talkies patrolled each of the four floors. Corridors were quiet except for the periodic sweeps made before the holidays. In my two weeks in Cardozo, these security procedures were taken for granted by students and adults, just as they are viewed as normal in nearly all low-performing urban high schools, including Glenville. Students and teachers interacted easily and sociably with uniformed and non-uniformed staff.

Pervasiveness of Posters and Slogans

I do not recall placards, posters, and photos urging students to achieve when I taught at Cardozo in the 1960s. Now, however, like Glenville in 2014, a profusion of slogans and posters plasters the hallways of every floor and classroom. A large bulletin board posted on the wall near the main office announces "SCHOLAR OF THE MONTH" and lists students for each grade. On another floor is a "COUNTDOWN CALENDAR" of months before the Comprehensive Assessment System (CAS) test—the standardized test measuring the degree of proficiency DC students achieve in reading, math, and other subjects, is administered. Running vertically beside this, in bold red letters, is the slogan: "LET'S KICK SOME CAS, CLERKS."

Elsewhere in the building purple and yellow banners hang from walls, proclaiming that "CLERKS S.O.A.R."—an acronym for "CORE VALUES of Safety, Organization, Achievement, Respect."

These signs all aim to motivate students to do well in school and think of why they come to school, that is, to achieve success not only in school but in life. As at Glenville and in nearly every urban high school I have visited over the past quarter-century, such cheerleading was ubiquitous.

The Grammar of Schooling

Although Cardozo, originally a ninth- to twelfth-grade high school, was restructured in 2013 to incorporate middle school grades to become the sixth- to twelfth-grade Cardozo Educational Campus, the basic structure of the age-graded high school has remained the same for the past fifty years. The primary means of organizing teachers into departments has also remained unchanged over the decades.

One change that has occurred, however, has been the creation and dissolution of smaller school communities or schools-within-a-school. There were none before the early 1990s. Over the past two decades, this has been an on-again, off-again organizational change within this age-graded, departmentally organized high school.

The TransTechAcademy for tenth-graders, for example, was formed in 1992. It was designed to attract students who wanted to work in local transportation and technology-related occupations. At about the same time, the federally funded Project Accord, which aimed at increasing the employability of youth who were identified as potential dropouts, was established. This school-within-a-school provided computer-assisted instruction in reading and math, mentoring, and internships in local companies for a selected group of students.[22]

In the mid-1990s, school district officials reshuffled Cardozo because of persistent low academic performance. Under new principal

Reginald Ballard—who ended up staying eleven years, the longest-serving school leader since 1955—Cardozo was split into four more schools-within-a-school or career-focused "learning communities": Explorers (for ninth-graders); TransTech (retained); Sports Management; and Fine Arts, Humanities, and International Studies. This structural change accorded with the prevailing reform ideology of improving school performance through smaller schools.[23]

By 2014, however, Project Accord was gone, as were the experimental Explorers, Sports Management, and Fine Arts, Humanities, and International Studies learning communities. TransTech continues and now incorporates students pursuing Science, Technology, Engineering, and Math (STEM); as of 2013, it had graduated nearly six hundred students). The Academy of Construction and Design, where students learn carpentry, architecture, and heating and air-conditioning, opened in 2005 and continues today. The Academy of Information Technology opened in 2014.[24]

Within age-graded high schools, the school day is divided into class periods during which students take the different courses that will fulfill graduation requirements. So the daily schedule for teachers and students changed as school officials converted the large comprehensive high school into a cluster of smaller schools-within-a-school. For example, in 1992, students and teachers followed a seven-period day on Mondays and Fridays, with each class lasting forty-seven minutes. But on Tuesday, Wednesday, and Thursday, there would be morning and afternoon "flex periods" of ninety-five minutes each, during which teachers could allocate time for students to do their homework, offer remedial help for individual students, and add enrichment activities for those students already doing well. Between the early 1990s and today, the daily schedule changed repeatedly, moving from shorter to longer periods and back again.

In 2014, the school day runs from 8:45 a.m. to 3:15 p.m. There are A and B schedules of four periods running between eighty to ninety minutes. Each day is either A or B schedule. There is also a forty-five minute "0 period" for electives and activities in the early morning. In the age-graded, departmentalized high school, the duration of time that students sit in classrooms with one teacher can vary, as it has over the decades at Cardozo. But these periods, whether they are forty-five or ninety minutes long, are linked to credits for graduation—called *Carnegie units*—and teachers must certify that each student has completed the content and skills covered in the course.[25] These regularities continue in 2014.

Extracurricular Activities

Both then and now, a rich array of afterschool activities was available to Cardozo students. Over the decades, athletic teams, after-school clubs, and other activities ebbed and flowed, especially as women's sports emerged. The ramshackle building and athletic facilities, however, shaped the extracurricular program and pride in school for decades. The dilapidated swimming pool, basketball court, and football stands forced teams to play elsewhere in the city. There were years that the baseball, football, and basketball teams soared to city championships and school pride rose, but turnover among students, and athletic staff and the state of the facilities made such achievements more difficult. A winning record could not be sustained over multiple years. Nonetheless, even with all of the changes over time and the adverse conditions (including turnover of students, faculty and administration as well as athletic staff), faculty and coaches fielded teams, put on plays, published newspapers and yearbooks, and conducted after-school programs in many, if not all, years.[26]

To sum up all these changes, I offer an at-a-glance comparison of Cardozo then and now in table 5.1.

CHANGES IN THE CITY AND ITS SCHOOLS

What is missing from this description of teaching history at Cardozo High School, features of the school, and comparisons with an earlier period are the larger contexts in which Cardozo operated then and

TABLE 5.1   Summary of then and now at Cardozo High School*

	1963–1967	2013–2014
School grades	9–12	6–12
Number of students	2,000	681
▪ Minority (%)	99	68 black/31 Latino
▪ Poor (%)	Neighborhood designated as poor to receive federal projects	99 (free and reduced-price lunch)
▪ Special education (%)	NA	28
Number of faculty	79 (1967)	60
▪ Minority (%)	85	80 (author estimate)
Graduation rate (%)	50 (author estimate)	38
College enrollment (%)	35 (author estimate)	30 (author estimate)
Curriculum offerings	Honors, College Prep, General, Vocational Tracks	Career and College Readiness Academy; Health and Sports Academy
Advanced Placement courses	0	8 (English Literature, World History, Biology, Chemistry, Calculus, Statistics, French, Spanish)
Daily school schedule	Eight periods of 45 minutes	Four 80–90-minute periods a day
Technology access for teachers and students	Classroom blackboards, films and projectors, filmstrips and projectors, audio recorders	Interactive whiteboards and five new desktop computers in each classroom; teacher laptops
Testing	No state or district tests; teacher designed classroom tests	District administered Comprehensive Assessment System for grades 2–10 in reading, math, science, and health; teacher-designed tests
Consequences for low academic performance	Student failing course and retention in grade or subject; no school penalties	Identified as low-performing school for four years; received "corrective action"; restructured in 2008 and 2013
Extracurricular programs	Sports, Drill Team, Chess Club, cheerleaders, drama, student newspaper, yearbook, etc.	Sports, Drill Team, band, online literary and artistic journal, Chess Club, etc.
Roaming in hallways	Students wandered halls during classes	Aides periodically sweep halls to round up tardies; uniformed security walk halls during class time
Discipline	Referral to administrators, paddling, suspension	Referrals to administrators; in-school and out-of-school suspensions
School security	Teachers and administrators	Metal detectors at only entrance to school; uniformed and non-uniformed aides; school aides with radios

*Information comes from author's direct observation of high school for a week in November 2013 and a week in May 2014. Also see Cardozo High School website for current school information at: http://www.cardozohs.com/; http://profiles.dcps.dc.gov/pdf/454_2013.pdf; Emma Brown, "At Cardozo School, High Hopes for a Cultural Transformation to Match Physical One," *Washington Post*, August 26, 2013.

now. Those macro-contexts all had their effect on the micro-contexts in which Cardozo teachers worked in the 1960s as they do now.

The Cardozo principal, teachers, staff, and students in 2013–2014, like their predecessors, as in Glenville, responded to demographic, political, economic, and societal changes that had occurred in the nation, the city, and the schools. Cardozo's organization, curriculum, and instruction profoundly influenced what occurred when teachers taught history.

Broken Promises and the DC Schools

In their book, *Dream City*, Harry Jaffe and Tom Sherwood describe one of presidential candidate Bill Clinton's campaign stops:

> [In 1992, President-elect] Bill Clinton picked a block on Georgia Avenue in the heart of what once was a thriving black business community ... The incoming leader of the world's most powerful nation spoke with the shop owners and local politicians, promised Georgia Avenue and the city more jobs, more credit, safe streets, better housing. Then he departed in a sea of secret service agents. After Clinton finished his talk on Georgia Avenue, a middle-aged black man in the crowd asked: "Haven't we heard all that before?" [27]

Reflecting on this incident, the authors conclude that one "had to agree" with the unnamed commentator: "LBJ promised self-rule in 1967. Nixon promised to rebuild the riot zones in 1968 [i.e., damaged property following the assassination of Martin Luther King, Jr.] and George H.W. Bush in 1989 orchestrated a cocaine bust across from the White House and declared war on drugs." [28] Those presidential promises over the years tried to convert two separate and distinct Washingtons—the federal and the local—into one city. They failed.

Federal Washington stretches from the White House to the Capitol and includes museums, monuments, and government buildings. Along Pennsylvania and Constitution Avenues and the National Mall stand the Department of Justice, the Environmental Protection Agency, the National Archives, the Federal Trade Commission, and Smithsonian Institution. The Federal Triangle anchors official Washington. In Capitol Hill cafes, Georgetown restaurants, and K Street hotels, mostly white policy elites—executive agency officials, business leaders, US senators and representatives, lobbyists, and think tank pundits—gather to discuss and plan strategy and tactical moves.[29] These are the people who run official Washington. In doing so, they influence but do not control the DC mayor's office, city council, public schools, and local black policy elites.

Local Washington, "the city beyond the monuments," has had until the past few years a largely black population, living in such neighborhoods as Petworth, Fort Dupont, Southwest, Brookland, Cardozo, and Trinidad. The vast majority of earners in these neighborhoods work in DC and surrounding suburbs for global corporations, family businesses, and local and federal governments. They shop, dine, play sports, and go to parks in DC and suburban Maryland and Virginia. Their children go to nearby schools or, in later decades, enroll in charter schools. They seldom show up in the *Washington Post* or *Washington Times* (they do appear, however, in the *Washington Afro American* and *Washington Informer*). It is when presidents make promises during campaigns as Clinton did in 1992 that both local and federal Washington come together for a kiss and part company until the next time.

And those promises that presidents made? Congress converted some of those presidential promises into dollars and actions. Local Washington finally got self-rule in 1973, but as of 2014, the city still does not have two senators and one congressman who can vote in the House of Representatives. The damaged buildings and vacant lots left by the 1968 riots were slowly rebuilt or cleared for new office buildings and convention centers in the 1970s and 1980s. And slowly but erratically, federal and local Washington came together in reforming public schools—almost a national pastime—as one president after another entered the White House and one Congress after another looked down on the city they both loved and dallied with.

But operating DC public schools in the twenty-first century still involves negotiating a tangled swamp of overlapping authorities. New mayors, city council members, superintendents, school board members, federal legislators, and successive presidents arrive and push favorite reforms, making and unmaking district policies. When their initiatives flop, they point fingers at one another. The jumble of contentious oversight authorities nearly guaranteed that the DC schools complicate the lives of administrators, teachers, and students when I began teaching at Cardozo and now, a half-century later.

Two experts on D.C. school governance described the situation this way:

> In recent years, the Board of Education (both appointed and elected), a number of US Senate and US House of Representative committees, the DC city council, DC Financial Control Board, a state education office, the mayor, the DC Chief Financial Officer, two charter school boards, many superintendents (appointed by different authorities), and unions have all played key roles in education policy making and school management. At almost any point in time, overlapping areas of responsibility provided all players with reason to blame each other when things went wrong, and they left none of the players with sufficient power to demand quality performance.[30]

This patchwork governance increased the complexity of administering schools ("Which of my bosses do I listen to?") and teaching ("How much, if any, of this new policy do I have to put in my lessons?"). To this Rube Goldberg contraption called DC governance, add dramatic shifts in the city's population, significant governmental interventions, and high turnover among district and school leaders. All of this filtered down into DC schools and classrooms.

Demographic Changes

Between the 1940s and the 1960s, the city had gone from majority white to majority black. When I began teaching at Cardozo in 1963, nearly 55 percent of DC's 765,000 residents were black. School population, however, ran more than three-quarters black; Cardozo's black population accounted for 99 percent of the student body.

By 1970, blacks made up 71 percent of the city's residents.[31] However, in every decade since the early 1950s, a slow but steady white and black exodus to the Maryland suburbs drained the city's overall population, which had fallen to 572,000 in 2000. And as the population shrank, its schools became starkly segregated. In 2005, for example, 91 percent of black students attended schools that were over 70 percent black.

Beginning in the 1990s, another shift in population emerged. The black majority started to shrink as Hispanic and white residents moved into hitherto black neighborhoods. By 2010, only 62 percent of DC residents were black. In 2011, the white and black population of Washington was nearly the same as in 1960.

Government Decisions

In 1954, the US Supreme Court ruled in *Bolling v. Sharpe* that the DC schools had to be desegregated. That judicial decision produced the first wave of reform that washed over the DC schools into the early 1960s. Following the Kennedy-Johnson years and in subsequent decades, reforms deluged the DC schools. With each new administration, both Democratic and Republican crusaders came to town touting favorite reforms (governance changes, better teachers and curriculum, school-community collaboration, expanded parental choice, and on and on). Appointed and then elected mayors came and went, desperately trying to fix the schools.[32]

One persistent problem was the lack of DC schools' control over expenditures. The city's schools had amassed annual deficits in the late 1980s and early 1990s that could not be ignored by either the city government or Congress. Moreover, embarrassing stumbles by school officials made front-page reading in DC media: not enough certified teachers to staff classrooms, fire code violations preventing public schools from opening on time each September, lack of textbooks, student test performance perpetually lagging behind most urban districts, and special education students ill-served. To correct these festering problems, Congress appointed a new Board of Financial Control in 1995 to take over the schools for four years.[33]

When the DC Control Board, as it was called, took over, one member compared the DC schools to "a Third World country where there is little or no money available for education."[34] It stripped the elected board of education of its authority, transferring powers to a new board of trustees, and fired superintendent Franklin Smith. A retired Army general, Julius Becton, was appointed to run the schools.

Becton served two years and departed, and the DC Control Board appointed his deputy, Arlene Ackerman, an experienced urban administrator, to the post. In 2000, Ackerman resigned after two years, the year that the elected board of education resumed its fiscal and managerial authority over the public schools. Even after that Fiscal Board disappeared and the resurrected board of education hired new superintendents who initiated more rounds of reforms, both school chief and school board struggled with the mayor and council over funding these initiatives.

Reforms continued to pour down after the DC Control Board disappeared and the board of education resumed control of the system. Within a few years, President George W. Bush and Congress intervened in two ways. First was the enactment of the No Child Left Behind Act (NCLB) in 2001, which required all states and the District of Columbia to install standards-based testing and for schools and students to be held accountable for academic performance. Second, in 2004 Congress mandated that the DC schools offer parents vouchers to send their children to private schools, including religious ones. Here again, Congress's penchant for using the DC schools as a national laboratory to experiment with reforms returned.

The vouchers covered nearly seventeen hundred students from low-income families, becoming the only federally funded voucher program in the United States. When school officials objected to the $14 million program, congressional leaders threatened to reduce school district appropriations. That ended officials' public criticism. When journalists and researchers evaluated the program over the next decade, they found a lack of managerial controls, that schools accepting the vouchers were not accredited and, to the disappointment of administration and legislators, no improved academic achievement. Both NCLB and vouchers shaped the DC schools and teacher actions as subsequent school boards and superintendents came under the control of the mayor.[35]

Unlike Congress, DC mayors since 1967, when President Lyndon Johnson appointed Walter Washington, found themselves increasingly criticized for the abysmal performance of the school system. Potential voters complained to mayoral candidates that the school system was broken and demanded to know what exactly was going to be done about it. After being elected, mayors and city council members trying to deal with the board of education and turnstile superintendents seldom received standing ovations or Valentine Day cards from the voters who has put them into office.

Lacking authority over top school officials, city leaders pushed the idea that mayors should appoint school board members and the superintendent—as was done in New York City, Chicago, and Baltimore. In 2000, Anthony Williams was elected mayor after disastrous two-term mayor Marion Barry and his ineffective successor Sharon Pratt Dixon. Williams decided that his office had to exert more control over the schools, since he would end up being blamed for Barry's and Dixon's failings anyway. He sought that authority from the city council, which granted it in 2007. However, by that time, Adrian Fenty had whipped Williams in the previous year's election, and it was Fenty who exercised mayoral control over the schools. Fenty fired Clifford Janey, superintendent since 2004, and appointed Michelle Rhee, a Teach for America alumna and head of the New Teacher Project, as chancellor for the DC schools.

Rhee's brief stint as chancellor advanced both a reform agenda sharply focused on teachers and principals that even went beyond what national reformers advocated. Keep in mind that one version of school reform, largely market-driven since the late-1990 and early 2000s, dominated urban schools across the nation. Its platforms—mayoral control, raising academic standards, more testing, developing portfolios of schools from which parents could choose including vouchers and charter schools, anti-union rhetoric and action, and accountability for students and teachers were on both Republican and Democratic reformers' to-do lists.[36]

What had been a conservative reform agenda aggressively pushed by Republican governors, state legislators, and George W. Bush (2001–2009) soon merged with the Democratic school reform agenda of Barack Obama (2009–2013) to incorporate mayoral appointed superintendents (later called *chancellors*), charter schools, attacking collective bargaining agreements, and test score-driven evaluations of schools and individual teachers. [37]

And Michele Rhee's tenure with the DC schools became a poster child for those market-driven, results-oriented reformers. Rhee fired teachers and administrators, closed schools, introduced a new evaluation system—called IMPACT—where student test scores primarily determined teacher effectiveness. These and other actions led to a steep loss in teacher trust for their chancellor. Rhee served for only three years. When Fenty lost his bid for reelection in 2010, Rhee resigned. Newly elected mayor William Gray appointed Rhee's deputy, Kaya Henderson, the new chancellor in 2011. [38]

Turnover in Leadership

Between 2004 and 2011, there were three school chiefs. Such rapid entering and exiting undercut sustainability of any single reform aimed at classrooms while corroding teacher trust in their district and school leaders. But that kind of turnover was par for the course in DC.

Superintendent firings and resignations had run high since Carl Hansen became superintendent in 1958. Between then and 2011, thirteen school chiefs have held the post (not counting the eight interim appointees who served until the board of education named successors). The average tenure of these superintendents was just over three and a half years. The longest-serving school chiefs were Carl Hansen (1958–1967) and Floretta McKenzie (1981–1988).[39]

Each school chief, charged by the board of education to improve schools, brought in his or her preferred reforms. One sought to centralize district office functions, while another pushed to decentralize the same set of tasks. One directed all teachers to align district curriculum standards to their daily classroom objectives and to list them on the chalkboard. Another, eager to sort out effective from ineffective teachers, introduced a systemwide teacher evaluation process linked to how well their students did on tests. And on and on.

Consider Barbara Sizemore, a superintendent imported from Chicago in 1973 and exported—that is, fired—two years later. Six months after she was appointed, she brought to the board of education her plans to improve schooling in the DC schools:

- "Restructuring of the schools so that students of different ages and abilities can be taught in the same classroom.
- Decentralizing the school system into six administrative regions with the use of PACTS [Parents, Administrators, Community Residents, and Teachers and Students working together] as the means to accomplish decentralization.
- Curricular changes: Multi-lingual instruction; combinations of like disciplines being taught together; emphasis placed on concepts rather than facts; and flexible time sequences."[40]

Within fourteen months, after much internal squabbling, her top administrators resigned and the board of education, tired of constant bickering with Sizemore, fired her.

Longtime *Washington Post* columnist William Raspberry, looking back on his coverage of the DC schools, reflected on the many superintendents he had seen come and go over the years when yet another superintendent—Clifford Janey—was appointed in 2004:

The point is that a newspaper career spanning nearly a dozen superintendents, and as many more acting superintendents, has taught me not to expect very much from the next school chief, however credentialed or well meaning. Aside from [Vince] Reed and Floretta

McKenzie, I have trouble thinking of any in the long succession of short-term administrators who made much of a difference in the local schools.[41]

Principals entered and left schools at an equally high rate. Consider Cardozo High School principals exiting and entering the schools over the past half-century. Since 1963, when I arrived at Cardozo, there have been twelve principals. That translates into an average tenure of just over four years per principal. This average is a bit misleading, however. Geraldine Johnson and Reginald Ballad served eight and eleven years, respectively; the average is dragged down by the four principals who served three or fewer years.[42] The current principal, Tanya Roane, who presided over the 2011–2013 renovation, the reconstitution of the high school, and expansion to a grade 6–12 school, has been in the post since 2011.

Consequences of such principal and superintendent turnover often drained staff morale, lowered odds that reforms would be sustained, and created cynicism among civic and business leaders, parents, and teachers about comprehensive plans and innovations that successive newcomers brought to the district and Cardozo. As a result of governmental decisions and high leader turnover, uncertainty grew and infected principals and teachers with suspicion of new policies and procedures. Disaffection with reform after reform led many school staffs to hunker down and continue to do what they have been doing in schools and classrooms year after year.

IN THE CLASSROOM, PART 2

I bring this chapter to an end with a description of another Cardozo history teacher's lesson. Readers will note the similarities and differences between the two Cardozo history teachers I have already described.

World History with Burt Taylor

Burt Taylor, a tall, stocky man in his late twenties, with a trim mustache and goatee and wearing a beige shirt and bright tie with casual dark pants, is completing his fifth year as a world history teacher at Cardozo High School. After graduating college, he served in the US Army for three years. While he was in Afghanistan, his mother sent him Frank McCourt's *Teacher Man* and urged him to consider teaching after he left the service. He did. In 2007, he joined Teach for America. After his five weeks of training in Philadelphia, he was assigned to Cardozo High School in 2009. He completed his two-year commitment and has taught three additional years.[43]

While he did not major in history as an undergraduate, he says he has had a "passion for reading and studying history since I was a kid." The African American and Latino high school students he faces for eighty- and ninety-minute sessions four times a day, while bringing with them "many challenges," have made teaching at Cardozo "rewarding."[44]

Taylor teaches mostly tenth- and eleventh-graders. I observed the world history class that he teaches immediately after the lunch period. As we stand in the hallway before class, the PA blares a reminder that all teachers are to stand outside of their classroom as students pass to their next period. Some students say hello to Taylor and he smiles and shakes hands or nods in a response.

As students enter, they pick up their Daily Participation Grade sheet. When class starts, fifteen students (enrollment is twenty-five) are present, sitting at pods of three desks scattered around the spacious room. Written on the whiteboard is the DC curriculum standard that this lesson addresses and objectives for the day. An agenda for the lesson is on the IWB. Along the sides of the room are posters, placards, and bulletin boards holding student work, upcoming assignments, and photos of historical figures. In the rear of the classroom are five new computers.

The activities that unfolded in this lesson, the numbers of students attending, instructional materials Taylor used, and student participation were, he said, "typical" of other world history classes he is teaching this semester.[45]

The materials Taylor uses are drawn from a pool of lessons available online from the Stanford History Education Group. He has liked and used other lessons offered by SHEG.[46] I asked him how he came to this website: Was it from district or school professional development? A fellow teacher? The text? None of these. Basically, he told me, "I did it myself," he said. One night, he had stumbled onto the website, liked it for the focus on concepts, primary and secondary sources, and how historians read documents. He ended up adapting some of those lessons to his classroom.[47] "I am not a big fan of texts," he explained, "They shy away from controversy." He does use the textbook, however, for maps, charts, and graphs.[48]

The lesson I observed was the "Invasion of Nanking."[49] Taylor used primary and secondary sources: photos, excerpts from Japanese and Chinese accounts of the invasion, and then a final selection from an eminent historian of Chinese history on what happened in the city in 1937. He sought to get across the idea that textbooks contain biases and express points of view, and that students need to be critical thinkers, like detectives, to figure out the biases and perspective buried in the text.

On the whiteboard in front of room, Taylor had listed each activity the class would do in today's lesson with times allotted for each. A stopwatch alarm on his desk would ding periodically to end each activity. Here's how the lesson unfolded.

For the students' warm-up activity, Taylor projects a photo with no caption on the IWB, along with directions and questions for the students: "List what you see in photo. What questions do you have? What conclusions do you have?" He walks around the room to see what students are writing and marks each student's Daily Participation Grade sheet. The sheet has a section set aside for "Warm Up" and two boxes that Taylor can check off: "Partial" and "Good to Go."[50]

Taylor then asks students what they have written down about the photo. On the IWB, he compiles what they say. He calls students by first name and a few who raise their hands (few questions call for choral responses). Students use clues in the photo to conclude that it shows a post-battle scene in an Asian city many years ago.

Taylor tells students that the photo was taken in Nanking in 1937, after the Japanese invaded China. "We are," he says, "going to figure out what happened in Nanking in that year." He then gives a ten-minute mini-lecture—he asks students to take notes—on the background of the invasion and what happened in the 1930s in Japan. Of the fifteen students, thirteen are writing as Taylor lectures. He then tells the class that they will read two different paragraphs from textbooks about the invasion of Nanking and challenges them to figure out which description came from a Japanese textbook and which from a Chinese textbook.

To insure that students know the geography of the photo and sources, he has them go to a shelf holding a classroom set of world history texts and turn to a map of Japan, China, and the region. He asks questions about location of the countries. At this point, Taylor tells class that he will ask a "trick question" about the photo and the text excerpts, so they should "pay attention" to what he says and what they read.

He then segues to a small group activity. Students move quickly into three-person groups made up of a designated "reader," "materials manager," and "discussion leader." This is a familiar activity to them. Taylor calls on "material managers" to come up to desk and get textbook excerpts. He then tells "readers" to read aloud to their group each excerpt, labeled A and B. Students are to underline unfamiliar words and try to figure out what each means. The "reader" in the group near me trips over "atrocity" and discusses it with other group members. Taylor, carrying a clipboard on which he notes each student's participation, comes by and listens in to back-and-forth among the three students.

Afterward, he asks each group to decide whether paragraphs A and B were from the Japanese or Chinese text. "Discussion leaders" in each group worked to get agreement about texts—one group was excited enough to give each other fist bumps on completing their choices.

Taylor records the student votes: of the fifteen, eight think A is the Japanese text, and seven think it is Chinese. He then asks individual students to give the reasons why they voted as they did, using the text to support their answer. Eight of the students enter this discussion. Taylor offers the class another chance to vote and many cross over from their original vote, agreeing that excerpt A came from a Japanese textbook.

The teacher now asks: "Which of these two textbook accounts do you trust?" Students raise hands, and Taylor calls on students who have not yet participated in whole-group discussion. After one student said she distrusted A, he asks her to underline the sentences that led to her conclusions and why she had little faith in that account. By and large, students agreed that you cannot trust either one, because the different sides wanted to portray the Nanking invasion as either common wartime practice or a deliberate massacre. When Taylor asks the students what they have learned so far, many respond with variations of: there are at least two sides to listen to when something occurs; you cannot believe that textbooks tell the "truth" about the past.

"I'm going to have you now work as historians do," Taylor tells the class. Then he calls for "materials managers" to come up to desk to get a final reading, written by historian Jonathan Spence about the Sino-Japanese war and the Nanking incident. "Readers" spring into action, and the "discussion leaders" lead exchanges in the group to determine what the historian contributed to their earlier decision on texts A and B. For the ten minutes of this final activity, Taylor listens to each group, asks and answers student queries, and jots notes on his clipboard. The alarm bell rings to end the activity.

Taylor asks students what they learned from reading the historian's account and texts A and B. Answers vary a great deal among those who raise their hands to reply. The teacher also calls on a few students who have not raised their hands. Most students feel that the historian's view of the invasion of Nanking is most accurate because he used Chinese, Japanese, and non-Asian primary sources. Taylor nods his head, and says the historian "corroborated" his account of what happened with other sources, essential for anyone writing about the past.

At this point, seventy minutes into the lesson, with a few minutes left, I left the room to see another history teacher teach.[51]

Did the macro-context of Washington, DC, with its gaggle of over-sight agencies, constant intrusions by federal and city authorities, and unanticipated demographic changes over the interim decades since the mid-1960s seep down into the micro-context of Cardozo High School? Yes. As in Glenville, the external context did influence what happened at Cardozo.

Standards-based reforms, testing, and accountability regimes building up over three decades of market-inspired school reform yielded policies and procedures that did influence what teachers did in classrooms, especially during and after Chancellor Michelle Rhee established the IMPACT teacher evaluation system and negotiated a new contract with the Washington Teachers' Union. Teachers' fear for their positions and hostility to school officials increased.[52]

And on the procedural side of teaching, DC policies obviously influenced teaching lessons. The Teaching and Learning Framework gave teachers a model of a "good" lesson as defined by the school district and accounted for the usual listing of standards and objectives on whiteboards, including pervasive use of initial warm-ups in lessons. Yet beyond these procedures, how the teacher taught, the organization and presentation of content and skills varied by teacher and how he or she taught, as did student responses in each of the three teachers' history classes.

One part of each history teacher's repertoire at Cardozo did differ from Glenville's history teachers. Cardozo teachers practiced elements of the New, New History, while three of the four Glenville teachers I observed did not. Topper, Faulkner, and Taylor all taught within a framework of the trying to get students to think historically, assess the value of primary and secondary sources, and construct their own accounts of what happened in the past. Of the three teachers, Taylor came closest to that concept of teaching history, while the others incorporated parts of this approach to varying degrees. At Glenville, by contrast, with the exception of some of what Lawrence Otter did, very little of this New, New History approach appeared in the practice of the teachers I observed or their syllabi and lessons.

Chapter 6 compares and contrasts history teaching at Glenville and Cardozo then and now and offers an answer to the central question of this book: *What has changed and what has remained the same in the content and pedagogy of high school history over the past half-century?*

CHAPTER 6

Stability and Change in Schools and History Classrooms— Then and Now

I put a dollar in a change machine. Nothing changed.
—George Carlin[1]

The quip could be coming from a disappointed reformer eager to improve public schools and classrooms but coming up with zilch. Unrealistic expectations and simple-minded views of change have haunted school reformers for over a century. Those hyped hopes and naive views explain why so often well-intentioned leaders often fall on their faces after adopted policies aimed at altering what happens daily in the nation's classrooms end up unimplemented. Smart, energetic decision makers frequently miss the complexity of change, of seeing that both continuity and change inhabit classrooms, schools, and districts. Like George Carlin, unfortunately, policymakers insert a dollar when they adopt policies and are disappointed when they see little change.

In this chapter, assessing what has remained stable and what has changed in these two urban high schools over the past half-century, I analyze each school's demography, size and organization, and students' academic performance. Following that analysis, I look beyond

159

the two high schools to compare and contrast what I observed and connect what I saw to macro- and micro-studies of contemporary teachers of history in the US over the past decade. Then I take a step back and see what patterns, if any, emerged for the two high schools and nationally over the entire period of five decades in the teaching of history.

WHY CHANGE?

The embrace of change (one can substitute *progress, reform,* or *improvement*) as an unalloyed good, particularly in public schools, is understandable. In the US, the idea of change is highly valued in the culture and daily life (e.g., high-fashion and automobiles get reworked annually, reinventing oneself is common, moving from one place to another is a national habit, standing in line overnight to buy the most recent technology is unremarkable). Change is equated with progress toward material or spiritual success (or both). Opposition to whatever planned change is proposed in a family, workplace, school, or community is often clothed in negative labels such as "resistance" or "supporting the status quo."[2]

The ideal of improving education has fueled myriad reform efforts over the past century. Reformers from both the political left and right have assumed that public school officials and practitioners oppose designed changes to keep things as they are. That assumption is in error.[3]

To dig a little deeper, there are two essential questions that come to the fore when examining change in US schools: *What are the goals of the changes?* and *In what ways have schools changed and in what ways have they remained stable?*

For over thirty years, policy elites—business, civic, philanthropic, and educational leaders—have lined up foursquare behind the ideas and sentiments of *A Nation at Risk* report which explicitly linked school improvement to national economic growth and stronger global competition in international markets. Increasing "human capital" (a.k.a. more high school and college graduates) has gripped policy elites like firefighters' jaws of life, driving reform-based policies to achieve these larger social and political aims. The economic purpose of public schooling has displaced traditional goals of civic responsibility, strengthening moral character, and improving the well-being of individuals and society.

In response, federal, state, and district policymakers have adopted expanded parental choice in schools, new curriculum standards, more standardized testing, tough accountability rules, and an unadorned affection for new technologies to equip the next generation with twenty-first-century skills. They have answered the question (What are the goals of the changes?) for over two generations of children. The fiscal, social, and educational costs of those reforms have run far more than George Carlin's dollar and yielded similarly paltry results.[4]

And how about the second question? In what ways have schools remained the same and in what ways have they remained stable? An obvious (and ignored) fact is that planned changes continually occur in districts, schools, and classrooms. Districts mandate different policies for schools to follow. Schools launch new programs. Teachers alter classroom tasks. In a word, change happens. But to most reformers, such changes do not make public theater or express their deeply felt hopes. They don't ring bells of joy, but tend to ignore actual changes as beside the point since such changes do not move the system of schools toward their desired goals.

Consider the New Orleans public schools. The past decade in New Orleans illustrates the direction in which reformers have moved to achieve their goal of binding schools to the economy through creating knowledgeable and skilled students who can gain entry-level jobs in the labor market.

No doubt exists that the city's schools have changed in the aftermath of Hurricane Katrina. The system has shifted from one of regular public schools operated by Orleans Parish School Board to the Recovery District—where forty charter organizations run fifty-eight schools, and only a handful continue to function as regular public schools. This restructuring has been applauded loudly by those reformers who see such changes as moving in the right direction—an entrepreneurial school system that they believe (though the evidence thus far is slim) will produce higher rates of attendance, graduation, and achievement in its over thirty thousand students than traditional Orleans Parish schools ever did. Others in New Orleans and elsewhere, however, see these dramatic changes as retrograde, dumping the goal of civic engagement in schools by destroying parental participation in schools and shrinking communities that heretofore looked to the neighborhood school for social glue, while creating a generation of graduates who see the sole purpose of tax-supported public schools as entirely vocational, that is, go to college and get a career.[5]

Yet even in New Orleans, there is an ever-present stability. Just because charter schools are new institutions, they still contain familiar regularities (and flaws) that mirror the schools they replaced. Charters are age-graded; their teachers follow daily routines; bell-schedules continue; employees are expected to abide by standard operating procedures from week to week. In short, stability is a defining trait of what occurs daily in organizations—even new ones.[6]

To maintain stability, however—and here is a contradiction—planned changes must occur. Continuity and change are flip sides of the same coin. The interdependency keeps organizations in balance. No classroom, school, or district is frozen in amber; they are constantly changing. Schools-within-a-school were created (recall that Glenville and Cardozo incorporated small schools over the past few decades); some have disappeared and some have remained. Mixes of student-centered and teacher-centered pedagogies evolved over time (again evidenced in Glenville and Cardozo) . Districts developed portfolios of school options from which parents could choose. Donald Schön's phrase *dynamic conservatism*, referring to organizations that "fight to remain the same," captures the nature of the frequent changes that strengthen institutional continuity in practice.[7]

What is too often overlooked in reformers' gusto for school improvement, however, is that planned changes vary in reach, magnitude, and pace. Consider the common types of planned changes—reforms—that can be made. Some are intended to create incremental changes (speedily or slowly) in the governance, organization, curriculum, or instruction (or some combination of these) of districts, schools, and classrooms. And some are intended to alter fundamentally (speedily or slowly) the structures and processes in all of those venues.

In the introduction, I distinguished between planned incremental and fundamental changes. *Incremental* changes—use of new computer devices in classrooms, having teachers act as student advisers for part of school day, new curriculum standards in history—added to the existing structures that shape schooling—what I called the "grammar of schooling." *Fundamental* changes designed by policymakers tried to alter the structures themselves—different funding mechanisms such as vouchers and charter schools, massive online instruction, schools-within-a-school, non-graded organization. Policymakers' adoption of these intended incremental and fundamental changes, however, did not mean that district administrators and classroom teachers automatically implemented them.

The gap between adoption of a policy and its implementation in classrooms (and there always is one) varies from an inch to a mile wide. There are many reasons for such gaps. There may be a lack of resources, the implementation design may be flawed, or policymakers may overlook—maybe ignore—the basic fact that teachers are gatekeepers who decide how much, if any, of a policy to put into practice and what to put into the closet. Teachers exercise constrained choice; that is, within each classroom, teachers determine how much they will teach, in what ways, and when. So the variation between Glenville and Cardozo High School history teachers then and now in how they taught and in how students responded reflected the limited but nonetheless crucial autonomy that teachers have when they close their classroom doors. Teachers, in short, are covert policymakers and exercise choice in both content and pedagogy when they determine what to accept, modify, and reject of those decisions made at school board meetings and in superintendent offices.[8]

Without this grasp of why Glenville teachers Mike Allison, Gary Hart, Barry Rabson, and Lawrence Otter differ from each other in their classroom lessons and their decisive role in determining the success of a policy change, whether incremental or fundamental, efforts to achieve improved classroom practices are futile. Moreover, that futility is compounded by a contradiction that lies at the very heart of school reform that policymakers too often fail to note.[9]

In their exuberant embrace of educational improvements, most contemporary policymakers disregard not only the reality that teachers, in their gatekeeper role, reach decisions in their lessons that make and unmake policy but also the enduring paradox at the core of tax-supported, compulsory schooling. Historically, public schools have been expected to conserve community and national values and traditions embedded in the goals of making citizens, preparing the next generation for the workplace, and enhancing the well-being of individual students and society. This expectation makes sense of the stability mentioned above. Yet these very same schools are also expected to give children and youth the knowledge and skills to make changes in their lives, communities, and yes, in those very values and traditions they have absorbed.[10]

This inherent conflict in values prizing both continuity and change helps explain the laundry list of contradictions that zealous reformers and ardent supporters of the traditional purposes for schooling have compiled about public schools:

- Schools are resistant to changes/schools adopt one fad after another.
- Schools change at a glacial pace/schools move at warp speed in embracing innovations.

These contrary complaints shed light on the paradox that, even after many changes are introduced into districts and schools, abiding routines and practices persist. In public schools, it is not change *or* stability; it is both at the same time. Coping with this contradiction in school reform requires policymakers and practitioners to recognize the conflict between conserving and changing beliefs and values as it plays out in the teaching of math, science, and history. Those conflicting tasks highlight the question that I asked at the beginning of this book: *What changed and what remained the same in the content and pedagogy in high school history over the past half-century?*[11]

In chapters 1 and 2, I described how I and other teachers taught history at Glenville and Cardozo High Schools between the late 1950s and mid-1960s. Because contexts matter in influencing what occurs in classroom lessons, I looked at the cities of Cleveland and Washington, DC, their school systems, and the two high schools before turning to the micro-view of the history classroom in each high school. In chapters 4 and 5, I used my observations after returning to those urban high schools in 2013–2014 to see what had changed and what had remained the same in each city, district, school, and history classrooms.

IN THE SCHOOLS—GLENVILLE AND CARDOZO THEN AND NOW

In comparing Glenville and Cardozo High Schools then and now, I saw clear signs of continuity mixed with changes crossing almost six decades.

Demography

For over a half-century, both schools remained minority and poor. Where Glenville in the 1950s did have a larger percentage of middle-class black families, by the mid-1960s, more low-income families had moved into the area, shifting the balance to a predominately poor, all-black high school, a condition that has lasted until the present day. Although Cardozo High School, on the other hand, remains majority black, the influx of immigrant families into adjacent neighborhoods in the past few decades has shifted the demographics so that today, one in three Cardozo students is Hispanic. The city's population has also undergone a dramatic shift with the entry of many young white professionals and families, shifting the district's population from majority black to majority white. That swing has yet to affect Cardozo's enrollment. In sum, both high schools have served minority families mired in poverty for over five decades (see appendix 3).

Size and School Organization

Enrollment at both high schools has shrunk dramatically over the decades so that by 2014, both schools hovered around seven hundred students, down from highs of over fifteen hundred students in previous decades. In both districts, new policies expanded school choice (e.g., magnets, alternative schools, and charters) giving parents opportunities to send their children to schools elsewhere in each district. Such choices cut each school's student population.

The schools have used different organizational designs over time to stabilize a changing demographic environment. Both remain age-graded schools, but have shifted at least once in their life cycle. Glenville was a tenth-to twelfth-grade high school until 1966. Then, after moving into a new building, it added the ninth grade and has remained a ninth- to twelfth-grade high school ever since. Cardozo had been a four-year high school since its move to the old Central High School in 1950. After district officials restructured the school in 2013, Cardozo became a six-year secondary school (grades 6–12) to attract students from nearby gentrifying neighborhoods. But they both continue as age-graded school organizations.

Both Glenville and Cardozo underwent internal reorganizations. In each case, district officials mandated the high school to create small schools and academies in the 1990s and since. Many were inaugurated and subsequently dropped or never fully implemented. In 2014, both schools still retain remnants of these schools-within-a-school (see appendix 3).

Allocating time to academic subjects in the daily schedule is also part of school organization and here again, the picture is more one of constancy than change. Glenville has maintained forty- to fifty-minute periods for nearly sixty years. Recently, Cardozo shifted from seven forty-five-minute periods to four eighty- to ninety-minute periods a day.

So we can say that organizational changes occurred. Whether these grade-level changes, establishing schools-within-a-school, and altering daily schedules one way or another make a difference in academic performance, no policymaker or researcher can say with any degree of confidence.[12]

Academic Outcomes

Over a half-century, the academic performance of Glenville and Cardozo High School students ran from mediocre to poor as measured by test scores, high school graduation rates, percentages of students dropping out, and number of students entering college. Of course, there were students in each high school who earned diplomas and went on to college (in 2013, for example, Glenville had two AP courses and Cardozo had eight). However, they were a small fraction of their class that had started in the ninth grade. Overall academic outcomes were consistently low. By 2014, under NCLB requirements, district officials had restructured both high schools not once, but twice, meaning that the principal and entire staff were replaced. In both instances, teachers could reapply for their old posts, but it was up to the principal which teachers rejoined the faculty.[13]

In the past half-century, many changes in demography, school size, school organization, and students' academic performance surely occurred. Demographic shifts in student population and reduced enrollments were unplanned changes. Planned changes included new grade levels at each school; alteration of daily time schedules; the reorganizing of each high school into schools-within-a-school; and two restructurings of each school as a result of persistently low academic performances. Although these changes are intended to be fundamental in nature, they turned out to be more like incremental changes because none of them altered the basic grammar of schooling.

Underlying, and undermining, those supposed fundamental changes was a regularity in school processes that went undisturbed. Students and subjects designated by grade level continued. Each school remained organized by departments. Teachers had separate classrooms, twenty-five to thirty students were enrolled in each class, students entered and left each class as bells marked the beginning and end of the period. Students were still required to sit in classes for a specified time in order to pass courses required for graduation. All of these regularities in schooling permeated what students, teachers, and administrators did between 8 a.m. and 3 p.m., five days a week for the thirty-six weeks of the school year. So after all of these intended "fundamental" changes in each high school, the grammar of schooling put into place in the early twentieth century was still alive and thumping in 2014.[14]

THE NATIONAL PICTURE

Are Glenville and Cardozo High Schools similar to other urban high schools across the nation in terms of demography, school size, organization, and students' academic performance? Yes, they are.

Like so many other urban schools, Glenville and Cardozo High Schools are in the lowest quartile of public schools across the country. Low academic performance, high dropout rates, just over half of students earning diplomas, and falling enrollments demonstrate remarkable parallels. Repeated efforts to reverse the cycle of failure have fallen short time and again. A few years ago, urban schools that had 60 percent or less of their students earning diplomas were labeled "dropout factories." Of all high schools in the nation, 15 percent fell into that category, including Glenville and Cardozo.[15]

Under NCLB, five years of not meeting Adequate Yearly Progress requires a school to make fundamental changes—a *restructuring*—in its operation. District officials can go for an organizational *reconstitution* (for example, close down the school and reopen it as a charter school); they can also choose less onerous alternatives called *transformation* and *turnaround* options. The latter choices required dumping the principal and staff. The lowest of the low-performing schools—the bottom 5 percent—became eligible in 2009 for federal School Improvement Grants.

Low-performing Glenville and Cardozo faced these choices when they repeatedly failed to meet AYP.

Anyone who would gamble that restructuring would make failing urban high schools rise into the first or second quartile of US schools would face odds running 70:1 against. The persistence of dwindling academic achievement in low-performing urban high schools throughout the nation over decades is both stunning and wretched. The experiences of Glenville and Cardozo High Schools are heartbreakingly similar to the national picture. Both high schools have been restructured twice within a decade (Glenville also received federal School Improvement Grants, although Cardozo did not). In both schools, over decades, planned changes occurred in staffing, curriculum, reorganization of the larger school into smaller ones, and introduction of new technologies yet those intentionally designed changes, whether implemented incrementally or in one fell swoop (restructuring) have not reversed chronic low performance. Even with district support and efforts by school principal and staff, failure persisted.

The grim consistency of the data on how hard it is to turnaround failing schools is overwhelming—another sign that no fundamental change had occurred in such schools regardless of the hyped-up language reformers used.[16]

What is unclear, however, is whether these features of failing urban high schools persist because of demographics and the influence of poverty on schooling and student outcomes or whether it's because these schools continue year after year under the shadow of the grammar of schooling. Or is it some combination of poverty and regularities in age-graded schooling of children and youth? In short, are the historical metrics of these low-performing urban high schools, including Glenville and Cardozo, also metrics of poverty's influence on schools operating within the grammar of schooling?

Amid that uncertainty about what causes urban schools to perform so poorly, I turn to what ways history teachers in these schools over the past half-century continued and changed familiar classroom practices.

TEACHING HISTORY AT GLENVILLE AND CARDOZO THEN AND NOW

Teaching History a Half-Century Ago

In chapters 1 and 2, I summarized what I had reconstructed of my own teaching and that of other history teachers from the late 1950s through the mid-1960s. In chapter 1, I recalled that as a novice teacher at Glenville, I hewed closely to the then dominant pattern of teacher-centered instruction, leaning heavily on the textbook, lecturing, leading guided discussions of content, going over homework assignments, and assigning students occasional projects. As I gained classroom experience and experimented with materials on explicit teaching of thinking skills and using primary sources in what was then called Negro history, I slowly incorporated small group work, student-chosen research projects, more student participation in discussions, debates, and reports to class. I gradually developed a hybrid of teacher- and student-centered techniques that I carried with me to the Cardozo Project in Urban Teaching.

At Cardozo High School (recounted in chapter 2), working with history interns who had served overseas in the Peace Corps, I brought my Glenville lessons about ethnic and racial content, using primary sources, and critical thinking skills to bear. The blending of teacher- and student-centered activities became the model of teaching in our classrooms and was enhanced by a chance convergence with the national flowering of inquiry approaches, using primary sources, and asking the questions historians ask in the New Social Studies. That accidental merger may not have been attributable to divine providence, but it was close.

Although the sample of social studies teachers teaching history classes at the two schools is small (just twenty-plus teachers, including interns), I compared and contrasted what I experienced then with studies of US social studies classrooms between the 1950s and 1970s. The overriding patterns of teacher-centered instruction I saw in my

Glenville and Cardozo classrooms and those of peers and interns were similar, but not identical, to those of teachers across the country whose schools and classrooms had been studied and documented by scholars of the day.[17]

Teaching History Now

Since the 1990s, efforts to teachers teach history in ways that get students to think, read, and understand the past as professional historians do has coalesced into a multifaceted movement, not as widespread as the New Social Studies was in the 1960s, but still expanding into classrooms across the country as I write. In chapter 3, I called this the *New, New History* movement.

As I noted, this current reform of history teaching mirrored earlier efforts during the New Social Studies in the 1960s and scattered initiatives in the original New History of the early twentieth century.[18] Previous reforms tried to disrupt the tedious pattern of lecture, textbook, homework so characteristic of how teachers taught history. This century-long unfolding of reform efforts—up to the current day—to alter how teachers teach history is the background context. The foreground context is that Glenville and Cardozo High Schools in 2013–2014 continue to serve minority and poor families.

In turning now to the social studies teachers teaching history at Glenville and Cardozo whom I observed and interviewed in 2013–2014, again the sample is small (seven in total). What I observed in both schools, over a score of lessons, was a dominant pattern of teacher-centered, history textbook, and test-bound instruction, especially at Glenville, with occasional hybrid lessons that blended student- and teacher-centered instruction. At Cardozo, however, there were also instances of lessons using primary source materials derived from the New, New History on a daily basis. At Glenville, only Lawrence Otter had students work on a newspaper project and used a textbook reflecting the New, New History that paid attention to primary and secondary sources, including awareness of bias. In sum, just four teachers (one teacher at Glenville, and Cardozo's three history teachers) taught with varying degrees of effectiveness the content and skills consistent with the New, New History.

At Glenville, of the four teachers I observed (the entire department), all taught squarely within the teacher-centered tradition and conventional ways of teaching history through the textbook, homework, in-class worksheets, guided whole-group discussions recalling facts, and multiple-choice tests. That said, depending on the teacher, students' responses varied from strong engagement with content (Mike Allison's and Lawrence Otter's classes) to apathy and persistent clock-watching (Gary Hart's and Barry Rabson's classes). Allison and Otter had developed hybrid versions of teaching where I observed lessons and materials reflecting student choices and voices. The four teachers' syllabi, interviews, and direct observation showed me that none of the teachers directly taught students to read like historians, do historical thinking, or evaluate sources they used. Indirectly, Allison (students closely inspecting photos of civil rights movement events) did so and Otter (students creating a historical newspaper of a particular decade in the twentieth century) came closest to representing the New, New History in both content and ways of teaching.

In these teachers' classes, however, I did note that the textbooks they periodically used in world history and US history contained many primary sources, thoughtful essential questions, and tasks that called for critical thinking skills.[19] All the Glenville teachers, except for Lawrence Otter, used those texts sparingly.

At Cardozo High School, the situation differed. From my observations, interviews, and review of class materials of the three teachers I observed in their world history and US history lessons, I found that all three clearly fell into the teacher-centered instruction pattern with varied student participation in classroom activities. Within the confines of an eighty-minute period, all three had students analyze primary sources, use printed worksheets that focused on a divisive question, take a stand on the issues, and provide evidence to support their position.

Mike Topper, a first-year teacher, was the least experienced of the three. Shelves and boxes in his world history classes held interactive notebooks and texts that proudly featured primary sources.[20] Topper also prepared lessons that asked students to read like historians. But his students ranged from those who were borderline out-of-control to those who were apathetic and hostile to his teaching efforts. In general, they were inattentive when he lectured or asked questions.

That was not the case with his colleagues. When I watched veteran teacher Kerry Faulkner's US history class working on their end-of-semester research papers, I saw that most were engaged, even anxious about completing the paper on its due date. From my observations in Faulkner's classroom and in the library, it was evident that distinguishing between primary and secondary sources and writing were critical for the completion of the research paper. In class, Faulkner made clear that their paper had to answer a central question and have a logical argument supported by evidence. Students understood these elements of the final paper, as their answers to my questions in the library showed. Moreover, the syllabus Faulkner distributed earlier in the semester to students and parents was chock-full of historical questions, opportunities for analyzing primary and secondary sources, and materials connecting history to the present that would give advocates of the New, New History goose bumps. The textbook for the US history course, *The American Vision: Modern Times*, contained primary sources and exercises that guided students to read and think like historians.[21] To the best of my knowledge, Faulkner had not participated in any professional development for reading and thinking like a historian; rather, through his own observations of teachers he admired, research he had selectively sampled, and experience in his own teaching, he had come up with a meld of teacher- and student-centered activities that included what many in the New, New History movement would have applauded.

Only Burt Taylor used an actual lesson drawn from the inventory of the Stanford History Education Group. A five-year veteran drawn from the Teach for America program, Taylor's "Invasion of Nanking" unit orchestrated a tightly controlled, timed set of activities into a hybrid lesson combining teacher- and student-centered activities. The class thoroughly gripped students. Student participation exceeded anything I had seen in either Glenville or other Cardozo history lessons.

I saw this lesson at the end of the spring semester, and it was clear to me that the students had been trained during this course to do such document analyses through small-group work and whole group instruction. As noted in chapter 5, Taylor had used SHEG lessons before, downloading them from the Internet after finding them in the course of his own search for materials, rather than learning of them through any district or school-based professional development on historical reading, thinking, and understanding.

In sum, I concluded that in this small sample of history teaching at Glenville and Cardozo urban high schools, all of the teaching fell within the historical framework of teacher-centered, content-driven instruction with the clear development of hybrids. At Cardozo, the New, New History was evident in the classes of all three teachers I observed and interviewed. Just a glimmer, however, appeared among the four teachers who formed the history department at Glenville.[22]

TEACHING HISTORY ACROSS THE NATION IN THE EARLY TWENTY-FIRST CENTURY

To what degree did Glenville and Cardozo history classrooms echo patterns of teaching across the United States? Keep in mind that in 2003 (the latest figures I could find) there were about fifty-seven thousand history teachers nationally. Also note that no large-scale surveys of these teachers' teaching practices have been done since the mid-1990s. The data I use to answer this question comes from surveys done of small samples of this population, student descriptions of history teaching, firsthand accounts from history teachers, research studies of small groups and individual teachers, and my own research and experience in many high schools observing social studies teachers, most of whom taught history. Without apologies, I note that this effort to answer the question is a sketchy first pass only. Far more data is needed to give a national picture of history instruction in the past decade when the movement for the New, New History has emerged.[23]

The Incomplete Mosaic of History Instruction

The baseline of how teachers taught history up until the 1990s is the familiar pattern of teacher-centered instruction with slow growth of blends with student-centered activities. The sequence of activities that history teachers designed and students encountered included lectures, note taking, textbook assignments, tests, and occasional small group work and projects. A small minority of teachers departed from this pattern, but the vast majority stayed within its boundaries.[24]

In 1994–1995, the National Center for Education Statistics published *What Happens in Classrooms? Instructional Practices in Elementary and Secondary Schools*, a national survey of nearly four thousand teachers, including self-reports from social studies teachers. Over 90 percent of the teachers surveyed taught in age-graded elementary and secondary schools.

The picture that emerges nearly duplicates what social studies teachers—the majority of whom teach history courses—have done in the twentieth century up through the aftermath of the New Social Studies. In 1994–1995, social studies teachers reported that in a typical week:

- 78 percent lectured
- 88 percent led question-answer sessions
- 91 percent asked students recall questions
- 96 percent led whole-group discussions
- 61 percent worked with small groups
- 31 percent had students work on projects[25]

In 2009, a national random sample of twelve hundred social studies teachers, half of whom taught US or world history, responded to a survey that gave the following snapshot. Of the random sample, 74 percent reported that they made a presentation or led a discussion to the entire group in "every class" or "almost every class." Students used the textbook 75 percent of the time for lessons. Just under 40 percent of teachers reported that they used small groups during lessons.[26]

The picture of mostly teacher-centered, content-driven classroom activities revealed by the second survey, a decade and a half after the earlier national survey, suggests that the dominant pattern of teacher-centered instruction heavy on delivering content, although allowing for hybrids, persisted. Direct evidence of use of materials where students learn to read, think, and write as historians, however, is missing from these surveys, since the designers of the questionnaire did not address the issue.

Yet by the early 2000s, using primary sources in classrooms and students learning the kind of questions historians ask of sources, seeking corroboration, and creating arguments with accompanying evidence to answer historical questions had become "best practices" for training novice history teachers and a model for newcomers and veterans to teach students history. Some of the Teaching American History (TAH) grants throughout the first decade of the twenty-first century focused on NNH skills in developing materials and training teachers.[27]

How Many Teachers Teach the New, New History?

Answering the question of what percentage of teachers over the decades have used lessons crafted to simulate how historians read, think, write, and come to understand the past is tough. No national studies that cover the classroom practices of the nearly sixty thousand social studies teachers in the United States have been done since the mid-1990s. But there are data fragments, even slivers, that can be assembled into a mosaic from which emerges a shadowy picture of how teachers have taught and are teaching history.

I have already described what I found among Glenville's and Cardozo's seven teachers. Three Cardozo teachers actively used primary sources, taught students how to analyze such sources, and raise questions that historians would ask about Reconstruction in the United States, the Great Depression, and the Egyptian Pyramids. My data, however, consists of splinters. Much more data is needed to amass a recognizable picture.

Here are a few other shards. Data on materials that teach students how to read, write, and think like historians comes from Advanced Placement courses that have been taught since the mid-1950s. Recall the opening of chapter 3, where Edwin Fenton describes teaching AP history at Pittsburgh's Taylor-Allderdice High School in 1960. The Document-Based Question (DBQ), a way of analyzing a primary source, was part of the AP exam in 1973. The question was designed, in the words of one of its authors, to make students "become junior historians and play the role of historians" for the hour they worked on it. Those who took AP history courses, then, were clearly exposed to materials and tasks that replicated the work of historians. However, no AP history course was taught at Glenville High School in 2013–2014. At Cardozo High School, one of the three teachers I interviewed had taught AP US History periodically but not in 2013–2014.[28] So those high school teachers in urban high schools nationally who teach AP history courses teach at least one section of AP students and as well as other history classes—already use hybrids of teacher-centered instruction for a College Board–centered, textbook-bound curriculum heavily geared to how historians read, think, and write. The vast majority of history teachers, however, do not teach AP courses.

Another sliver of data comes from the view afforded by the large-scale effort undertaken by the Reading Like a Historian Project at Stanford University under the leadership of Sam Wineburg. That project has recorded nearly 2 million viewers (all 50 states and 127 countries) who have downloaded these free curriculum materials since they were first posted in 2009. Just in 2014, there were more than 630,000 visits to the website to copy over 100 different lessons for US and world history courses. Moreover, Wineburg and his team are now providing professional development to history teachers in big city and suburban school districts on how to use these and similar lessons to add interactive pieces to lessons and do classroom assessments.[29]

Downloaded lessons, though, do not necessarily transfer to classroom use. Finding out the degree to which these lessons and similar ones designed by teachers are used weekly, occasionally, or not at all requires studies of history teachers' classroom practices. I have not yet located such studies. It is worth noting that it was not until the New Social Studies had already exited stage right from the passions of the 1960s and early 1970s that academic studies of teacher use NSS materials were completed. It may take equally long for studies on SHEG lessons or similar materials for students to appear. This far, no researcher has documented use of these materials apart from AP history courses that have embedded document-based questions and the work habits of historians.[30]

What little data there is about the degree to which history content and pedagogy have moved from textbook-bound conventional pedagogy to the inquiry-, primary-source-driven historical approach comes from scattered small reports of social studies teachers, again through surveys rather than direct observations, interviews, and examination of classroom materials. Like the above fragments, they add a few more chipped tiles to the mosaic of teacher use of New, New History materials.

One national study (2004), for example, used a random sample of social studies teachers to determine the purpose of and the classroom use of primary sources. The authors concluded that although respondents acknowledged the importance of using historical sources and having students do historical inquiry, " . . . teachers' actual use of both classroom-based and web-based primary sources was somewhat low."[31] A similar report of social studies teachers in one Virginia county found that teachers "report that they are only occasional users of historical primary sources; however, when they do use these sources, they obtain them primarily from textbooks and the web."[32]

My own studies add another shard to add to the fragmentary picture that emerges from bits and pieces. Over the past five years, apart from my study of Glenville and Cardozo High School history teachers, I have visited fifteen teachers' classrooms, observing twenty-one lessons and examining classroom materials. These visits took place mostly in Northern California as part of different studies I was doing on technology use and at the invitation of these teachers. Clearly, the sample was non-random, but I offer it as another piece of evidence. Eight of these fifteen teachers (four of whom taught AP history) used primary sources and questioned students to get at historical thinking on a particular topic.[33]

Finally, over the years, researchers have published individual case studies of novice and experienced history teachers using the New, New History approach. In many instances, such case studies were exemplars of how to convert textbook-bound lessons into ones that included historical thinking skills. These studies made the simple point that as hard as it may appear to social studies teachers to alter their teacher-centered, content-driven pedagogy given the contexts in which they teach (e.g., state tests, accountability regulations, age-graded school, and poverty-ridden neighborhoods), this approach can be successfully used within the framework of existing public schools, including those located in cities. It is clear that these teachers are exceptions, not the rule. None of the studies finds that the profiled teachers and lessons are the norm for history teachers, although authors imply they should and can be.[34]

What Do the Pieces Tell Us? History Teaching Now

Do all of these splintered tiny tiles add up to a clear picture of history teaching in 2015? Hardly. While historians, teacher-educators, and researchers are leading a small-scale reform of history teaching, no single study or group of studies has yet determined the degree to which the content and practices in US classrooms have changed in the desired direction. What is clear, however, is that the historic pattern of teacher-centered instruction where lecture, whole group discussion, small-group work, reliance on the textbook and worksheets, homework, and tests persist as typical history lessons. The splinters of data I picked up in Glenville and the other high schools I visited in Northern California reflected the dominant national pattern of teaching history. I have not yet seen any accumulated, credible evidence that this pattern has substantially altered in most high schools in the past decade. Cardozo High School, however, did offer a different picture.

My observations and interviews of the three teachers there suggested that some small fraction of high school history teachers have adopted the approach of the New, New History in their hybrids of teacher-centered instruction.

There are indeed a portion of high school history teachers like those Cardozo teachers, who, while continuing to use largely teacher-centered approaches, have enthusiastically and credibly adopted historical inquiry through primary sources to teach students critical thinking skills as they learn how historians read, think, and write.

How large is that slice? I don't know. But I can make an informed guess based on earlier efforts to alter classroom content and practice. Consider previous large-scale reforms to alter the practice of teaching: the twentieth-century progressive movement to shift teaching from teacher- to student-centered pedagogy; the mid-century, academic-developed new curricula aimed at turning students into investigators in science, math, and history; and the Open Classroom movement of the late-1960s. In those national efforts to change how and what teachers did in their classrooms, I estimated that up to one out of four elementary school teachers adopted and adapted some version of the pedagogical reforms, while one out of five secondary school teachers doing the same.

I cannot look around a corner and see what will happen with the New, New History movement. While the Common Core standards emphasize awareness of sources and the cultivation of problem-solving and thinking skills, I cannot say to what degree that the standards have influenced the teaching of history. Sam Wineburg has made explicit the links between reading and thinking as a historian, and I would guess others have done the same. But whether that portion of history teachers who embrace this approach will continue to expand, crest, or shrink, I cannot yet say.

For now, based on these shards of evidence I have compiled and the analogies of the past, I estimate that between 15 and 25 percent of social studies teachers (including those teaching AP course) have adopted versions of teaching history as inquiry where primary sources are used at least once a week to help students learn how historians read, think, and write. However, although those teachers adopting different versions of this approach have, indeed altered the content of their lessons, they have not necessarily changed how they teach. Having students handle primary sources, ask questions of sources that historians ask, more often than not, still falls within some version of teacher-centered instruction.[35]

SO WHAT?

I have come to the end of this study of history teaching in two urban high schools separated in time by nearly six decades. My analysis of change and stability in the contexts of two cities, school district policies, school practices, and teacher lessons creates a picture—clear in parts, blurred in others. The mosaic reveals dynamically conservative organizations in which nearly three generations of teachers have taught history. Stepping back from this picture, fuzzy as it is, I ask readers to consider whether this inquiry into change and continuity in schools, the teaching of history then and now, have a larger meaning for reform-driven policymakers, practitioners, and researchers. I can sum this up into a single question: *So what?*

I ask this question to look for any relevance to, significance of, and implications for those policymakers, practitioners, and researchers who tirelessly seek to remedy school and classroom problems. These remedies often require planned changes, or reforms, in school governance, organization, curriculum, or instruction (or combinations thereof). This personal and scholarly inquiry into teaching history contains, I believe, important lessons especially for policymakers, but also for practitioners and researchers who seek improvements in public schools. I offer here four lessons that, in my judgment, account for the turmoil surrounding contemporary school reform and answer the "So what?" question.

Policymakers Erred in Framing the Problem of Failing Schools

Three decades of school reformers have operated under the assumption that all US schools are broken. Comparisons of international test scores and looking abroad for models of "good" schools have confirmed in the minds of policy elites that the US system of schooling in its totality—over 100,000 schools with 3 million-plus teachers serving over 50 million students—is badly damaged. Damaged schools, current reformers believe, harm the nation's economy. The economy is dependent on renewable "human capital," and when schools cannot deliver sufficiently knowledgeable and skilled graduates, they fail to keep the nation competitive in global markets. As a result, US prosperity is undercut

The *Nation at Risk* report that appeared in 1983 first made explicit this marriage between the economy and public schools. In response, state and federal policymakers mandated curriculum standards, testing, and accountability regulations and the No Child Left Behind law. Those reforms converted policy rhetoric into a national program of school improvement aimed at all classroom teachers.

Yet so much of the current reform agenda of improvement concentrates on urban schools such as Glenville and Cardozo High Schools. From calls for more charter schools to closing the white/black gap in academic achievement to restructuring failing high schools to recruiting better teachers, reformers end up trying to fix urban schools filled with minorities, not largely white middle-class and affluent suburban and exurban schools. Certainly, these reforms have affected white, affluent suburbs and distant exurban districts such as Beverly Hills, California, Northbrook, Illinois, and Prince William County, Virginia, but overall they have escaped the full brunt of these reforms.

The policy error, then, is in conflating two separate problems—academically low-performing urban schools and soft spots in the US economy—that policymakers attribute to one problem: broken US schools. That unexamined fusion of two distinct problems has been a policy virus that has infected school reforms in governance, organization, curriculum, and instruction over the past thirty years.

Policymakers Have Largely Ignored the Macro- and Micro-Context of Schooling in Making School and Classroom Decisions

What further complicates a shotgun marriage of separate problems and worsens the policy error is the lack of clarity about how much of this merged problem can be remedied inside schools and how much can be done outside schools.

Contemporary reformers have concentrated on solving the national economic problem and failing urban students from within schools. Giving parents more choices in schools, more efficient school governance, more demanding curriculum, added testing, coercive accountability, and a rigorously evaluated teacher corps unprotected by seniority and tenure rules capture contemporary policies aimed at improving US schools. The trickle-down effects of these federal and state policies have touched history lessons at Glenville and Cardozo.

Politically smart but myopic policymakers have concentrated on inside-school remedies—missing a key factor in the micro-context of the school and classroom. Present reformers have been blind to the *grammar of schooling*—the workplace in which students and teachers live six hours daily, 180 days a year. The structure of the age-graded school, its norms of progress and regress, isolation of academic subjects from one another, daily schedule, and separating teachers from one another in self-contained classrooms has generated regularities in teacher and student behaviors, attitudes, and values for well over a century. This "machinery of instruction" influences how teachers teach and what students learn.[36] Evidence drawn from studies done in schools over the past century and lessons observed at Glenville and Cardozo, past and present, make that connection clear. Yet much of the current reform agenda takes the grammar of schooling for granted. As part of the landscape that reformers traverse it is the background that few notice but all accept as normal.

Not only do current reformers disregard the age-graded school structures, separation of subjects, and the academic culture accompanying those structures, they discount what occurs outside the schools or the macro-context. Few current policymakers are inclined to look at factors that also influence student and teacher behavior, such as socioeconomic structures (e.g., residential segregation, unequal funding of schools), inequalities in income and wealth, and effects of policy elites—their power to shape reform agendas and decisions, make tax policy, and protect their financial and social interests. There are, of course, solid reasons for ignoring these structures. Making policies to change what is in schools is far easier politically than altering structures embedded deeply in the very socioeconomic system of democratic capitalism.

For now, current reformers—over the past thirty years—have framed the problem of schooling as a national one but in practice have focused most intently on failing urban schools while ignoring the macro- and micro-contexts in which schools and teachers operate daily. That is another policy error.

Teachers Are Policymakers

The policy-to-practice journey ends at the threshold of the teacher's classroom. As gatekeepers to their classrooms, teachers are de facto policymakers. They decide what content to teach and what practices to use in daily lessons. Yet top federal, state, and local decision makers see the policy formation and adoption stages as the be-all and end-all of getting teachers to change their classroom practices. The final stage of implementation is rhetorically important but policymakers too often exit the stage and let the policy go unmonitored as it wends its way into schools and classrooms.

That is another error in policy thinking and action. As gatekeepers, teachers are seldom included in the loop when policy is formed and then adopted. Only when policymakers see the critical importance of the implementation stage do they bring teachers in—often too late, because teachers' ideas and perspectives have been excluded from the first phase of policy formation. It is the same error that high-tech entrepreneurs eager to improve schooling and teaching make when they create devices and software for teachers and students to use, then get administrators' approval to pilot the hardware and software without a nod to teachers ideas and the realities they face. After all, the real customers—the users—are teachers, not administrators. Like CEOs of tech companies, policymakers engage in beta testing with reforms in governance, organization, curriculum, and instruction.

What distinguishes the New, New History movement is that the academics and practitioners who support it do recognize the pivotal role that teachers perform as gatekeepers by designing materials that accommodate the constrained workplace within which teachers and students find themselves. For example, the Stanford History Education Group explicitly developed lessons—tinkering with the language of primary sources to help English Language Learners and students whose reading skills are limited—that can be taught within the constraints of meeting state curriculum standards, fifty-minute periods, and in units that cover no longer than a day or two rather than a units. They have explicitly linked lessons to meeting Common Core standards in literacy and thinking skills. The popularity of these lessons, which can be freely downloaded from their website, are one marker of the wisdom of their insights—as well as awareness of the flaws in the New Social Studies of two generations ago. The trade-off is that the SHEG group accepts the existing confines of the age-graded school. Then again, these academics and practitioners are not in the policy position of altering the school workplace.[37]

Teachers Continue to Manage the Classroom Dilemma of Skills Versus Content

Both *heritage-* and *historical-*driven teachers wrestle with the tension over teaching content and teaching skills in their courses. Most history teachers value highly both subject matter ("students need to know the context of an event") content and skills ("students need to read closely sources and corroborate their accuracy"). They know that the two are inseparable. Yet the either/or conundrum pops up again and again. Across science, math, English, and social studies, classroom teachers weigh whether they are content-driven or skills-driven in their teaching. The popular (and false) dichotomy afflicts all academic subjects; it generates more emotional heat than incandescent light.

A *historical* lesson on the Homestead Steel Strike of 1892 or the Nanking Invasion in 1937, for example, is seemingly focused on skills used in examining a primary source for bias and close reading of a document. Yet the lesson would necessarily be chock-full of content. Thus, content versus skills is a false choice. The more appropriate question about teaching an academic subject like history is: where on a continuum of content at one pole and skills at the other pole, would history teachers place themselves? For example, history teachers committed to the *heritage* approach would place themselves on the content side of the continuum, yet still have lessons that get students to analyze documents and identify assumptions.

All teachers would have a center of gravity along that continuum. Some would be smack in the center, equally dividing their lessons into mixes of both, depending on their training and topic they were teaching; others would tilt toward the skills side. I, for one, would place myself near the center but clearly on the skills side of the continuum. Here's a reflection by an eleventh-grade history teacher who would locate herself on a different spot:

> I'm a fan of primary sources. But I'm not so much a fan of the "what do you think" form of history . . . I don't think asking kids to decide "who is more believable" or "which side is responsible" is a useful way to teach history. I'm not creating historians. I'm teaching history and—hopefully—showing kids that history isn't just a case of "what happened" . . . As you know, I believe strongly in teaching content while also teaching skills—particularly reading. And despite the occasional problems, the reading is going very well. I hope they remember the content, but I know they are spending more time actually reading.[38]

Another teacher from a private college prep school had this to say about the historical approach:

Are students in K–12 really ready to think like historians? We believe that learning content at this stage is of utmost importance rather than trying to force an analysis of primary source documents onto students. Yes, we introduce them to historical sources and ask them to read longer works of literature or non-fiction, but we often find the lack of content knowledge of basic historical periods—Western or otherwise—to be an impediment to the sort of analysis hoped for in the Common Core or DBQ [document-based-question] dynamic . . .

   In the end, we believe that asking a student to "read like an historian" a narrative of an ANZAC soldier at Gallipoli will be lost time unless the student has had the background knowledge of the British Empire, Australia or New Zealand, the Great War and Ottoman history.[39]

These teachers locate themselves at different points on the continuum of content and skills. Replacing a false dichotomy with a continuum, of course, would hardly erase the hard questions—here is where the dilemma enters—that continue to accompany decisions on history content and skills: To what degree should time—a scarce resource in a fifty-minute period—be set aside in lessons to acquire and strengthen skills while teaching historical content? To what degree should student acquisition of skills drive selection of content? Regardless of where history teachers place themselves on this continuum, the dilemma generating both the questions and their answers still remain highly contested in 2015.

In answering the question *So what?*, I bring to a close this personal and scholarly inquiry into the teaching of history in two urban high schools a half-century apart. At the very core of a tax-supported public schools in a democracy is the paradox of an institution committed to both conserving values and beliefs and simultaneously changing those prized values and beliefs as children and youth work their way through preK–12 years on to adulthood. Teaching history—as well as other academic subjects—contains that core contradiction and the struggles that policymakers and practitioners face in reconciling opposite expectations.

The constant tension between stability and change in public schools is not always pretty and often frustrating to those who seek improvement. Yet without the deep understanding of the paradoxical mission of US public schools and awareness of common policy errors and enduring dilemmas, chances of avoiding cyclical reforms and helping students, teachers, and the larger polity are slim.

APPENDIX A

Methodology

Three aspects of my methodology need elaboration:

1. How did I reconstruct my teaching of history at Glenville and Cardozo High Schools between 1956 and 1967?
2. How did I construct the teaching of history at Glenville and Cardozo High Schools in 2014?
3. In what ways did my skills as a historian and writing about my experiences in the past help and hinder the account I constructed.

How did I reconstruct my teaching of history at Glenville and Cardozo High Schools between 1956 and 1967?

The design of the book is basically two case studies that answer the question: *What has changed and what has remained the same in the content and pedagogy of high school history over the past half-century?* I used the common historical methodology of seeking out multiple primary and secondary sources to describe and analyze the macro- and micro-contexts—that is, national movements (e.g., civil rights, the New Social Studies), city and school district settings, and what happened during the decade I taught in Cleveland and Washington, DC.

Primary sources included district school board minutes, local newspaper articles, available school archives, and district and school reports and studies published in the late 1950s through the late 1960s.

I used secondary sources to establish national socioeconomic and political forces that influenced each city (e.g., the civil rights movement, demographic changes, shifts in the economic base). Other secondary sources included descriptions of how teachers taught elsewhere in the nation during these years. I tapped histories of Cleveland's and the District of Columbia's black communities, the political and socioeconomic forces at work in those cities in the 1950s and 1960s, and their links to changes in the two districts in those years.

These sources permitted me to recapture the macro-contexts within which my classroom teaching unfolded. I used a similar mix of sources to portray the micro-setting of my classrooms in each district and how history teachers in other locations taught.

For my teaching at Glenville and Cardozo High Schools between 1956 and 1967, I used the following primary sources:

1. Student study guides I created and used in my US history and world history classes at Glenville (two former students kept copies and sent them to me), lesson plans and readings I used in classes at Cardozo High School, and syllabi I wrote for social studies seminars I led for the Cardozo Project in Urban Teaching Interns.

2. Student assignments at Glenville that I had graded and commented on (one of the above students sent a packet of her work to me from 1960).

3. Personal journal I kept for 1961 to 1967.

4. Annual yearbooks from Glenville (*The Olympiad*) and Cardozo (*Purple Wave*) for the years I taught.

5. Glenville student newspaper articles for the time period.

6. Newspaper articles from the *Cleveland Press* and *Cleveland Plain Dealer* from the years I taught at Glenville; articles on Cardozo High School from the *Washington Post* and *Washington Evening Star*.

7. Cleveland School District documents, including board of education minutes, special reports, and memos.
8. District of Columbia documents, including board of education minutes, memos, and official reports. I also have in my possession Cardozo Project in Urban Teaching memos, internal documents, and correspondence from Joan Wofford, interns, and my letters to various people. In recent years, I have also kept e-mails written by former interns.

In returning to the two high schools I taught in a half-century ago, what methods did I use to describe what I saw and heard?

I spent two weeks at each high school. I visited Glenville High School November 12–15, 2013. The media center specialist set me up in a room adjacent to the library filled with yearbooks and uncatalogued issues of the student newspaper for the years just before, during, and after I taught there. For recent years, I found scattered issues of the yearbook for the years 1990–2010.

At Cardozo, I spent December 9–13, 2013, navigating the school library and storage closets for past and current school reports, evaluations, yearbooks, and student newspapers. The high school had just reopened after a two-year-long renovation of its facilities. Many materials had been tossed out or destroyed in the move to prepare for the renovation; some had been stored at other sites, but I could not locate any staff members who knew where they were.

I established a relationship with one veteran English teacher, Frazier O'Leary, who had become a local celebrity in his dedicated work with Advanced Placement English students. He had been at Cardozo High School since 1977. I interviewed him during the week, since he had seen many changes in principals, faculty, students, and staff. He introduced me to the school principal and two history teachers I could observe on my next trip to DC. One world history teacher invited me in to observe two of his lessons.

After some digging, I located a basement room containing issues of yearbooks from 1990 and 2010. There had been no yearbooks published for 2011 through 2013. I also visited the District of Columbia school collections at the Charles Sumner Museum and located newspaper clippings about Cardozo High School covering the years 1975–2007.

In the next round of visits, I observed lessons and interviewed teachers. I went to Glenville for the week of April 28–May 2, 2014. I interviewed the principal and three of the four social studies teachers. I observed a total of eight classes (forty-five-minute periods) of these four teachers. Overall, I spent an entire period in at least one class of each teacher. For one world history teacher, however, I observed three back-to-back classes, and I visited three different classes of the other world history teacher over two days. One of these teachers had invited me into his classes on my first visit to the school in November 2013 (but did not agree to be interviewed). None of the teachers had printed syllabi available for me or had posted any on the school website.

My final visit to Cardozo High School occurred during the week of May 19–23, 2014. I interviewed two history teachers and observed three classes (eighty-minute periods). Another teacher permitted me to observe two of his classes, but did not agree to an interview. In total, then, over two visits to Cardozo, I observed seven lessons of three history teachers. In preparation for the observations, I reviewed the syllabi that all three teachers had posted on the school website (http://www.cardozohs.com/).

What did I do when I observed classes?

In four of the fifteen classes (total from both schools), I was introduced as a professor who had taught at the school a half-century ago. In three of these classes, at the end of the lesson, the teacher invited students to question me about what teaching at Glenville and Cardozo was like then. A handful of students asked questions, and I answered them.

During each lesson I observed, I wrote out in longhand or typed on my laptop what teachers and students did during the class period. Each sheet of paper or laptop screen was divided into a wide column and a

narrow column. In the wide column, I diagrammed the seating organization of the classroom and recorded what was on whiteboards and
on the walls and bulletin boards. I noted the electronic devices available, their location in the room, and whether the lesson included their
use by students. After the lesson began, I would note every few minutes
what the teacher was talking about or doing and student responses
and actions they were engaged in. I also noted when the teacher seg-
ued from one activity to another and directed students to the next task.

In the narrow column, I commented on what I saw. That included
connections (or lack of connections) between what teacher said and
what students did. I scanned the classroom every few minutes and commented on whether some, most, or all students were on- or off-task and
my sense of how attentive students and teacher were to what was happening in the lesson.

The major advantage of this approach is being in the room and
picking up nonverbal and verbal asides of what is going on every few
minutes as well as noting classroom climate or ethos, which often goes
unnoticed. As an experienced teacher familiar with schooling historically and the common moves that occur in teacher-directed lessons, I
can also assess the relationship between the teacher and students—sub-
jectively, to be sure—that other observers using different protocols or
videos may miss or exclude.

But like any methodology to describe what happens in a lesson,
there are inevitable trade-offs between using protocols with trained
observers who seldom depart from the instrument, videotaping the lesson with or without commentary, the approach I used, and other methods of classroom observation. Each approach and in combination may
increase objectivity and subjectivity, but trade-offs must be made.

In this case, the major disadvantage of this way of observing history
lessons is the subjectivity and inevitable biases that any observer, including myself, brings to documenting lessons. To minimize my biases, I
worked hard to separate what I saw from what I interpreted—thus the
wide and narrow columns I used to record what happens during a lesson and my comments, respectively. I described objectively classroom

conditions in diagrams and descriptions of the physical space. I could record and not judge teacher and student interactions and behaviors. I could describe content and how it was used. But eliminating biases completely is impossible, so as in other approaches researching classroom lessons, some remain.

After observing classes, I conducted half-hour to forty-five-minute interviews with teachers at times convenient to them. After jotting down their history in the district, the school, and other experiences, I turned to the lessons and asked a series of questions about what happened during the period I observed. I asked what the teachers' goals were and whether they believe those goals were reached. Then I asked about the different activities I observed during the lesson (see interview protocol in appendix B).

In answering these questions, teachers gave me reasons they did (or did not) do certain things in lessons. In most instances, the teachers were eager to provide a rationale for doing what they did, thus communicating to me a cognitive map of their beliefs and assumptions about teaching, learning, and the content they typically teach. In all of the give-and-take of these discussions, I made no judgment about the success or failure of different activities or of the lesson itself.

In what ways did my skills as a historian and writing about my classroom experiences in the past help and hinder the account I constructed?

History is what historians say and can document of what happened in the past; memory is what individuals believe occurred in the past. So when a historian writes about what he or she has personally experienced, analytic skills, remembrances, and perceptions get entangled and sorting out one from the other becomes essential.

I have tried to disentangle documented facts, memories, perceptions, and analysis—particularly in identifying for the reader sources that may be unreliable but nonetheless usable because they add a dimension to the account that would be missing if this were another of my academic studies.

To be clear, then, this description of the way history was taught then and is taught now in two urban high schools is neither a memoir nor an autobiography; it is a combination of facts that can be documented by reliable sources (and I use endnotes to establish a factual basis for statements or raise doubts about what I and others have said and done) and my personal experiences of teaching history. It is neither an academic study of teaching history nor a personal recollection of then and now but a hybrid, or "unconventional history," of teaching a high school subject.[1]

I reconstruct my personal experiences as a history teacher at Glenville and Cardozo a half-century ago, documenting those experiences when I can, and then flip back to the academic researcher role, documenting in 2013–2014 how history teachers in those same schools, albeit in different contexts, teach history. In both instances, I compare and contrast my observations with how history teachers in other locations taught.

Moreover, I take my memories and those of former students and others to construct a story of how I taught history a half-century ago. I drew from my previous studies such as *How Teachers Taught* to give a context for how and what I taught from the mid-1950s to the late-1960s. As for how history is taught now in these two high schools, I draw from the current movement among social studies educators of teaching students the skills and concepts that working historians use in describing, analyzing, and interpreting the past.

This hybrid of memoir and history tries to combine two disparate impulses that have characterized my career as a high school teacher and historian. As Patrick Hutton put it: "What is at issue here is not how history can recover memory but, rather, what memory will bequeath to history."[2] Both history and memory, then, are necessary to recover what has occurred as policy decisions travel their rough, erratic path into classrooms. Those policies and practices are here filtered through the remembrance of one participant who was deeply involved in both teaching high school history and researching the history of education.

This hybrid study of teaching history then and now also reinforces my long-standing commitment to teachers and teaching as the core, the very essence, of public and private schooling in the United States. Understanding that centrality of teachers and teaching to the enterprise of formal schooling has been the mainstay of my academic work for the past forty years.[3]

So being a historian who also traffics in personal stories, I have had to be careful in how I documented my remembrances and those of my former students. Here are some examples of decisions I made on personal accounts:

- In chapter 1, I have cited student remembrances from my seven-year stint at Glenville High School. As a historian, I have to be clear that such decades-old recollections are neither representative of all of my students nor constitute even substantial fraction of those who were in my classes. The truth is that no more than twenty of my former Glenville students contacted me—fewer than 1 percent of the students I taught there. They have written about their experiences to me in e-mails and in published venues. Moreover, for even that tiny fraction of students, memories that are decades old are selective and often subject to bias. Yet I also know that perceptions and memories can direct a shaft of light on past events and experiences. Given these caveats, I have placed former students' recollections (for which I received permission to quote) in endnotes rather than the text to give readers the opportunity to judge the worth of their remembrances as a source of information about my teaching. For chapter 2 (Cardozo fifty years ago), I put recollections from former interns in the Cardozo Project in Urban Teaching in endnotes as well. In each instance, I contacted the writer of the e-mail and asked for permission to quote from it. I did include in the text, however, entries from two journals, one mine and the other kept by then-intern Dirk Ballendorf.

- A Cardozo Project in Urban Teaching intern told me and a group of others gathered in room 111 the following story (this incident recorded in my journal for September 27, 1963). He said a veteran Cardozo teacher gave him the following advice: "All you have to do is to keep 'em from killing each other in the classroom and give 'em Fs. Then you get them under control." The intern did not identify which teacher gave him the advice. Since I could not verify who had told him this, I did not use the story in the chapter on teaching at Cardozo High School.

All in all, creating this hybrid of the history of classroom teaching mixed with personal recollections has opened a new door, I believe, to a deeper and fuller description of what teaching history over a half-century ago was like in two different high schools.

The foregoing description of the methods I used in describing and analyzing the teaching of history then and now hardly removes the difficulties and dilemmas built into any reconstruction of the past. I wanted to be explicit in detailing the ways that I captured the past and compared it to the present.

Interview Protocol for Teachers and Questions on the Lesson I Observed

Interview Protocol for Teachers

1. How long have you been at Glenville/Cardozo?
2. Prior teaching experience?
3. What brought you to this school?
4. What is your daily teaching schedule?
5. What texts do you use for history courses?
6. What was your undergraduate major?
7. What do you like best about teaching here?
8. What do you like least about teaching here?
9. Under which principals have you worked here?
10. How often do you get evaluated in your teaching? Who does the evaluations? What do you think of the process?

Questions on the Lesson I Observed

1. How many students enrolled in the class? How many usually show up?

2. Why are you teaching the content I observed? Why these materials? Do you use multiple sources with students? Give an example.
3. How often do you use text? Your attitude toward text?
4. Was the student participation in lesson that I saw typical or atypical?
5. Which activities that I observed seem to work in this lesson? Why?
6. Why do you arrange the classroom furniture as you have?
7. Was the overall lesson I observed typical or atypical? What was different?

Glenville and Cardozo
High Schools Now

	GLENVILLE	CARDOZO
Year	2012–2013	2013–2014
School grades	9–12	6–12
Number of students	719 (down from 1,663 in 2003)	681 (down from 1,100 in 2008)
▪ Minority (%)	99	68 black/31 Latino
▪ Poor (%)	85 (free and reduced-price lunch)	99 (free and reduced-price lunch)
▪ Special education (%)	30	28
Number of faculty	24 (excluding counselors and special education teachers)	60
▪ Minority (%)	67 (2003)	80 (author estimate)
Graduation rate (%)	53	38
College enrollment (%)	40 (2011)	30 (author's estimate)
Advanced Placement courses	2 (Biology, Calculus)	8 (English Literature, World History, Biology, Chemistry, Calculus, Statistics, French, Spanish)
Daily school schedule	10 periods of 40 minutes	Four 80–90 periods a day
Technology access for teachers and students	2–3 computer labs in school; 2–3 desktop computers of different ages in most classrooms; each teacher has laptop	Interactive whiteboards and five new desktop computers in each classroom; teacher laptops
Testing	Ohio Graduation Test in reading, writing, math, science, and social studies; teacher-designed classroom tests	District-administered Comprehensive Assessment System for grades 2–10 in reading, math, science, and health; teacher-designed tests

(continued)

	GLENVILLE	CARDOZO
Year	2012–2013	2013–2014
Consequences for low academic performance	Has not met state standard for Adequate Yearly Progress since 2005; school put on Academic Watch and then Academic Emergency; restructured twice, becoming an Investment School in 2013	Identified as low-performing school for four years; received "corrective action"; restructured in 2008 and 2013
Extracurricular programs	Sports (male and female), Junior Reserve Officers Training Program (ROTC), Chess Team, Drill Team, student government, newspaper, Yearbook Club	Sports, Drill Team, band, online literary and artistic journal, Chess Club, etc.
Roaming in halls	Depending on period of day, students in hallways fairly constant during school day	Aides periodically sweep halls to round up tardies; uniformed security walk halls during class time
Discipline	Referral to administration, suspensions	Referrals to administrators; in-school and out-of-school suspensions
School security	Metal detectors at only entrance to school; uniformed security guards; school aides with walkie-talkies	Metal detectors at only entrance to school; uniformed and non-uniformed aides; school aides with radios

Notes

1. David Lowenthal, *The Heritage Crusade and the Spoils of History* (Cambridge, United Kingdom: Cambridge University Press, 1998), xi, xiii, 123.

2. Lawrence Cremin, *Transformation of the School* (New York: Vintage, 1961); Lawrence Cremin, *American Education: The Metropolitan Experience, 1876–1980* (New York: Harper & Row, 1988), 1–14, 223–231; Phil Boyle and Del Burns, *Preserving the Public in Public Schools* (Lanham, MD: Rowman and Littlefield, 2011).

   The conflicting purposes of both conserving community values and beliefs while becoming more modern and able to cope with an ever-changing culture and society can also be seen in respondents' answer to questions on change in the 2014 PDK/Gallup poll. Forty-two percent of respondents said change in elementary schools is needed, while 42 percent said no change is necessary. Twelve percent said elementary schools are changing "too quickly." Forty-nine percent of respondents said secondary schools were "not changing enough," 32 percent said these schools "don't need to change," and 14 percent said these schools were changing "too quickly." See "The PDK/Gallup Poll of the Public's Attitudes toward Public Schools," October 2014, http://pdkpoll.pdkintl.org/october/.

3. Norton Grubb and Marvin Lazerson, *The Education Gospel* (Cambridge, MA: Harvard University Press, 2004); Larry Cuban, "A Solution That Lost Its Problem: Why Centralized Policymaking Is Unlikely to Yield Many Classroom Gains," (Denver, CO: Education Commission of States, 2004); and Larry Cuban, *The Blackboard and the Bottom Line: Why Can't Schools Be Like Businesses?* (Cambridge, MA: Harvard University Press, 2004).

4. I have not found any historians who have documented their high school teaching experiences and then compared those earlier years to a later period in the same high school. I did, however, find Sherry Ortner's *New Jersey Dreaming: Capital, Culture, and the Class of '58* (Durham, NC: Duke University Press, 2003). An anthropoligist now, Ortner had graduated from Weequahic High School in Newark, New Jersey, in 1958. She located over two hundred graduates in her class (out of a class of just over three hundred) and had them complete a questionnaire followed up with over one hundred interviews. As the title indicates, her study of the high school that was 83 Jewish, 6 percent African American, and 11 percent of other backgrounds focused much more on the issue of social

class and ethnicity in describing and analyzing what happened to those graduates by the mid-1990s.

5. Larry Cuban, *The Managerial Imperative and the Practice of Leadership in Schools* (Albany: State University of New York Press, 1988), chapters 2, 4, and 6: Larry Cuban, *Frogs into Princes: Writings on School Reform* (New York: Teachers College Press, 2008), chapter 1.

For a study of these wars (what I mean by *war* is political controversy over what content is suitable to use in schools) before the 1960s, see Ronald Evans, *Social Studies Wars* (New York: Teachers College Press, 2004). In the 1960s, the New Social Studies produced new courses and attempted to import new pedagogies into classrooms, and war erupted over the project "Man: A Course of Study." In the 1990s, political controversy broke out over proposed new history standards for public schools that were later condemned by a Senate resolution. In 2014, school protests broke out over the revised Advanced Placement US History course in Colorado and elsewhere (see Chapter 3).

6. Quoted in Gary Nash, Charlotte Crabtree, and Ross Dunn, *History on Trial* (New York: Alfred Knopf, 1998), 45.

7. Jonathan Zimmerman, *Whose America? Culture Wars in the Public Schools* (Cambridge, MA: Harvard University Press, 2002); Sam Wineburg, "Crazy for History," *Journal of American History* 90, no. 4 (2004): 1401–1414.

8. I distinguish between two kinds of planned changes, fundamental and incremental, that have occurred in US schools over the past two centuries. By *fundamental* change, I mean altering the basic building blocks of US schooling; for example, requiring taxpayers to fund public schools and give access to all students, establishing goals for schooling (e.g., all students will be literate, discharge their civic duties, and be vocationally prepared for the labor market), and organizing curricula and instructional practices in age-graded elementary and secondary schools. These "building blocks" are structures that have defined public schools for the past two centuries. Changing them fundamentally means altering funding (e.g., vouchers, charter schools), governance (e.g., site-based management, mayoral control), organization (e.g., moving from an age-graded school to non-graded teams and entire schools), curriculum (e.g., New Math, "hands-on" science), and instruction (e.g., moving from teacher-centered to student-centered pedagogy). When I initially wrote about planned school change, I called these fundamental shifts in structure *second-order* changes. Often those who champion second-order changes in public schools talk about "real reform" or "transformation of schooling."

Incremental changes are amendments in current structures, not deep changes to or removal of these core components of schooling. In my earlier writings on school change, I had called these *first-order* changes. Such changes as creating new academic courses, extending the school day or year, reducing class size, raising teacher salaries, introducing new reading or math programs, etc., are designed to correct deficiencies and improve existing structures, and do not alter substantially the basic structures of public schools. They do not replace the goals, funding, organization, and governance of schools; they are add-ons. Many promoters of change in schools call such changes "tinkering," usually in a dismissive way, because they want "real reform" or fundamental reordering of existing structures. I drew the terms *first-order* and *second-order* from Paul Watzlawick et al., *Change: Principles of Problem Formation and Problem Resolution* (New York: W. W. Norton1974), 10–11, and Cuban, *The Managerial Imperative*, 228–232.

For an example of the use of the words *revolution* and *transformation* to mean fundamental change, see the 2012 TED talk in which Sir Ken Robinson, former director of the arts in schools project in England and professor at the University of Warwick, now an international adviser on education, said: "Every education system in the world is being reformed at the moment and it's not enough. Reform is no use anymore, because that's simply improving a broken model. What we need—and the word's been used many times during the course of the past few days—is not evolution, but a revolution in education. This has to be transformed into something else."

Leonard Waks has critiqued my use of *fundamental* as confusing the institution of education (the norms, practices, and values of public schooling and higher education) with organizational structures and procedures—districts, K–12 public schools, and classrooms. I am persuaded that Waks makes a valid criticism and, were I writing my initial distinctions a quarter-century ago with Waks's critique in hand, I would have rewritten the notion of *fundamental*. Nonetheless, distinctions in the magnitude, scope, and pace of planned changes in school organizations and educational institutions need to be made, and Waks provides a useful road map for making them. I leave it to others to determine whether the distinctions are helpful in analyzing planned school changes. See Leonard Waks, "The Concept of Fundamental Educational Change," *Educational Theory* 57, no. 3 (2007): 277–295.

9. The metaphor of *grammar* suggests rules that should be followed. For teachers working within age-graded schools, the rules do shape their behavior. For example, teachers are legally responsible for the students who are in their classroom for four to six hours a day. Leaving students unsupervised for a class period or more is risky because of accidents, fights, bullying, etc. Over the course of a school day, teachers must take attendance, maintain control over their classrooms, teach lessons they are certified to teach, assume other duties in the school as assigned by an administrator, and turn in student grades and reports to the administration. These duties and expectations derive from the grammar of schooling. See David Tyack and William Tobin, "The 'Grammar' of Schooling: Why Has It Been So Hard to Change?" *American Educational Research Journal* 31, no. 3 (1994): 453–479. Also see David Tyack and Larry

Cuban, *Tinkering Toward Utopia* (Cambridge, MA: Harvard University Press, 1995) and Larry Cuban, "What Happens to Reforms That Last?" *American Educational Research Journal* 29, no. 2 (1992): 227–251.

10. For an example of this triad of perspectives, see David K.Cohen,"A Revolution in One Classroom: The Case of Mrs. Oublier," *Educational Evaluation and Policy Analysis* 12, no. 3 (1990): 311–329.

11. Curricular reform wars in math and science over the past century also involve issues of what to conserve and what to change. Cycles of new standards in math (1960s, 1980s, 2010s) and science (1950s, 1980s, 2000s) capture the tensions between competing values in each academic subject. Retaining basic knowledge and skills versus applying math and science concepts and reasoning to everyday life are a few of the abiding tensions that have been embedded in curriculum reforms over the decades. See Alice Crary and Stephen Wilson, "The Faulty Logic of the 'Math Wars,'" *New York Times*, June 16, 2013, http://opinionator.blogs.nytimes.com//2013/06/16/the-faulty-logic-of-the-math-wars/; George DeBoer, "What We Have Learned and Where We Are headed: Lessons from the Sputnik Era," address to the symposium held at National Academy of Sciences, Washington, DC, October 4, 1997, http://www.nas.edu/sputnik/deboer.htm.

12. Jeremy Popkin, "Historians on the Autobiographical Frontier," *American Historical Review* 104, no. 3 (1999): 725–748.

13. Ward Just, *Exiles in the Garden* (Boston: Houghton Mifflin Harcourt, 2009), 251.

14. Cormac Mc Carthy, *The Road* (New York: Vintage, 2007), 10.

15. Mark Twain, cited in Walter Menninger, "Memory and History: What Can You Believe?" *Archival Issues* 21, no. 2 (1996): 103.

16. Cited in Menninger, "Memory and History," 102–103. A recent example of "false memories" and the role that vanity plays in needless embellishments of the past is the example of the nightly NBC news program with anchor Brian Williams who confessed that he had made up a story of being attacked by a rocket-propelled grenade in 2003 while flying in a helicopter in Iraq. Tara Parker-Pope, "False Memory vs. Bald Faced Lie," *New York Times*, February 10, 2015, D6.

17. Peter Novick, *That Noble Dream: The 'Objectivity Question' and the American Historical Profession* (New York: Cambridge University Press, 1988).

18. I also taught an additional three years at Roosevelt High School in the DC schools between 1967 and 1972.

CHAPTER 1

1. Leonard Moore, "The School Desegregation Crisis of Cleveland, Ohio, 1963–1964," *Journal of Urban History* 28, no. 2 (2002): 135–147. Within the school, I quickly learned from experienced colleagues that the district personnel department customarily assigned young, white, inexperienced teachers to mostly minority schools to see if they would survive.

2. Kenneth Kusmer, *A Ghetto Takes Shape: Black Cleveland, 1870–1930* (Champaign: University of Illinois Press, 1978), 157–173; David Van Tassel (ed.) *The Encyclopedia of Cleveland History* (Bloomington: Indiana University Press, 1996), 595–599.

3. Kusmer, *A Ghetto Takes Shape*, 170–171.

4. When I use the phrases *teacher-centered instruction* or *student-centered instruction*, I confer no positive or negative value to either. Nor do I think that one is superior to the other in effectiveness or quality of instruction. I am reporting on how I taught at this time, given the spectrum of teaching stretching from one pole (teacher-centered) to the other (student-centered) that I have described in *How Teachers Taught* and *Hugging the Middle* (New York: Teachers College Press, 2008).

5. I encountered the idea of teaching history as *heritage* in David Lowenthal, "Fabricating Heritage" *History & Memory* 10, no. 1 (1998): 5–24.

6. James Patterson, *Brown v. Board of Education: A Civil Rights Milestone and Its Troubled Legacy* (New York: Oxford University Press, 2001), 70–117.

7. In writing personally about how I taught history in the late 1950s and early 1960s, I used a few lessons that I still had in my files, course outlines, and textbooks from which I drew assignments. I also used archival sources such as school yearbooks, student newspapers, and records. Furthermore, when I contacted former Glenville students, two told me that they had kept materials from my classes. They sent me papers with my comments on them and tests, quizzes, and study guides that I had given to my classes in US history and world history.

8. David S. Muzzey, *History of Our Country* (New York: Ginn, 1955).

9. From time to time, I will cite student remembrances. Such decades-old recollections are by no means representative of all those who were in my classes. The truth is, no more than twenty of my former students in the years I taught at Glenville have contacted me—a tiny fraction of less than 1 percent. They have written about their experiences to me in e-mails and in published venues. Moreover, memories decades old are selective and often subject to bias. Nonetheless, what these students have to say, given these caveats, may be worthwhile to place not in the text but in these endnotes. I leave it to the reader to judge their worth as a source of information about my teaching.

Elbert Hendricks, for example, remembered a unit on the Civil War when he was in my class in 1959:

> *During the study of the Civil War at Glenville, Mr. Cuban (for this is still how I think of him) asked a question which I remember clearly. The question was what the effect of the underground railroad in alleviating pressure on the slave owners in the South . . . This is in any case what I remember. I put my hand up and gave the answer that what the underground railroad did was to remove the intelligent Negroes from the plantations and suppress a great deal of unrest that would have otherwise disturbed the order of the plantations.*
>
> *Mr. Cuban accepted my answer and built on it during the class. He said that it also provided a large number of motivated Negro recruits for the Union Army when the*

Civil War eventually did happen. I felt well rewarded personally for my answer and the incident gave me a great deal to think about at the time. The reasons is that I had never tried to think about history in this way and that intelligence (and training) can make a difference in everyday life for me personally and of course for Negroes in general.

Hendricks sent this e-mail to Carol Schneider Carstensen on June 6, 2001, and she forwarded it to me June 13, 2001. I received a subsequent e-mail from Hendricks on July 1, 2013. He had become a professor at the Technical University of Denmark in the Department of Electrical and Control Engineering. He retired in 2011 from teaching but still advises both undergraduate and graduate students. On March 3, 2015, while at a conference in Copenhagen, I had dinner with Hendricks and his son. It was a remarkable reunion after fifty-six years.

10. Former student Marsha Kindall Smith became a music teacher and later a university music educator and wrote of her experiences at Glenville High School. She described four of her teachers, of whom I was one. She said of me:

    Larry Cuban, my tall history teacher, made history alive and relevant with small group discussions and paper-mache art projects. When he excitedly engaged us about history, Mr. Cuban talked faster and walked around the room with his eyes growing bigger and bigger. Although he gave us more Dittos than any other teacher, I was intrigued by the numerous perspectives of history gleaned from various sources. I eagerly anticipated each class because Mr. Cuban asked questions that made me think and made me more aware of authenticity in research materials. Because he was the first White teacher to teach me Negro history, as it was called at that time, I was impressed with his knowledge and social consciousness. In the early 1960s, Negro history was not in the textbooks . . ." (Marsha Kindall Smith, "On My Journey: Minority Teachers and Teaching Beyond the Curriculum," *Mountain Lake Reader*, Spring 2004, 1–20).

11. For reconstructing how I taught in these years, I used study guides from three different units I taught (and papers I assigned) in US history that former student Carole Schneider Carstensen had kept since she took my course in 1959. I also have student recollections from these courses that five former students had sent to me over the years. For world history, Patricia Ryan Paulsell sent me copies of papers she had written, lecture notes she had taken in my classes, and notebooks that she had kept from 1960.

    Back issues of the *American Heritage* were available from 1954 in the Glenville high school library. Historians and journalists authored most of the magazine articles. Civil War historian Bruce Catton was founding editor. Published initially by Forbes and then taken over by the National Geographic Society in 2008, it suspended publication in 2013.

12. Benjamin S. Bloom, ed., *Taxonomy of Educational Objectives: Book 1:Cognitive Domain* (New York: David McKay, 1956); the taxonomy was soon adapted to the asking of oral and written questions in classrooms. For an example, see http://wwild.coe.uga.edu/pptgames/resources/bloom_questions.pdf.

13. In US history, I also introduced debates on current topics, as I describe later in the chapter. Lawrence Young remembered the following:

    In 1959, you were . . . social studies teacher to some of us . . . At the time a young Jack Kennedy was campaigning against Richard Nixon for the presidency. While I was aware of politics and elections, I must admit I paid little attention to issues and gave what little attention I paid to slogans—"I Like Ike," etc. I can distinctly remember you making a point of dividing the room equally between the candidates and challenging us to come up with a rationale for voting for either of them. A lot of debates focused on personality or looks . . . However the seed was planted that elections and politics were important for every citizen and deep understanding of issues paramount. I and other classmates became registered voters at the first chance and I have voted in every primary and general election since, no matter where I lived." (E-mail communication with author, July 30, 2013)

14. I have no documentation in my records, student recollections, or other sources that can tie down whether it was 1956 or 1957.

15. A few students got back in touch with me after they learned that I was writing about my experiences at Glenville. For example, former student Marv Bullock e-mailed me:

    Well, yesterday, while listening to NPR, I heard a name I first remember hearing back in 1958. His name was Ho Chi Minh. He was of many back then as a world figure that I became familiar with, not just name, by face recognition, too. As I recall there was an effort to familiarize students with the names and faces of world leaders. Pictures of their faces were taken from magazines like Life, Look, Time, and Newsweek, etc. The teacher would flash the pics to us in class as part of a test. Of course I could recognize all shown. I recall Dag Hammarskjold, secy of the UN, my first contact with anything or world figure of that nature. (E-mail communication with author, October 17, 2013. Used with permission.)

16. For the Sam Sheppard murder trial, see http://en.wikipedia.org/wiki/Sam_Sheppard; for the *$64,000 Question* scandal, see http://en.wikipedia.org/wiki/The_$64,000_Question.

17. Daniel Willingham, "Critical Thinking: Why Is It So Hard To Teach?" *American Educator* (Summer 2007), 8–19, http://www.aft.org/pdfs/americaneducator/summer2007/Crit_Thinking.pdf.

18. David Perkins and Gavriel Salomon, "Transfer of Learning," *International Encyclopedia of Education*, 2nd ed., 1992, http://learnweb.harvard.edu/alps/thinking/docs/traencyn.htm.

19. On current proponents of historical thinking, see Sam Wineburg, *Historical Thinking and Other Unnatural Acts* (Philadelphia: Temple University Press, 2001); Bruce VanSledright, *The Challenge of Rethinking History Education* (New York: Routledge, 2011); Bruce Lesh, *"Why Won't You Just Tell Us The Answer?" Teaching Historical Thinking in Grades 7–12* (Portland, ME: Stenhouse Publishers, 2011); Linda Levstik and Keith Barton, *Doing History*, 4th ed. (New York: Routledge,

2011); Avishag Reisman, "Reading Like a Historian: A Document-Based History Curriculum Intervention in Urban High Schools," *Cognition and Instruction* 30, no. 1 (2012): 86–112; Sam Wineburg, Daisy Martin, and Chauncey Monte-Sano, *Reading Like a Historian* (New York: Teachers College Press, 2013).

20. For a romp through history of classroom devices, see Jeff Dunn, "The Evolution of Classroom Technology," April 18, 2011, http://www.edudemic.com/classroom-technology/.

21. In 2008, a convicted Soviet spy who had served seventeen years in prison admitted that Julius Rosenberg had been a courier for the USSR but that Ethel was not involved. By then, decoded cables had been released to the public leading to the conclusion that Julius Rosenberg had indeed been a Soviet spy. See Sam Roberts, "Figure in Rosenberg Case Admits to Soviet Spying," *New York Times*, September 11, 2008, http://www.nytimes.com/2008/09/12/nyregion/12spy.html?_r=1&; also see http://articles.baltimoresun.com/1995-07-12/news/1995193002_1_soviet-union-venona-rosenbergs. I had later encounters with Carol after she graduated from Glenville. My family and I had moved to Washington, DC, where I taught at Cardozo High School, training returned Peace Corps volunteers to teach in urban schools (see chapter 2). After a few years of directing the program, I returned to classroom teaching at Roosevelt High School. By that time, Carol, in her early thirties, had become a social studies teacher, married, and moved with her family to DC, where her husband worked for the US Department of Justice. She was assigned to Roosevelt in 1969. The next year, I became Director of Staff Development for the DC schools and established an Innovation Fund for teachers. Carol and Sherry Lanoff, another Roosevelt teacher, applied for a grant. A committee of DC teachers chose their proposal to team-teach an interdisciplinary course of English and US history. In 1972, I returned to Roosevelt to teach, and remember many intellectually exciting meetings with Carol and Sherry. Our paths parted after I went to graduate school and Carol and her family eventually moved to Madison, Wisconsin. We continued to exchange annual holiday cards, and in the 1990s, when my daughter went to the University of Wisconsin, I reestablished contact with Carol. By that time, she was a member of the Madison school board—a post she served in for eighteen years before retiring in 2008.

22. I wrote to Carol and sent her what I had remembered about my experience with her about the Wexley book. She replied on September 4, 2013: "My memories are similar to yours (though maybe there are a few minor differences). I remember how impressed I was that a teacher would actually 'learn' from a student. It gave me a heady feeling that I had the ability to actually impact my world . . ."

23. I relied on two sources for describing dominant teacher-centered patterns of history instruction in the 1950s and early 1960s. Both reported the familiar sequence of activities of lecture, textbook assignments, guided

question-and-answer discussions of text, and tests. One researcher surveyed one hundred randomly selected teachers in California, and another did a survey of nearly 1,100 teachers in Indiana (80 percent of all U.S. history teachers in the state). Richard Gross, "Trends in the Teaching of United States History in the Senior High School," (unpublished PhD dissertation, Stanford University, 1951) and Maurice Baxter, Robert Ferrell, and John Wiltz, *The Teaching of American History in High Schools* (Bloomington: Indiana University Press, 1964).

24. His obituary in the *Encyclopedia of Cleveland History* is as follows: James O'Meara, Jr. (5 May 1908–14 Nov. 1988) earned an international reputation in education, law and labor. Born in Cleveland to James and Anna (Freidel) O'Meara, he graduated from the Cleveland public schools and received an M.A. and Ph.D. from John Carroll University. He began a 39-year teaching career in the Cleveland Public Schools . . . He was admitted to the bar in 1941, and subsequently earned his J.D. in 1968 from Marshall Law School.

In 1934, he became a charter member of the Cleveland Teachers Union. Over the course of his career, O'Meara held leadership positions in the Cleveland Teachers Union, the Ohio Federation of Teachers, and the American Federation of Teachers . . . His involvement in civil rights activities led to service on the Civil Rights Committee of the Cleveland AFL-CIO, the Ohio Civil Rights Commission, the United Negro College Fund Committee and the Urban League . . . (http://ech.case.edu/cgi/article.pl?id=OJEJ).

25. Martin Mayer, *Where, When, and Why: Social Studies in American Schools* (New York: Harper Colophon Books, 1962), 157–160. How accurate is Mayer's account of the lesson I taught? Here is where my memory and a journalist's account conflict. While Mayer captured the key elements of the discussion, my memory of the class and Mayer's description still differ. Of course, there are solid reasons why our two accounts differ. For one, Mayer was a journalist and reported what he saw and heard while having to retain readers' attention using the art and craft of a non-fiction writer. For me, a historian recalling one lesson I taught decades ago revealed gaps in my memory.

Looking back a half-century, how can I remember this one lesson out of thousands that I have taught in different high schools? One reason is that Mayer's version was published and simply reading it in print fifty years later jogged my memory so that I could even recall some students' names. A second reason that this summary lesson on the causes of the Civil War stayed in mind for years was because of the uncommon way that I had brought together conflicting historical interpretations. I did recall how that lesson had resonated strongly with students.

Yet there are holes in my memory simply because it was so long ago. Mayer's account filled in some of them just like a parent's retelling of a story about a child's experience growing up becomes the "truth." Telling the difference between Mayer's account and what I remember, however, becomes nearly impossible simply because memory is a trickster.

Nonetheless, as I can recall, in less than a thousand words, Mayer caught the main elements of a twenty-minute teacher-led discussion. Skilled writers create drama. Mayer did that at two points. The first time was when I prodded students to explain how a minority of white slaveholders could convince the majority of small non-slaveholding farmers to fight for the Confederacy. I used a paradoxical statement to provoke students to become aware of the centrality of race in the South. So I pushed students, and Mayer picked that up.

The second instance of drama was when a student role-played a planter and referred to slave rebellions. I followed up with the phrase "white supremacy" and then nudged students to leap ahead to the post-Civil War years and Jim Crow laws. That is when the student delivered the one word—*segregation*. In ending the vignette of the lesson on that note, Mayer dramatically brings the lesson to a close. I remember that moment well, even recalling the tingles that ran up my back when the student made the connection. All that is missing from his account is a clanging bell ending the period and students exiting the classroom talking about the connections between white supremacy before and after the Civil war.

But the period did not end then. The bell rang undramatically minutes later after the discussion ended and after I, undramatically, gave the assignment for the next day.

Furthermore, Mayer omitted the hard work of beginning and ending a lesson. I endured rough spots in the early part of the forty-five-minute period, such as handling tardy students, collecting homework, taking head counts to determine which students were absent, etc. He also left out the tedious question-and-answer review with students of the previous day's lesson. In Mayer's description, everything seemed milkshake smooth. It was not.

26. Some readers may ask whether the principal or other administrator watched me teach and evaluated my performance. In the seven years I taught at Glenville, I do not recall any such evaluations or discussions of my lessons.

27. *Culturally deprived* was the educational phrase used in the late-1950s and early 1960s to describe minority and poor urban students. For a summary of what I said, see *Scholastic Teacher*, December 12, 1962.

28. *Negro in America* was published in 1964 and reissued in 1971 as *The Black Man in America* (Glenview, IL: Scott Foresman, 1971).

29. That $5,000 annual salary, accounting for inflation since then, would be equal to $38,600 in 2014. See http://www.dollartimes.com/inflation/inflation.php?amount=5000&year=1963

CHAPTER 2

1. Eve Edstrom, "Slum Children a New Challenge to Peace Corps Group," *Washington Post*, September 8, 1963, E2.

- I also taught three years at Roosevelt High School after leaving Cardozo High School, but I decided to focus on the latter for the following reasons:
- What I did at Glenville continued to evolve in the next four years at Cardozo.
- The city and district school contexts were the same for Cardozo and Roosevelt.
- The years 1963–1967 years were at the height of the War on Poverty, whose funds underwrote much of our work at Cardozo High School.

Cardozo High School opened in 1928 as a segregated business education school closely connected with local companies in what was then called the "colored" community. The school was named for Francis L. Cardozo, who was born a slave and attended the Universities of Glasgow and Edinburgh in Scotland. Following the Civil War, he became South Carolina's highest elected official. Cardozo came to Washington in 1878 as an appointed official and, after a few years, became principal of the District of Columbia Colored High School. He served the school between 1884 and 1896. One part of the high school was the business department, which Cardozo directed as part of his duties. After he died, the business department became a separate school named after him. As a vocational school within the "colored" division of the DC schools, Cardozo High School prepared office workers, salespeople, bookkeepers, and secretaries.

The original building became overcrowded, and in 1950, the school board approved its move to the previously all-white, nearly empty Central High School perched on a hill overlooking the city. The high school has been in that location ever since. The school, renovated in 2013, is now a sixth- to twelfth-grade secondary school. The nickname for Cardozo sports teams over decades, hearkening to its birth as a vocational school, has been "the Clerks." See http://en.wikipedia.org/wiki/Francis_Lewis_Cardozo; http://www.universitystory.gla.ac.uk/biography/?id=WH24164&type=P; Alison Stewart, *First Class: The Legacy of Dunbar, America's First Black Public High School* (Chicago: Lawrence Hill Books, 2013), 37; and Cardozo High School website, http://www.cardozohs.com/apps/pages/index.jsp?uREC_ID=187561&type=d.

2. I used the following primary and secondary sources in describing the DC schools and the city between 1963 and 1967: *Primary sources:* Washington, DC, School Board minutes, articles from the *Washington Post, Washington Evening Star*, and the *DC Gazette. Secondary sources:* Constance Green, *The Secret City: A History of Race Relations in the Nation's Capital* (Princeton, NJ: Princeton University Press, 1967); Haynes Johnson, *Dusk at the Mountain* (New York: Doubleday, 1963); Carl Hansen, *Danger in Washington* (West Nyack, NY: Parker Publishing Company 1968); Harry Passow, *Toward Creating a Model Urban School System: A Study of the Washington, DC Public Schools* (New York: Teachers College, Columbia University, 1967); Larry Cuban, *Reform in Washington: The Model School Division, 1963–1972"* (Washington, DC: US Office of Education, National Center for

Educational Research, December 1972); Larry Cuban, *Urban School Chiefs Under Fire* (Chicago: University of Chicago Press, 1976); Floyd Hayes III, "Politics and Educational Policy-making in Washington, DC: A Community's Struggle for Quality Education," *Urban Education* 25 (1990): 237-257.

3. Bethany Rogers, "'Better People, Better Teaching': The Vision of the National Teacher Corps, 1965-1968," *History of Education Quarterly* 49, no. 1 (2009): 347-372; Judy Aaronson, "Recruiting, Supporting, and Retaining New Teachers: A Retrospective Look at Programs in the District of Columbia Public Schools," *Journal of Negro Education* 68 no. 3 (2000): 335-342.

4. Cuban, *Urban School Chiefs Under Fire*, 30-33.

5. Statistics from Passow, *Toward Creating a Model Urban School System DC,* 46; *The Secret City*, 334.

6. Hugh Scott was appointed in 1970. Since then, Michelle Rhee (2007-2010) has been the only non-black superintendent.

7. Federal judges had appointed black men and women to the school board for decades. That changed in 1967 when an executive order from President Lyndon Johnson abolished the Board of Commissioners and appointed a mayor, deputy mayor, city council, and board of education. Shortly thereafter, all of those local posts became elected positions.

8. Steven Diner, "The Governance of Education in the District of Columbia: An Historical Analysis of Current Issues," *Studies in DC History and Public Policy*, Paper No, 2 (Washington, DC: University of the District of Columbia, 1982); Mary Levy, *History of Public School Governance in the District of Columbia*, Washington Lawyers' Committee for Civil Rights, January 2004, http://www.dcpswatch.com/dcps/0401.htm#1.

9. Carl Hansen, *The Amidon Elementary School: A Successful Demonstration in Basic Education* (Englewood Cliffs, NJ: Prentice Hall, 1962), viii.

10. Julius Hobson, an activist in school and city politics railed against segregation, poverty, and divided governance in Washington for decades. As a parent and activist, he sued the DC schools for the inequities inherent in the four-track system, and in 1967, Federal District Judge Skelly Wright ordered the abolition of tracking in the DC schools because it accounted for the resegregation of DC students and low academic achievement. Wright concluded that, "[A]ll of the evidence in this case tends to show that the Washington school system is a monument to the cynicism of the power structure which governs the voteless capital of the greatest country on earth." When the board of education refused Hansen's recommendation to appeal the Wright decision, he resigned. Quote from Hansen, *The Amidon Elementary School*, 151.

Favoring home rule and statehood for Washington, Hobson was eventually elected as a City Council member and continued his scorching criticism of the schools, city government, and Congress—" I sleep mad," he used to say—until the day before he succumbed to cancer in 1977. See Cynthia Gorney,

"Julius Hobson, Sr., Activist, Dies at Age 54," *Washington Post*, March 24, 1977, http://www.washingtonpost.com/wp-dyn/content/article/2007/06/10/AR20 07061000956.html.

For Skelly Wright quote, see *Hobson v. Hansen, 269 F. Supp. 401 (DC 1967)*.

11. Cuban, *Urban School Chiefs Under Fire*, 34–38.

12. Ibid., 36.

13. Interview with Carl Hansen, August 28, 1973.

14. Ibid., 35.

15. John F. Kennedy, inauguration speech, January 20, 1961, http://www.ushistory .org/documents/ask-not.htm.

16. There is, as one would expect, a backstory to this effort to tap a different pool of candidates for urban schools, break the cycle of poverty and crime through the school, and create a teacher education program for urban schools.

Joan Wofford, a twenty-eight year-old English teacher in Newton, Massachusetts, and her husband, Jack, moved to DC in 1962, after he was appointed clerk to a district federal judge. Jack's brother, Harris, was special assistant to President Kennedy. I mention these connections because how the project was conceived and put into practice depended heavily on family and political ties that people had then (and now) and their perceptions of what the problems of urban schooling were and the necessary solutions to those problems.

Wofford began teaching at Cardozo in 1962. She was the second white teacher at the school of sixteen hundred–plus students. Principal Bennetta Washington, who hired her, was well known in black elite educational and social circles in the District. She and her husband (Walter Washington, who became the first presidentially appointed mayor of DC in 1967 and served as first elected mayor until 1979) had a full range of political and social contacts within the District that crossed racial lines.

After a year of teaching honors English at Cardozo and working on the yearbook with students, Wofford came to see that how students were taught, the materials they used, and the distance between faculty, students, and community conspired to make Cardozo a school where students dropped out in droves.

Wofford's ties through her husband to key figures in the Kennedy administration and the principal's contacts in the black elite community became the fertile background for the proposal to the President's Committee on Juvenile Delinquency (headed by Attorney General Robert Kennedy) for a grant to bring ten returning Peace Corps volunteers to Cardozo to learn to teach, get certified by the district, and receive a master's degree from Howard University—all in one year.

Wofford was to be the master teacher in English. In the summer of 1963, both Wofford and Washington looked around for a master teacher in history. A friend recommended that Wofford get in touch with me. I agreed to an interview, and shortly thereafter, Washington appointed me. This backstory of the CPUT comes from the correspondence, memos, and personal conversations I have had with each one of the designers of the project (documents in author's possession).

17. Application for Training Grant under the Juvenile Delinquency and Youth Offense Control Act to U.S. Department of Health Education, and Welfare, April 1, 1963, pp. 5–6.

18. Cardozo Peace Corps Pilot Project in Urban Teaching, "Special Memorandum to Peace Corps Volunteers," May 10, 1963 (in author's possession).

19. Overall, I taught and administered programs in the schools from 1963 to 1972. I taught in DC for seven years: four at Cardozo and three at Roosevelt High School. I administered the Cardozo Project for two years while I was teaching. I then served as the first districtwide Director of Staff Development for the system from 1968 to 1970.

20. Dirk Ballendorf was a returned Peace Corps volunteer who had served two years in the Philippines. He interned under me in the 1963–1964 school year and stayed on for a second year as a resident teacher. Dirk went on to earn a doctorate from Harvard and then served in the national Peace Corps as director in Micronesia. Shortly thereafter, he became a professor at the University of Guam, specializing in the history of Micronesia. He published extensively on this and related subjects. He died in 2013 at the age of seventy-three. His ex-wife found a journal he kept of his first year at Cardozo and allowed me to use it as a source. A full description of Ballendorf's career can be found at http://en.wikipedia.org/wiki/Dirk_Ballendorf.

21. Dirk Ballendorf, journal entry, October 23, 1963.

22. Dirk Ballendorf, journal entry, November 17, 1963.

23. From my journal entry for, December 4, 1964, taking data from Model School Division proposals for reform of Cardozo High School and its feeder schools.

24. Larry Cuban, "The Cardozo Peace Corps Project: Experiment in Urban Education," *Social Education*, December 1964, 447–448; my favorite PA announcement was from the assistant principal following a rash of fire alarms: "Disregard all bells. There will be no fire drills unless the building is on fire" (author's note, March 4, 1966).

25. Cuban, "The Cardozo Peace Corps Project," 448–449.

26. In the previous chapter, I referred to Edwin ("Ted") Fenton as the person who invited me to write *The Negro in America*. I stayed in touch with him over the next few years and exchanged materials as he had started a project at Carnegie Institute of Technology focusing on social studies subjects, including US history. See Edwin Fenton, *Teaching the New Social Studies: An Inductive Approach* (New York: Holt, Rinehart and Winston, 1966). I invited Fenton to one of the supervision seminars where interns were joined by Cardozo faculty. From my

October 21, 1964, journal entry:

> *Yesterday's seminar with Ted Fenton was excellent. His point about the importance of having models in one's head is correct. He ably reinforced what Joan and I have been doing for a year. Interns and regular faculty heard our views for so long and now a person with prestige says the same thing.... [R]egular faculty who attended were visibly impressed. I had interns from both groups come over the house for dinner with Ted and my family.*

And from February 1, 1965:

> *Dick Brown from Project Social Studies in Chicago spent the day with us in classes and seminar.*

Brown moved to Amherst, Massachusetts, and headed up the Amherst Project that developed history units. He was there between 1964 and 1972. I visited their project in July 1965, where one of the CPUT interns in history had been hired to write units for that project (as had I).

Jerome Bruner (*The Process of Education: Toward a Theory of Instruction* [Cambridge, MA: Harvard University Press, 1962]) laid out a rationale for the inductive method in having children and youth discover the structure of disciplines, including history. All of that can be taught in an intellectually honest way to both children and youth. In an afternoon seminar for all interns conducted on October 18, 1965, Joan Wofford and I devoted over two hours to parsing what Bruner said and how it applied, if at all, to the lessons we were creating.

On September 17, 1966, our Supervision seminar was devoted to educational objectives taken from Benjamin S. Bloom, *Taxonomy of Educational Objectives, Handbook I: The Cognitive Domain* (New York: David McKay, 1956). From my journal:

> *I passed out Bloom's condensed taxonomy. A few bursts of discussion erupted but a general calm pervaded, I think, mainly due to [interns'] complete immersion in classroom. I was purposely dogmatic, authoritarian, and argumentative [about the taxonomy] something against which they could rub, rebel, or deny. Whatever they do [with the taxonomy], I wanted them to think about what was said. We'll see . . .*

27. Janice Landreau, a former intern who went on to pursue a career in teaching, had this to say about the seminars on teaching she attended in 1966–1967:

> *I guess the primary lesson I'd like to thank you for was your insistence upon inductive learning, I think you called it—finding out where the student is before you arbitrarily introduce something to him. Over the years, I can't begin to tell you how that has served me in becoming a better teacher. I cannot begin any kind of lesson at any level without some kind of connecting to where the student is, what he already knows, what he thinks. Just last week I used maps of the spread of Christianity and the spread of Islam to introduce the Crusades to a sixth grade world history class—the kids saw the problem at once when they spotted Jerusalem in the center of both worlds . . . (e-mail, December 4, 2005).*

28. See Bill Plitt, "Teacher Dilemmas in a Time of Standards and Testing," *Phi Delta Kappan*, December 2004, 745–748.

29. Chapter 1 lays out in more detail the failure of my Glenville students to transfer thinking skills to textbook content and units I taught on slavery, the causes
of the Civil War, Reconstruction, and industrialization of the United States.
See Bill Plitt, "Teacher Dilemmas in a Time of Standards and Testing," *Phi
Delta Kappan*, December 2004, 745–748.

CHAPTER 3

1. Edwin Fenton, "Working with High Schools: A Professor's Testimony," *School
Review*, 69, no. 2 (1961): 157–168. As described in chapter 1, I met Fenton in
1962 at a meeting of the National Council of Social Studies where he invited
me to write *The Negro in America*. Fenton and I stayed in touch by mail and occasional phone calls when I worked with the Cardozo Project in Urban Teaching
(1963–1967). When he developed a multivolume text on US history for "slow
learners," he hired Sam Bryan, a social studies intern whom we had trained,
to be one of the teacher-writers in the project. After 1970, I lost direct contact
with Fenton but stayed abreast of his work in the New Social Studies.

2. Fenton was amazingly prolific during and after the New Social Studies. In
1970, in a response to an article about textbooks in *Social Education*, he stated
that he "contributed to, written, or edited some sixty-four books of readings,
textbooks, audiovisual kits, teacher's manuals . . . I have worked closely with
about twenty house editors employed by five major publishing companies . . . "
Edwin Fenton, "Letters to the Editor," *Social Education*, January 1970, 5–7.

3. William Goetz, "The New Social Studies: The Memoir of a Practitioner," *Social
Studies* 85, no. 3 (1994): 100–105. In this excerpt, I did not use the extensive citations that Goetz included in the article. Unlike William Goetz, my participation in the New Social Studies was peripheral. As a history teacher at Glenville
High School, I had prepared new materials including primary sources for my
classes that caught the eye of Edwin Fenton. At Cardozo High School, I shared
materials from other New Social Studies Projects and invited some of the leaders to meet with history interns.

4. Thomas Bender, "The New History—Then and Now," *Reviews in American History* 12, no. 4 (1984): 612–622; Michael Whelan, "James Harvey Robinson, the
New History, and the 1916 Social Studies Report," *History Teacher* 24, no. 2
(1991): 191–202.

   Missing from most lists of these New Historians is Mary Sheldon Barnes,
an assistant professor of history who taught at Stanford University from 1892
to 1896. Barnes and husband Earl wrote a history text for eighth–graders in
1891; and in 1896, she published *Studies in Historical Method*, where she described
the use of primary sources as the mainstay in teaching history in secondary
schools. This was well before Robinson and Beard and a cadre of social scientists became identified as the New Historians. Highly critical of fact-by-fact
"recitation" and conclusions memorized from the text, Barnes argued that the

main aim of history is the "development of the student's abilities to observe, to weigh evidence, to generalize, and to exercise creative historical imagination." Robert Keohane, "Mary Sheldon Barnes," in *Notable American Women, 1607–1950: A Biographical Dictionary*, vol. 1, ed. Edward James et al. (Cambridge, MA: Harvard University Press, 1971), 92–93; also see Larry Cuban, *How Scholars Trumped Teachers: Change Without Reform in University Curriculum, Teaching, and Research, 1890–1990* (New York: Teachers College Press, 1999), 118–119.

5. Hazel Hertzberg, "History and Progressivism: A Century of Reform Proposals," *Historical Literacy: The Case for History in American Education*, ed. in Paul Gagnon (New York: Macmillan, 1989), 69–99; David Saxe, *Social Studies in Schools: A History of the Early Years* (Albany: State University of New York Press, 1991); Ronald Evans, *The Social Studies Wars: What Should We Teach the Children?* (New York: Teachers College Press, 2004).

6. Arthur Zilversmit, *Changing Schools: Progressive Theory and Practice, 1930–1960* (Chicago: University of Chicago Press, 1993); Larry Cuban, *How Teachers Taught: Constancy and Change in American Classrooms, 1890–1990*, 2nd ed. (New York: Teachers College Press, 1993).

7. See, for example, Barbara Stern, ed., *The New Social Studies: People, Projects, and Perspectives* (Charlotte, NC: Information Age Press, 2010).

8. Edwin Fenton, "The New Social Studies: Implications for School Administration," *Bulletin of National Association of Secondary School Principals* 51, no. 317 (March 1967): 62–76; Edwin Fenton, *Teaching the New Social Studies in Secondary Schools: An Inductive Approach* (New York: Holt, Rinehart and Winston, 1966); John Haas, *The Era of the New Social Studies* (Boulder, CO: Social Science Education Consortium, Inc., 1977), 70–84.

A personal aside: In 1966, while teaching and administering the Cardozo Project in Urban Teaching, a Scott, Foresman editor contacted me and asked me if I would like to write a US history textbook that would be published as a series of paperbacks and not the familiar three-pound, single volume text. I said yes, and over the next five years, I and coauthor Philip Roden, a teacher at Evanston (Illinois) High School, authored five paperback volumes, each one of about 175 pages, collectively called *The Promise of America.*

Conceptualizing the book as one that would engage students, get them to think about how the past informs the present, how historians interpret sources, and develop basic thinking skills was an exciting adventure for me. I wanted very much to capitalize on my experience of creating lessons at Glenville and Cardozo with content that motivated students and turned history into detective stories with endings that students could figure out for themselves.

Phil Roden and I developed lessons around ordinary people in the past whose lives were linked to social and political movements and key events—a forty-niner prospecting for gold in California, a Polish immigrant working in the Chicago pork plants, and what it was like to live in early twentieth-century

New York City tenements. We used fiction—for example, a passage from Stephen Crane's *The Red Badge of Courage* in the Civil War unit—lyrics from protest songs sung by late-nineteenth-century farmers, and cartoons pointing to the devastating effects of the Industrial Revolution on children.

We connected the past to the present. Within a chronological framework, we would insert links to the present. For example, in the background of the Spanish-American War (1898), we included primary sources that got at the tension between national self-interest (acquiring colonies) and national ideals (democratic government), connecting both to the war in Vietnam. And we built critical thinking skills into the content of history. Our questions following readings, photos, cartoons, and charts aimed for comprehension, analysis, and evaluation.

Promise of America came out in 1971 and sold well in high schools and junior high schools, especially for students designated as "slow learners" or "underachievers." By the late 1970s, however, back-to-basics and traditional instruction had seized US schools; reformers had turned their backs on open classrooms, student-centered activities, the New Social Studies, and connecting the present and the past. The hardback, single-volume three-pound textbook returned to history classrooms. Sales for the series dropped to zero by the end of the 1970s.

9. Edwin Fenton, "Curricular Experiments in the Social Sciences," *Proceedings of the Regional Conference on the Social Sciences in College Education*, University of California, Los Angeles, November 7, 1964, 7.

10. Richard Brown, "Learning How to Learn: The Amherst Project and History Education in the Schools," *Social Studies* 87, no. 6 (1996): 267–273. In the summer of 1966, Brown hired Phyllis Jackson, a former social studies intern in the Cardozo Project in Urban Teaching, and me to write units for the Amherst Project.

11. William Weber, "The Amherst Project: School-College Partnerships in 1960s History Education," n.d. (in author's possession). Peter Dow, *Schoolhouse Politics: Lessons from the Sputnik Era* (Cambridge, MA: Harvard University Press, 1991); Ronald Evans, *Social Studies Wars: What Should We Teach the Children?* (New York: Teachers College Press, 2004). For the controversy in the 1930s over textbooks written by Harold Rugg, professor at Teachers College, Columbia University, see Evans, *Social Studies Wars*, 75–84.

12. David Cohen and Bella Rosenberg, "Functions and Fantasies: Understanding Schools in Capitalist America," *History of Education Quarterly*, 1977, 17(2), p. 121.

13. Southwest Educational Research Laboratory, "What Works Clearinghouse," *Research Exchange*, 2003, 8(2), at: http://www.ncddr.org/products/researchexchange/v08n02/2_whatworks.html.

14. Ronald Evans, *Social Studies Wars: What Should We Teach the Children?* (New York: Teachers College Press, 2004), 96–148; Geoffrey Scheurman and Keith Reynolds, "The 'History Problem' in Curricular Reform," in Stern, *The New Social Studies*, 341–360; Dow, *Schoolhouse Politics*; Haas, *The Era of the New Social Studies*.

15. Mark Krug et al., *The New Social Studies: Analysis of Theory and Materials* (Itasca, IL: F.E. Peacock Publishers, 1970); William Goetz, "The New Social Studies"; Scheurman and Reynolds, "The 'History Problem' in Curricular Reform"; Edwin Fenton, "Reflections on the 'New Social Studies,'" *Social Studies* 82, no. 3 (1991): 84–90; (May/June 1991): 84–90; Edwin Fenton Papers, "Georgia Textbook Controversy," Box 17, folder 13, Carnegie Mellon University; Larry Kraus, "The Fight over MACOS," in *The New Social Studies*, 309–339.

16. I put quotation marks around "good" citizenship and citizen because academics, parents, practitioners, and taxpayers interpret the phrase in different ways.

17. Robert Barr, James Barth, and Samuel Shermis, *The Nature of the Social Studies* (Palm Springs, CA: ETC Publications, 1978).

18. Fenton, *Teaching the New Social Studies in Secondary School*, 151; Barr, Barth, and Shermis, *The Nature of the Social Studies*, 70–91. For early efforts to get students to imitate social scientists, see ibid., 67–70.

19. Barr, Barth, and Shermis, *Teaching the New Social Studies in Secondary School*, 99.

20. Saxe, *Social Studies in Schools*; Robert Barr, James Barth, and Samuel Shermis, *Defining the Social Studies* (Washington, DC: National Council for the Social Studies, 1977).

21. Kevin Vinson and E. Wayne Ross, "In Search of the Social Studies Curriculum: Standardization, Diversity, and Conflict of Appearances," in *Critical Issues in Social Studies Research for the 21st Century*, ed. William Stanley (Greenwich, CT: Information Age, 2001), 39–71.

22. Hertzberg, "History and Progressivism."

23. James Shaver et al., *An Interpretive Report of on the Status of Pre-College Social Studies Education Based on Three NSF-funded Studies* (Washington, DC: National Council for the Social Studies, 1978), 3.

24. Haas, "The Era of the New Social Studies."

25. Peter Dow, "The Past as Prologue: The Legacy of Sputnik," *Social Studies* 83, no. 4 (1992): 164–171; Barry Beyer, "Gone but Not Forgotten: Reflections on the New Social Studies," *Social Studies* 85, no. 6 (1994): 251–255; Goetz, "The New Social Studies"; Fenton, "Reflections on the 'New Social Studies'"; Scheurman and Reynolds, "The 'History Problem' in Curriculum Reform."

26. One example is how Edwin Fenton, a key figure in NSS, responded to one of these events. After visiting scores of NSS projects across the nation, Fenton gave a talk to the New York State Council for the Social Studies entitled 'The New Social Studies Reconsidered" on April 9, 1968. He explained why he had changed his mind about key elements of the NSS. He began his talk this way:

> *I wrote a speech for tonight two weeks ago. I threw it away on Thursday (the day of Martin Luther King's assassination). In the perspective of the last ten days, the old arguments about the new social studies seemed unimportant. I have spent most of my time since Thursday thinking about what I wanted to say to you tonight and a number of hours yesterday and today typing out this speech.*

Fenton went on to talk about Vietnam casualties on both sides, and listed areas that the NSS had neglected (e.g., "slow learners"). In this speech he called for more "teacher involvement and teacher militancy." Edwin Fenton Papers, Box 1, folder 33, Carnegie Mellon University.

27. Over the past four decades, I would hear from teachers who were still using NSS paperbacks and lessons well into the late 1990s. Here, for example, Arthur Pease, a retired social studies teacher from Lebanon High School in Lebanon, New Hampshire, recollects his years as a teacher and the NSS materials he used in his classes during his career (in a comment on a post I had written on NNH):

> As a first-year teacher, I used the Fenton US History text with college-bound Juniors … While there were some great lessons in all of these programs, the thing I learned that stood me in good stead for 40 years was that no one method\text\theory works all the time with all students. "Variety is the spice of life" is a hackneyed cliché but it is still true in terms of materials and methods!
>
> For my whole career, I picked and choose from Fenton, the Amherst Project, Larry's "Promise of America" programs, the High School Geography Project, the great little paperback unit books from the Harvard project, Sociology and Psychology materials and others I've forgotten.
>
> The "New Social Studies" gave those of us coming of age as teachers a wonderful set of resources and if we didn't slavishly used them in lock-step but carefully selected lessons that fit our goals, we could provide students with great lessons … ("The New History in the 1960s (Part 3)," Larry Cuban on School Reform and Classroom Practice [blog], November 24, 2014, http://larrycuban.wordpress.com/2014/11/24/the-new-history-in-the-1960s-part-3/#comment-33306.)

28. David Labaree has written about the "educationalizing" of US social, economic, and political problems; that is, policy elites turning to public schools, initially in rhetoric and then in mandated policies aimed at solving problems ranging from alcohol and drug abuse, teenage pregnancies, and obesity to installing courses to teach elementary and secondary school students how to code so that they will become computer scientists. See "The Winning Ways of a Losing Strategy: Educationalizing Social Problems in the United States," *Educational Theory* 58, no. 4 (2008): 447–460.

29. Ellen Leininger,"Underlying Concepts and Controversy," *Elementary School Journal* 79, no. 3 (1979): 167–173; Valerie Lee and Douglas Ready, "U.S. High School Curriculum: Three Phases of Contemporary Research and Reform," *Future of Children* 19, no. 1 (2009): 135–156.

30. Rodger Bybee,"Science Curriculum Reform in the United States," 1995, http://www.nas.edu/rise/backg3a.htm; Alan Schoenfeld, "The Math Wars," *Educational Policy* 18, no. 1 (2004): 253–286;Evans, *Social Studies Wars*, 149-160.

31. In 1989, the National Council of Teachers of Mathematics released its curriculum standards stressing problem solving and reasoning. In the same year, the

American Association for the Advancement of Science published *Science for All Americans* and in 1993 produced *Benchmarks for Scientific Literacy* that laid out basic learning goals in science for all students. Recapturing interest in history arose at this time also with the creation of the Bradley Commission on History in Schools, funded by the Lynde and Harry Bradley Foundation, in 1987. The seventeen commissioners were a group of prominent historians including two academic specialists in social studies and five secondary school teachers. The Commission began work shortly after the appearance of Diane Ravitch and Chester Finn's *What Do Our 17-Year-Olds Know? A Report on the First National Assessment of History and Literature* (New York: Harper & Row, 1987). The story of the Bradley Commission and its recommended guidelines for teaching history is in chapter 2 of Gagnon *Historical Literacy*, 16–47. Ravitch and Finn had started the Educational Excellence Network in the early 1980s, which then morphed into the Thomas B. Fordham Foundation, which Finn heads. The Bradley Commission called itself a "program of the Educational Excellence Network." See "Checker Finn Opposes the 'For-Profit Model in Education,'" *Diane Ravitch's Blog*, November 4, 2012, http://dianeravitch.net/2012/11/24/checker-finn-opposes-the-for-profit-model-in-education/; Hertzberg, "History and Progressivism"; Kenneth Jackson and Barbara Jackson, "Why the Time Is Right to Reform the History Curriculum," in Gagnon, *Historical Literacy*, 3–15; Linda Symcox, *Whose History? The Struggle for National Standards in American Classrooms* (New York: Teachers College Press, 2002); Gary Nash, Charlotte Crabtree, and Ross Dunn, *History on Trial: Culture Wars and the Teaching of the Past* (New York: Alfred Knopf, 1998).

32. Symcox, *Whose History?* 40–96; Diane Ravitch, *National Standards in American Education* (Washington, DC: Brookings Institution, 1995).

33. Gagnon, *Historical Literacy*; Jackson and Jackson, "Why the Time Is Right." Another way of making the point about "school history" being tedious, boring, and out of touch with what most Americans want to know about the past comes through in the uncommon survey of public opinion about American's interest in history. Survey results revealed that Americans were deeply interested in the past. They read popular histories, visited sites, and wanted to know more about the past—but not the "school history" kind of knowledge. See Roy Rosenzweig and David Thelen, *The Presence of the Past: Popular Uses of History in American Life* (New York: Columbia University Press, 1998).

34. Nash, Crabtree, and Dunn, *History on Trial*; Symcox, *Whose History?*; Evans, *Social Studies Wars*.

35. Nash, Crabtree, and Dunn, *History on Trial*, 232.

36. Ibid., 6.

37. Ibid., 205.

38. Ibid., 177. Quote from Dale Kildee (D-MI), cited in ibid., 227.

39. Joel Westheimer, "Politics and Patriotism in Education," in *Pledging Allegiance:*

The Politics of Patriotism in America's Schools, ed. Joel Westheimer (New York: Teachers College Press, 2004), 171–188.

40. Nash, History on Trial, 205.

41. David Lowenthal, *The Heritage Crusade and The Spoils of History* (New York: Cambridge University Press, 1996), xi, xiii, 123. Bruce VanSledright calls this approach the "collective-memory project"; see *The Challenge of Rethinking History Education* (London: Routledge, 2011), 12.

42. Michael Birnbaum, "Texas Board Approves Social Studies Standards Perceived Liberal Bias," *Washington Post*, May 22, 2010. Of course, many national leaders, past and present, have used history to convey the story that best fits the current government. The United States hardly stands alone in trying to convey a national story that will inculcate pride in its youth and instill loyalty to the government. For Britain, see Richard Evans, "Michael Gove's History Wars," *The Guardian*, July 13, 2013, http://www.theguardian.com/books/2013/jul/13/michael-gove-teaching-history-wars; for East Asia, see "Textbook Cases, Chapter 10," *The Economist*, July 5, 2014, http://www.economist.com/news/asia/21606332-which-democracies-join-east-asias-history-wars-textbook-cases-chapter-10. For other nations wrestling with the degree to which nationalist (read citizenship) feelings color treatments of the past, see Tony Taylor and Robert Guyver, eds., *History Wars and the Classroom: Global Perspectives* (Charlotte, NC: Information Age Publishing, 2012).

43. *Federal Register*, vol. 66, No. 100, May 23, 2001, 28429, at http://www.gpo.gov/fdsys/pkg/FR-2001-05-23/pdf/01-12931.pdf.

44. Phyllis Weinstock et al. *Teaching American History Evaluation: Final Report* (Washington, DC: Office of Planning, Evaluation, and Policy Development US Department of Education, 2011), viii–xi. One critic of TAH (also a grantee of the program) leveled serious complaints about the program's direction, quality, and outcomes. See Rick Shenkman's description of a talk that Stanford University Professor Sam Wineburg gave at the 2009 meeting of the Organization of American Historians: http://historynewsnetwork.org/article/76806.

45. Sam Wineburg, Daisy Martin, and Chauncey Monte-Sano, *Reading Like a Historian* (New York: Teachers College Press, 2013); Linda Levstik and Keith Barton, *Doing History*, 4th ed. (London: Routledge, 2011); VanSledright, *The Challenge of Rethinking History Education*; Bruce Lesh, *"Why Won't You Just Tell Us The Answer?" Teaching Historical Thinking in Grades 7–12* (Portland, ME: Stenhouse Printing, 2011).

46. The overarching goal for history education, according to Levstik and Barton is "preparing students for participation in a pluralist democracy," *Doing History*, 9. Sam Wineburg and his coauthors say directly, "Put simply, the skills cultivated by *Reading Like a Historian* provide essential tools for citizenship" (Wineburg, Martin, and Monte-Sano, *Reading Like a Historian*, x).

47. ETS listed the changes they made in the framework and exam; see https://secure-media.collegeboard.org/digitalServices/pdf/ap/ap-us-history-fact-sheet.pdf.

48. Karen Tumulty and Lyndsey Layton, "Changes in AP History Trigger a Culture Clash in Colorado," *Washington Post*, October 5, 2014, http://www .washingtonpost.com/politics/2014/10/05/fa6136a2-4b12-11e4-b72e-d60a92 29cc10_story.html; Julie Williams quote comes from her Facebook page, September 23, 2014, https://www.facebook.com/julieforjeffco/posts/15143185288 13222. A view of the AP US history course over the past half-century is provided by Luther Spoehr, formerly a student who took the AP course in the 1960s and ended up teaching the course in high school for eighteen years while also being a reader of AP exams and consultant to the College Board. See Spoehr, "Advanced Placement U.S. History: A Fifty-Year Classroom Perspective," *History News Network*, http://historynewsnetwork.org/article/156803.

    Conservative politicians in Oklahoma, North Carolina. Texas, Georgia, and South Carolina have also written legislation and protested the AP US history course. See Adam Lerner, "AP U.S. History Controversy Becomes a Debate on America," *Politico*, February 21, 2015, http://www.politico.com/story/2015/02/ ap-us-history-controversy-becomes-a-debate-on-america-115381.html.

49. Josh Edelson, "Colorado Students Protest Moves To Change AP History Courses," *Bloomberg Business*, October 9, 2014, http://www.bloomberg.com/bw/ articles/2014-10-09/colorado-students-protest-moves-to-change-ap-history-classes.

50. Jack Healy, "After Uproar, School Board Scraps Anti-Protest Curriculum," *New York Times*, October 3, 2014, http://www.nytimes.com/2014/10/04/us/after-uproar-colorado-school-board-retreats-on-curriculum-review-plan.html?_r=0.

51. I call it the "New, New History" to distinguish it from the early-twentieth-century New History, and to emphasize the way it echoes the New Social Studies of the 1960s as well as the New History.

52. Beginning in the mid-1990s, both academics and teachers completed research studies that included descriptions of classroom lessons using the historical approach.

    For academics, see, for example, Peter Sexias, "Parallel Crises: History and the Social Studies Curriculum in USA," *Curriculum Inquiry* 25, no. 3 (1993): 235–250; Terri Epstein, "Makes No Difference If You Are Black or White? African-American and European-American Adolescents' Perspectives on Historical Significance and Historical Sources," paper presented at annual meeting of American Educational Research Association, New Orleans, LA, 1994; Linda Levstik and Keith Barton, "'It Wasn't a Good Part of History': National Identity and Ambiguity in Students Explanations of Historical Significance," *Teachers College Record* 99, no. 3 (1998): 478–513; Jere Brophy and Bruce VanSledright, *Teaching and Learning History in Elementary School* (New York: Teachers College Press, 1997); Sam Wineburg, *Historical Thinking and Other Unnatural Acts* (Philadelphia: Temple University Press, 2001); S. G. Grant, *History Lessons: Teaching, Learning, and Testing in U.S. High Schools Classrooms* (Mahwah, NJ: Lawrence Erlbaum Associates, 2003).

Teachers who have written about their work include Bob Bain, "Into the Breach: Using Research and Theory to Shape History," in *Knowing, Teaching, and Learning History*, ed. Peter Stearns, Peter Sexias, and Sam Wineburg (New York: New York University Press, 2000), 331–352; Lesh, *"Why Won't You Just Tell Us the Answer?"*

Occasionally, an academic became a classroom teacher and studied how students learned history. See, for example, Suzanne Wilson, "Mastodons, Maps, and Michigan: Exploring Uncharted Territory While Teaching Elementary School Social Studies," Elementary Subjects Center Series, no. 24 (East Lansing, MI: Institute for Research on Teaching, Michigan State University, 1990).

53. Wineburg's dissertation (the committee was Shulman, historian David Tyack, and psychologist Dick Snow) dealt with how students and historians read history texts. Suzanne Wilson was the University Distinguished Professor in the Department of Teacher Education at Michigan State University from 1991 to 2013. She has since joined the faculty at the University of Connecticut; Pam Grossman began at the University of Washington in 1988 in Teacher Education and became full professor there until 2000, when she went to Stanford University. She stayed until 2014, when she was appointed Dean of Education at University of Pennsylvania.

I focus on Sam Wineburg for two reasons. First, he is clearly a thought leader in reading and thinking like a historian. Other academics and teachers cite him repeatedly. His early work in the field, awards given by professional associations, and influence as a writer and speaker have been substantial. Second, as I knew Ted Fenton in the early 1960s and his work and mine coincided when I was at Cardozo High School, I also have known Wineburg for over a quarter-century. When he was a graduate student at Stanford University, I was one of the historian-subjects he interviewed for his dissertation. We have stayed in touch over the years, and since his return to Stanford in 2002, we have had many conversations about career, the status of history education, writing, and his work in the field. For this chapter, I interviewed Wineburg (January 15, 2015). I also have e-mails he sent to me (he has given me permission to quote from them), articles he and doctoral students have written, textbooks, and videos of interviews and speeches he has given. His résumé is at https://ed.stanford.edu/faculty/wineburg.

Wineburg completed his dissertation in 1990. Drawing from that work, he published "On Reading of Historical Texts," *American Educational Research Journal* 28, no. 3 (1991): 495–519 where he compared how high school students and academic historians read historical documents, both fiction and nonfiction.

54. In 2008, "Why Historical Thinking Matters," an interactive presentation on the Battle of Lexington that Wineburg and his colleagues had designed, won the American Historical Association's James Harvey Robinson Prize for an Outstanding Teaching Aid.

55. Avishag Reisman, "The Document-Based Lesson: Bringing Disciplinary Inquiry into High School History Classrooms with Adolescent Struggling Readers," *Journal of Curriculum Studies* 44, no. 2 (2011): 233–264; and "Reading Like a Historian: A Document-Based History Curriculum Intervention in an Urban Classroom," *Cognition and Instruction* 30, no. 1 (2012): 86–112. Partners of the Stanford History Education Group are listed and described on website; see https://sheg.stanford.edu/partners. Wineburg's Curriculum and Instruction Course for social studies teachers in the Secondary Teacher Education Program at Stanford University is at https://gse-step.stanford.edu/sites/default/files/educ268_2014_0.pdf.

56. On the number of downloads and where they originated, email communication to author from Joel Breakstone, January 23, 2015.

57. See https://en.wikipedia.org/wiki/Lev_Vygotsky.

58. Email to author from Sam Wineburg to Larry Cuban, June 15, 2013. Richard Shavelson and Ed Haertel were colleagues of Wineburg and experts on assessment and tests.

59. David Tyack and William Tobin, "The 'Grammar' of Schooling: Why Has It Been So Hard to Change?" *American Educational Research Journal* 31, no. 3 (1994): 453–479.

60. Without federal funding, Fenton launched the "slow learner" project in 1967, a four-year social studies curriculum for grades 8 through 11. Holt, Rinehart, and Winston published the eighth-grade text, *The Americans*. (New York: Holt, Rinehart, & Winston, 1970). Fenton papers, Box 4, folder 22, Carnegie Mellon University.

61. See Wineburg, Martin, and Monte-Sano, *Reading Like a Historian*. A large yellow circle is stamped on the cover saying "Aligned with Common Core State Standards."

62. Sam Wineburg, "Choosing Real-World Impact over Impact Factor," *Chronicle of Higher Education*, August 26, 2013; interview with Wineburg, January 15, 2015.

CHAPTER 4

1. School policy prohibits cell phones in class. That policy is publicized in numerous wall posters on each floor of the three-story building, and many classrooms also display the No Cell Phone placard. If a student refuses to put away a phone or give it to the teacher, the teacher can blink and let it go or call a security aide. That occurred in the teacher's third-period class when a uniformed aide entered the room and removed a student.

2. All names are fictitious. I observed four straight classes that Hart taught on November 13, 2013. The lesson described here records what I saw in one of the four classes. However, a few of the actions described in this vignette occurred in another period (e.g., the cell phone incident occurred in second period; the PA announcements happened in third period).

3. District policy is that teachers are to list the Ohio state standard for each lesson. The teacher's written evaluation by principal or downtown supervisor includes whether or not the standard appears somewhere in the classroom. Hart explained that procedure to me after I asked about the standard listed on the board.

4. Roger Beck et al., *Modern World History: Patterns of Interaction* (Boston: Houghton Mifflin, 2008).

5. Public announcements (PA) occur throughout the school day. During the ten-minute homeroom period (10:08–10:18, which is part of the 3rd period) students and administrators cluster their announcements about after-school club meetings, varsity sport games, deadlines for submitting college applications, etc.

6. In the US history class (twenty-nine students) the entire forty-minute period was spent going over vocabulary, concepts, sample questions, and critical thinking skills that have been on previous years' Ohio Graduation Test (OGT). The students would take the OGT in the spring. From the OGT manual:

   > The OGT in social studies contains 32 multiple-choice, four short-answer and two extended-response test questions that measure student achievement related to the seven academic content standards (http://education.ohio.gov/getattachment/Topics/Testing/Ohio-Graduation-Test-OGT/2011-Family-Guide.pdf.aspx).

   There was a special text dedicated to covering the above knowledge and skills. Hart prepared overhead transparencies of vocabulary items on the subject of imperialism covered on pages 24–25 of the textbook. In a subsequent interview with a central office administrator in charge of social studies, the supervisor told me that the main job social studies teachers have is "to teach what is on the OGT. State standards tell teachers what content and skills to teach, and the OGT covers the standards." (Interview with administrator, November 14, 2013).

7. Details of Cleveland's teacher evaluation system can be found at http://www.clevelandmetroschools.org/Page/2767.

8. I observed Mike Allison's lesson on May 1, 2014. I saw another African American history class and a lesson he taught to his US government class the next day.

9. This PA announcement springs from the current district reform described later in the chapter, where low-performing schools were to be restructured into "Investment Schools." A few days earlier, the principal told me that she had been reappointed to the Glenville post, and now teachers had to reapply.

10. In the two other classes I observed Allison teach, there were twelve and twenty-two students, respectively. He basically used the same techniques of cards with questions and answers at the beginning of the class and then photo slides. The level of student engagement, the repartee and rapport with students, and prodding them to think about what they said were just as evident in these lessons as the period that I observed with eight students.

11. Mark Schug, "Teacher Centered Instruction: The Rodney Dangerfield of Social

Studies," in *Where Did Social Studies Go Wrong?* eds. J. S. Leming, L. Ellington, and K. Porter (Washington, DC: Fordham Foundation, 2003), 94–110; Larry Cuban, *How Teachers Taught* (New York: Teachers College Press, 1993).

12. A half-century ago, when I taught at Glenville the grammar of schooling was in place, but I did not know enough to note its influence on my daily teaching. In the mid-1950s, I took for granted the daily bell schedule to change periods, room 235 in which I regularly taught, and students moving through the school year absorbing content and skills as measured by the tests I gave. They were the regularities of a high school of which I took little notice. Not until I began to study the history of schooling in the early 1980s did these deep background structures and routines become visible to me as an important context shaping how I and other teachers taught.

13. Thomas Peters and Robert Waterman, *In Search of Excellence* (New York: Harper and Row, 1982); *A Nation at Risk: The Imperative for Educational Reform* (Washington, DC: National Commission on Excellence in Education, 1983), http://en.wikipedia.org/wiki/A_Nation_at_Risk.

14. Ronald Edmonds, "Program of School Improvement: An Overview," *Educational Leadership* 40, no. 3 (1982): 4–11.

15. For seven correlates that the Center for Effective Schools concentrated on, see http://ces.ou.edu/7_correlates_effectiveness.html.

16. Glenville football team under Coach Ginn and his associates have established an enviable reputation in Cleveland for discipline, hard work, and attention to academics. See Pete Thamel, "Ted Ginn: A Life Greater Than Football," *New York Times*, October 9, 2009, http://thequad.blogs.nytimes.com/2009/10/09/a-life-greater-than-football/?_php=true&_type=blogs&_r=0.

17. William Henderson, "Demography and Desegregation in the Cleveland Public Schools," *New York University Review of Law and Social Change* 26, no. 4 (2002): 460–557. For 2010 population, see http://quickfacts.census.gov/qfd/states/39/3916000.html.

18. Henderson, "Demography and Desegregation."

19. Ibid.

20. Todd Michney, "Race, Violence, and Urban Territoriality," *Journal of Urban History* 32, no. 3 (2006): 404–428; Leonard Moore, *Carl Stokes and the Rise of Black Political Power* (Urbana: University of Illinois Press, 2002): 79–99.

21. Henderson, "Demography and Desegregation"; for 2012 data, see Ohio department of Education district profile at: http://odevax.ode.state.oh.us/htbin/F2012-DISTRICT-PROFILE.COM?irn=043786.

22. For the story of demographic, social, economic, and political changes in these decades, I have drawn from: Kenneth Kusmer, *A Ghetto Takes Shape: Black Cleveland, 1870–1930* (Urbana: University of Illinois Press, 1976); Wilbur Rich and Stephanie Chambers, "Cleveland: Takeovers and Makeovers Are Not the Same," in *Mayors in the Middle: Politics, Race, and Mayoral Control of Urban Schools*, ed. Jeffrey

Henig and Wilbur Rich (Princeton, NJ: Princeton University Press, 2004), 159–190; Stephanie Chambers, *Mayors and Schools: Minority Voices and Democratic Tensions in Urban Education* (Philadelphia: Temple University Press, 2006); Moore, *Carl B. Stokes and the Rise of Black Political Power*; Henderson, "Demography and Desegregation"; Leonard Moore, "The School Desegregation Crisis of Cleveland, Ohio, 1963-1964," *Journal of Urban History* 28, no. 2 (2002): 135-157.

23. Chambers, *Mayors and Schools*, 76. Between 1956 and 2011, there were thirteen superintendents who presided over the Cleveland schools. The longest-serving superintendents have been Paul Briggs (1964-1975) and Barbara Byrd-Bennett (1998-2006). Apart from these two, the superintendency has been a revolving door. (List of superintendents compiled by author.)

24. Chambers, *Mayors and Schools*, 69-77. For a description and analysis of Cleveland's voucher plan in its early years, see Frederick Hess and Patrick McGuinn, "Muffled by the Din: The Competitive Noneffects of the Cleveland Voucher Program," *Teachers College Record* 104, no. 4 (2002): 727-764. In 2002, the US Supreme Court decided in *Zelman v. Simmons-Harris* that the pilot voucher program—which permitted public funds to go to parents who chose religious schools—was constitutional. See http://edition.cnn.com/2002/LAW/06/27/scotus.school.vouchers/index.html and http://en.wikipedia.org/wiki/Zelman_v._Simmons-Harris.

25. List of superintendents compiled from newspaper articles, Board of Education documents, and district reports (in author's possession). Krupansky decision can be found at: http://blog.cleveland.com/pdextra/2011/06/robert_b_krupanskys_order_for.html.

26. Beginning in the 1990s, small high schools and schools-within-a-school had become a popular strategy; these were funded by private donors and state and federal agencies. For portfolio strategy, see Thomas Toch, *High Schools on a Human Scale: How Small Schools Can Transform American Education* (Boston: Beacon Press, 2003), http://www.clevelandmetroschools.org/cms/lib05/OH01915844/Centricity/Domain/409/HighSchoolChoicesBookLR.pdf.

27. Thomas Ott, "School Improvement Grant Program Has Positive Impact on Cleveland Schools," *Cleveland.com* (blog), February 13, 2011, http://blog.cleveland.com/metro/2011/02/school_improvement_grant_progr.html

28. Interview with Jacqueline Bell, April 29, 2014.

29. For Cleveland Plan, see http://www.clevelandta.org/pdf/ClevelandPlan ExecutiveSummary.pdf; for Investment Schools, see: http://clevelandmetro schools.org/Page/2713.

30. Superintendent turnover as described above exceeded principal turnover. Since I taught at Glenville, there have been nine principals, with an average tenure of over six years—a reasonably stable term for a principal. Five of those principals have served six to ten years (including Jacqueline Bell). However, during the early to mid-1980s, three principals served one or two years each, reflecting the turmoil in both the city and school district. (compiled from yearbooks, newspaper articles,

board of education documents, and district reports in author's possession).

31. The class observation occurred on April 28, 2014; I interviewed the teacher that day during his lunch period at a nearby McDonald's.

32. The textbook students use is: Edward Ayers et al., *American Anthem* (New York: Holt Rinehart and Winston, 2009). It is one of the texts often cited as exemplary for the New, New History. Stanford University Professor Samuel Wineburg, a leader in the current movement to have students read and think like historians, is senior consultant to Ayers and his authors.

33. Exit passes are ways that teachers can determine quickly and briefly what students know and understand in the lesson. As a form of assessment, it is often used by teachers to see whether what has been taught has been learned. See Robert Marzano, "The Art and Science of Teaching: The Many Uses of Exit Passes," *Educational Leadership* 70, no. 2 (2012): 80–81.

34. I observed Lawrence Otter's class on April 28, 2014. The single computer was in constant use during the period I observed. However, Otter told me that his biggest issue is not access to computers, since the class uses the school's computer lab often, but access to a working printer. The printer on the third floor where his classroom is located is broken, so he and students must travel back and forth to the second floor to use a printer there.

35. Otter told me that he lists the standard and objective because the district requires it, but notes, "It is all for show."

36. Ayers et al., *American Anthem*.

37. In 1969, I returned to the then new Glenville building to see some former colleagues. On the day I was there, large gates clanged down at the end of one period, and a group of security aides went through the halls on each floor, rounding up students to be taken to the office and detention room. Roaming in halls during classes preceded Otter's arrival at Glenville in the early 1980s.

38. Thomas Dee and Brian Jacob, *The Impact of No Child Left Behind on Students, Teachers and Schools* (Washington, DC: Brookings Institution, Center for Education Policy Analysis, 2010), 149-207, http://cepa.stanford.edu/content/impact-no-child-left-behind-students-teachers-and-schools; Steven Sawchuk, "NCLB's Classroom Effects," *Education Week*, November 26, 2008, http://blogs.edweek.org/edweek/teacherbeat/2008/11/nclbs_classroom_effects.html; Larry Cuban, "Hugging the Middle," *Educational Policy Analysis Archives*, 2007, http://epaa.asu.edu/ojs/article/view/49; Jason Grissom, Sean Nicholson-Crotty, James Harrington, "Estimating the Effects of No Child Left Behind on Teachers' Work Environment and Job Attitudes," *Educational Evaluation and Policy Analysis* 20, no.10 (2014): 1-20.

39. For the pedagogical continuum, see Larry Cuban, "How Have Teachers Taught?" *Larry Cuban on School Reform and Classroom Practice* (blog), August 16, 2009, http://larrycuban.wordpress.com/2009/08/16/how-do-teachers-teach-2/.

CHAPTER 5

1. Interactive whiteboards are connected to a computer, a projector, and software through cables or wireless. Slides and video clips stored on laptop or desktop computer can be projected onto the whiteboard. There is also a pen function—an optical sensor permits the pen (or finger) to write in different colors on the whiteboard. Every academic classroom at Cardozo High School had an IWB.

2. I observed Mike Topper's second period world history classes on December 12, 2013, and May 21, 2014. This account combines events that occurred in both lessons; the history content is taken from the December observation.

3. Before the ninety-minute period began, I asked Topper about the token system, and he told me that it is really a "warning" system for misbehavior. He does not use tokens anymore.

4. As part of the district instructional guidance for and evaluation of teachers, called the DCPS Teaching and Learning Framework Resources Overview, there is a template for every lesson taught in a District of Columbia classroom. See http://dcps.dc.gov/DCPS/Files/downloads/TEACHING%20&%20LEARNING/Teaching-Learning-Framework/DCPS-Teaching-Learning-Framework-Binder-Resources-September-2009.pdf. In the framework, the template for the warm-up says: "Teacher hooks students to the content, activates students' prior knowledge, and introduces the objective" (p. 13).

5. The text the class uses is Jackson Spielvogel, *World History: Modern Times* (New York: McGraw-Hill, 2004). The eleven-hundred-page, five-pound book contains many graphics, photos, charts, and sidebars with vignettes of historical personalities. Accompanying each unit in the book is a "Primary Source Library." There is a set of the texts in the classroom for students to use when the teacher assigns pages to read and questions to ask in a lesson. "3-2-1" is an acronym for a teaching technique that gets students to summarize a reading and think about its meaning. Students were familiar with the technique and had used it for readings in the text and in primary sources. Each student would write on one sheet of paper: "Three things you learned from reading; two things you have found interesting; one question you still have."

6. The lesson template mentioned above states that teachers must have the curriculum standard and daily objective displayed for all students to see. When evaluators—the school principal or DCDC master educators (former teachers hired by the district to observe and evaluate other teachers) make for either scheduled or unannounced visits, they expect to see this information posted.

7. Bloom's Taxonomy is part of the DCPS Teaching and Learning Framework (pp. 4–6). The district expects all academic teachers to sort out the content and skills they teach and use the language of the taxonomy in stating their daily objectives.

8. Students use interactive notebooks to take notes on lectures, create responses to those ideas, comment on textbook passages, and often include drawings

and cartoons they have created. These notebooks often end up as portfolios of student work. For ten years, I team taught a Social Studies Curriculum and Instruction course at Stanford University for graduate students preparing to become teachers. My partner was Lee Swenson, who had developed the idea of an interactive notebook. He showed our students and me how to use it in daily teaching. We incorporated the notebook activity into our syllabus for the course (see http://www.teachtci.com/pdf/webinar_handouts/Managing__ the_Notebook_Secondary.pdf). In Topper's ninth-grade world history class, the term *interactive notebook* was used, but I did not find out exactly how Topper used the notebooks beyond student note-taking during short lectures and answering questions from particular textbook pages.

9. Level 1 questions—factual recall of dates, events, and people—are classified as such according to Bloom's taxonomy. I assume that Topper has taught the taxonomy to students earlier in the semester. Whether the students understand the clarification about the questions they are expected to answer, I do not know.

10. Cardozo school rules include: no cell phones used during class; no hats worn in classrooms; and students must wear uniforms—gray polo tops and khaki pants or skirts for grades 6–8, purple polo tops and khakis for grades 9–10, and black polo shirts and khakis for seniors (see Cardozo website: http://www.cardozohs.com/apps/pages/index.jsp?uREC_ID=207589&type=d&pREC_ID=408163). No street clothes are allowed; loaner shirts are available to students who break rules. In the two weeks I was in the school, I noted that about half of the students wore uniforms.

11. Exit Passes are described in chapter 4.

12. Mike Topper (pseudonym), Department of Social Studies, Ninth-Grade Academy, "Syllabus for World History I, 2013–2014," 1. (In author's possession.) I cannot give web link to syllabus because it would reveal the teacher's actual name.

13. Interview with Kerry Faulkner, May 19, 2014.

14. Kerry Faulkner, "US History w/ Mr. Faulkner: Syllabus 2013–2014." On one page, Faulkner has a grid showing Dates, Units, Standards and Time Periods, Common Core Skills, and Assessments. So, for the recently completed "Civil Rights" unit, Faulkner listed the standard: "11.11. Students analyze the origins, goals, key events, and accomplishments of Civil Rights movement in the United States," followed by a listing of the people, events, and other movements that will be covered. (In author's possession).

15. Ibid.

16. For a description of the renovation, see: http://www.dcstudentsctf.org/PDFs/JOBS_MayJun2013.pdf. Also see Emma Brown, "At Cardozo School, High Hopes for a Cultural Transformation to Match Physical One," *Washington Post*, August 26, 2013, http://www.washingtonpost.com/local/education/at-cardozo-school-high-hopes-for-a-cultural-transformation-to-match-physical-one/2013/08/26/e4801764-0c38-11e3-8974-f97ab3b3c677_story.html. According to Brown's

article, the Cardozo makeover also raised hopes that low-income students of color would work harder in a renovated building.

17. When I began teaching at Cardozo in 1963 the name "Cardozo," engraved into stone over the main entrance, did not fully cover the original name of "Central High School."

18. *Reconstitution* is one of the remedies for persistently low academic performance mandated by the federally funded No Child Left Behind act and Race to the Top initiative. Glenville High School was also reconstituted through Ohio's adoption of Race to the Top requirements and its School Improvement Grants, one of which went to particular Cleveland high schools, including Glenville. Under Mayor Jackson's Cleveland Plan, Glenville was again reconstituted. See chapter 4.

19. Emma Brown, "With 'Reconstitution,' DC Officials Hope for School Turnaround," *Washington Post,* June 10, 2013.

20. Statistics from Emma Brown, "Middle Schools Present Vexing Problem for DC Leaders as Parents Choose Other Options," *Washington Post,* February 17, 2014, http://www.washingtonpost.com/local/education/middle-schools-present-vexing-problem-for-dc-leaders-as-parents-choose-other-options/2014/02/17/29b95e24-93ef-11e3-83b9-1f024193bb84_story.html.

21. A description of the shooting and trial of the former students can be found at: http://news.google.com/newspapers?nid=1798&dat=19710114&id=4RMfAAAAIBAJ&sjid=CI0EAAAAIBAJ&pg=7523,2204113.

22. Like Cleveland and most other urban districts, DC administrators joined the small high school movement. Schools-within-a-school mushroomed throughout the city. Academies, magnets, and theme-dominated small schools proliferated, either as stand-alone small schools or as part of converted large high schools. At Cardozo, different principals sought private and federal funds to underwrite TransTech Academy, the Academy of Construction and Design, and the newly established Academy of Information Technology as schools-within-a-school in the larger building.

23. See Mary Anne Raywid, "Current Literature on Small Schools," *ERIC Digest,* 1999, ED425049 1999-01-00; Cardozo High School News and Announcements, "Retirement Celebration for Reginald Ballard," http://www.cardozohs.com/apps/news/show_news.jsp?REC_ID=289125&id=0.

24. Information on current Cardozo academies can be found at http://www.cardozohs.com/; for the Academy of Construction and Design, see http://www.dcstudentsctf.org/foundation/GroundBreaking.htm.

25. *Cardozo Senior High School Student Handbook, 1991.* The flex schedule (no page numbers) follows page 13. (In author's possession.) For Carnegie units and their persistence in US high schools, see David Tyack and William Tobin, "The 'Grammar' of Schooling: Why Has It Been So Hard To Change?" *American Educational Research Journal* 31, no. 3 (1994): 453–479.

26. For the past decade of wins and losses in football, see http://www.maxpreps .com/local/team/records/year_by_year_results.aspx?gendersport=boys,football &schoolid=1c8fed20-3a08-4e2e-9864-e0318e9bf322. For basketball, see http:// www.maxpreps.com/local/team/records/year_by_year_results.aspx?gender sport=boys,basketball&schoolid=1c8fed20-3a08-4e2e-9864-e0318e9bf322. For baseball, see http://www.maxpreps.com/local/team/records/year_by_ year_results.aspx?gendersport=boys,baseball&schoolid=1c8fed20-3a08-4e2e- 9864-e0318e9bf322.

27. Harry Jaffe and Tom Sherwood, *Dream City: Race, Power, and the Decline of Washington, DC* (New York: Simon & Schuster, 1994), 13.

28. Ibid.

29. Mark Leibovich, *This Town* (New York: Blue Rider Press, 2013) describes the power elites' unrelenting search for power, approval, and glory at cocktail parties, funerals, and celebrity events in federal Washington over the past few decades.

30. Division of Behavioral and Social Sciences and Education of National Research Council, *A Plan for Evaluating the District of Columbia's Public Schools* (Washington, DC: The National Academies Press, 2011), 13.

31. All statistics come from following sources: US Bureau of Census at https://www .census.gov/statab/hist/HS-07.pdf; http://en.wikipedia.org/wiki/Demographics_ of_Washington,_DC#Population; Parents United for DC Public Schools, "Separate and Unequal: The State of the District of Columbia Public Schools Fifty Years after *Brown* and *Bolling*," March 2005, 8–9. www.washlaw.org/pdf/ Separate_and_Unequal_Report.pdf.

32. The longest-serving DC Mayor was Marion Barry. A former civil rights activist, Barry ran for and was elected to the DC Board of Education in 1971, serving as president of the school board before he left in 1974 to run for city council. He served on the city council until 1979, when he was elected mayor. He left office in 1991 after being arrested by the FBI on cocaine charges. He was convicted and served six months in prison. He ran for mayor again in 1995 and was reelected. From 2005 until his death in November 2014, he again served on the city council representing the Anacostia neighborhood. As mayor, Barry worked with the school board and superintendents erratically, seldom making a signature change in the public schools. See Jaffe and Sherwood, *Dream City* and Wikipedia entry at: http://en.wikipedia.org/wiki/Marion_Barry#DC_Board_ of_Education_.281971.E2.80.931974.29. For cited examples of reforms, see *A Plan for Evaluating the District of Columbia's Public Schools*, 31–32.

33. Another governance change occurred in 1996, when the city council created the DC Public Charter Board to authorize charter schools. In 1996, there were two charter schools; by 2013, there were sixty, enrolling 43 percent of all district students. See District of Columbia Public Charter School Board, "Facts about DC Public Charter School Board and Charter Schools," October 2013, http://www .dcpcsb.org/data/files/fast%20facts%20-%20october%202013%5B1%5D.pdf.

34. David Vise, "DC Control Board Takes Charge of Public Schools," *Washington Post*, November 16, 1996, A01; District of Columbia Financial Responsibility and Management Assistance Authority, "Children in Crisis: A Report on the Failure of the DC Public Schools," November 12, 1996. (Washington, DC: Responsibility and Management Assistance Authority, November 1996).

35. Spencer Hsu and Justin Blum, "DC School Vouchers Win Final Approval," *Washington Post*, January 23, 2004, A01; US Department of Education, *Evaluation of the DC Opportunity Scholarship Program*, NCEE-2010-4019 (Washington, DC: US Department of Education, National Center for Educational Evaluation, 2010); Lyndsey Layton and Emma Brown, "Quality Controls Lacking for DC Schools Accepting Federal Vouchers," *Washington Post*, November 17, 2012, http://www.washingtonpost.com/local/education/quality-controls-lacking-for-dc-schools-accepting-federal-vouchers/2012/11/17/062bf97a-1e0d-11e2-b647-bb1668e64058_story.html.

36. Stacy Khadaroo, "For Obama, Split Looms Over Education Reform," *Christian Science Monitor*, December 18, 2008; Paul Tough, "No, Seriously: No Excuses," *New York Times Magazine*, July 7, 2011. Few Democrats, however, supported voucher initiatives.

37. Joseph Viteritti, "The Federal Role in School Reform: Obama's 'Race to the Top'" *Notre Dame Law Review* 87, no. 5 (2012): 2087–2120; Lyndsey Layton, "Overhaul of Education," *Washington Post*, September 20, 2012.

38. June Kronholz, "DC's Braveheart," *Education Next*, 2010, http://educationnext.org/d-c-s-braveheart/; Clay Risen, "The Lightning Rod," *The Atlantic*, November 2008, http://www.theatlantic.com/magazine/archive/2008/11/the-lightning-rod/307058/.

39. Lists of principals and superintendents compiled from school yearbooks, newspaper articles, board of education documents, and district reports. (In author's possession).

40. Quoted in Hugh Scott, *The Black School Superintendent: Messiah or Scapegoat?* (Washington, DC: Howard University Press, 1980), 97.

41. William Raspberry, "School Superintendents Aren't All That Important," *Washington Post*, August 16, 2004, A17.

42. I located each principal from Cardozo yearbooks, *Washington Post* articles, personal contacts, and student newspapers.

43. Frank McCourt, *Teacher Man: A Memoir* (New York: Scribner, 2006).

44. I observed Taylor's world history class on May 19, 2014, and interviewed him at the end of the school day. He had to leave before I completed the interview, so he offered to finish with a follow-up phone call. We spoke on May 29, 2014. All quotes come from these interviews.

45. In a letter to parents and guardians, Taylor had written the following:
    I am pleased to have your child in my World History and Geography II class. Your child will find that I am a tough but fair teacher who has planned an exciting and

productive school year. I am writing this letter to introduce myself to you . . .

    My love of history and passion for education brought me into the classroom. I have been teaching at Cardozo Senior High School since 2009. My particular style of teaching is based on three things: setting high expectations for EVERY (original emphasis) student; showing students respect and expecting it in return; and last, but certainly not least, parental involvement. I believe when parents and teachers work together, a student can accomplish anything." (In author's possession.) I cannot give web link to letter and course syllabus because it would reveal actual name of the teacher.

46. "Stanford History Education Group: Charting the Future of Teaching the Past." See http://sheg.stanford.edu/world. SHEG made available individual world history lessons such as the "The Invasion of Nanking," the one that Burt Taylor found when surfing the web. For elaboration of SHEG, see chapter 3.

47. Quotes from Taylor come from two interviews.

48. Spielvogel, *World History*. This is the same text used in Topper's class.

49. See http://sheg.stanford.edu/invasion-nanking.

50. The Daily Participation Grade sheet amounts to ten points for each student that period. It has three sections: The first is the warm-up described in text: "Ready?" The next section, "Resolute?" refers to taking notes, participating in class, and assignments. There are three choices for Taylor to check off: "Partial," "Almost There," and "Good to Go!" The last section is "Respectful?" and covers "no electronics and good behavior," with the same three boxes to check as "Resolute?"

51. Burt Taylor left Cardozo High School in June 2014 and is now working at the US Department of Education.

52. Bill Turque, "Rhee Has Asked How to Regain Teachers' Trust, Principals Say," *Washington Post*, October 28, 2009, http://www.washingtonpost.com/wp-dyn/content/article/2009/10/27/AR2009102702108.html. At a leadership meeting of DC principals, a participant quoted Rhee as asking the group, "What can I do to regain the trust of my teachers? I don't understand why everyone is so afraid." Two of the three teachers I observed and interviewed specifically mention the distrust they had felt about the new evaluation system. They all felt it was unfair because working at Cardozo, an academically low-performing school, made it very difficult for them to be judged as a highly effective teacher. A veteran English teacher (nearly thirty years at Cardozo) who I had interviewed for background mentioned the distrust and unfairness as well.

CHAPTER 6

1. "Funny Comedian Quotes and Videos," http://funnycomedianquotes.com/funny-quotes-and-jokes-about-change.html.

2. Robert Nisbet, *The History of the Idea of Progress* (Piscataway, NJ: Transaction Publishers, 1995); Henry Perkinson, *The Imperfect Panacea: American Faith in*

Education, 4th ed. (New York: McGraw-Hill, 1995).

3. For a recent and typical example of this genre of critique, see Jeff Livingston, "3 Ways to Radically Remake U.S. Schools and Education," *U.S. News and Report*, February 5, 2013.

4. Norton Grubb and Marvin Lazerson, *The Education Gospel* (Cambridge, MA: Harvard University Press, 2004); Larry Cuban, "A Solution That Lost Its Problem: Why Centralized Policymaking Is Unlikely to Yield Many Classroom Gains" (Denver: Education Commission of States, 2004); and Larry Cuban, *The Blackboard and the Bottom Line: Why Can't Schools Be Like Businesses?* (Cambridge, MA: Harvard University Press, 2004).

5. Lyndsey Layton, "In New Orleans, Major School District Closes Traditional Public Schools for Good," *Washington Post*, May 28, 2014, http://www.washington post.com/local/education/in-new-orleans-traditional-public-schools-close-for-good/2014/05/28/ae4f5724-e5de-11e3-8f90-73e071f3d637_story.html; Alan Greenblatt, "New Orleans District Moves to All-Charter System," *nprEd*, May 30, 2014, http://www.npr.org/blogs/ed/2014/05/30/317374739/new-orleans-district-moves-to-an-all-charter-system.

6. Seymour Sarason, *Charter Schools: Another Flawed Educational Reform* (New York: Teachers College Press, 1998).

7. Donald Schön, *Beyond the Stable State* (New York: Norton, 1973), 32; "Introduction," in *Explaining Institutional Change*, ed. James Mahoney and Kathleen Thelen (New York: Cambridge University Press, 2009), 1–37.

8. I elaborated on the idea of teachers having constrained choice in content and pedagogy in their lessons and as gatekeepers at the classroom door in *How Teachers Taught* (New York: Teachers College Press, 1993), 260–264. The literature about implementation is rich in examples of policies and their implementation that would be disheartening to either current or prospective policymakers. Some key studies over the decades: Jeffrey Pressman and Aaron Wildavsky, *Implementation* (Berkeley: University of California Press, 1973); Paul Berman and Milbrey McLaughlin, *Federal Programs Supporting Educational Change*, vol. VIII, *Implementing and Sustaining Innovations* (Santa Monica, CA: RAND, 1978); Meredith Honig, ed., *New Directions in Education Policy Implementation* (Albany: State University of New York Press, 2006); Charles Payne, *So Much Reform, So Little Change* (Cambridge, MA: Harvard Education Press, 2008); Joseph McDonald et al., *American School Reform: What Fails and Why* (Chicago: University of Chicago Press, 2014).

For nearly half a century, researchers have documented that top-down policy formation and adoption seldom spurred practitioners to put policies into classroom practice in ways that bore much resemblance to what policymakers intended. Rather, as policy traversed district and school offices into classrooms, teacher made adaptations and adjustments to it.

9. David Tyack and William Tobin, "The 'Grammar' of Schooling: Why Has It Been So Hard To Change?" *American Educational Research Journal* 31, no. 3 (1994): 453–479; Stephen Thornton, *Teaching Social Studies That Matters* (New York: Teachers College Press, 2004).

10. An obvious example of conserving and changing traditions can be seen within the overall purpose of public schooling to inculcate citizenship. That purpose is shared by the social studies and history. However, there have been arguments for decades about what kind of citizenship is preferred for students and all Americans. See Joel Westheimer, *What Kind of Citizen?* (New York: Teachers College Press, 2015).

11. In math, historic tensions between teaching students to master the skills and procedures of arithmetic, algebra, and geometry—the "basics" (conserving the knowledge and skills) and learning how to reason and solve problems mathematically (the New Math) of the 1960s; math standards of the late 1980s, etc. See George Stanic, "The Growing Crisis in Mathematics Education in the Early Twentieth Century," *Journal for Research in Mathematics Education* 17, no. 3 (1986): 190–205; Alan Schoenfeld, "The Math Wars," *Educational Policy* 18, no. 1 (2004): 253–286; Elizabeth Green, "Why Does Everyone Hate the New Math?" *New York Times Magazine*, July 27, 2014, 23–27, 40, 42. For science, historic tensions have existed in the various reform efforts to alter its content and pedagogy. One thrust of these reforms over the past century has been to have students know bodies of organized scientific knowledge (conserving basic knowledge in biology, chemistry, and physics) and to create a "science for living," where the knowledge is relevant to students' lives and all students become scientifically literate. Of the two aims, the former has dominated curricula since the late nineteenth century, the latter has been evident in periodic bursts of reforms since the 1950s. But the conflict continues even today. See John Rudolph, *Scientists in the Classroom: The Cold War Reconstruction of American Science Education* (New York: Palgrave Macmillan, 2002); Richard Duschl, "Science Education in Three-Part Harmony," *Review of Research in Education* 32 (2008): 268–291; Mahoney and Thelen, "Introduction"; Schön, *Beyond the Stable State*; Herbert Kliebard, "Success and Failure in Educational Reform: Are There Historical 'Lessons?'" *Peabody Journal of Education* 65, no. 2 (1988): 144–157; David Paris, *Ideology and Educational Reform* (Boulder, CO: Westview Press, 1995).

12. Regional Education Laboratory West, "Research on Grade Span Configurations," 2011, http://relwest_production.s3.amazonaws.com/documents/pdfs/000/000/233/original/REL_West_website_Grade_Span_Configuration.10.2013.pdf?1400083900. For schools-within-a-school, see Valerie Strauss, "How Much Bill Gates Disappointing Small School Effort Really Cost," *Washington Post*, June 9, 2014.

13. Since NCLB was enacted, both high schools regularly missed meeting their

Adequate Yearly Progress targets. Each school was cited for low performance, leading to restructuring (*reconstitution*, as it was called in DC) twice.

14. I have laid out the different ways that continuity in districts and schools often trumps policymaker designs for incremental and fundamental changes in Larry Cuban, "Curriculum Stability and Change," in *Handbook of Research on Curriculum*, ed. Philip Jackson (New York: Macmillan, 1992), 216–247.

15. Robert Balfanz et al., "Building a Grad Nation: Annual Update 2013," http://www.civicenterprises.net/MediaLibrary/Docs/Building-A-Grad-Nation-Report-2013_Full_v1.pdf.

16. Tom Loveless, *The 2009 Brown Center Report on American Education: How Well Are American Students Learning?* (Washington, DC: The Brookings Institution, 2009), 19–25; Debra Viadero, "Research Doesn't Offer Much Guidance on Turnarounds," *Education Week*, August 4, 2009; William Mathis, "NCLB's Ultimate Restructuring Alternatives: Do They Improve the Quality of Education?" (East Lansing, MI: Great Lakes Center for Research and Practice, 2009); Andy Smarick, "The Turnaround Fallacy," *Education Next* 10, no. 1 (2010), http://educationnext.org/the-turnaround-fallacy/. For an account of turnarounds in DC, see Emma Brown, "With 'Reconstitution,' DC Officials Hope for School Turnaround," *Washington Post*, June 10, 2013.

17. Larry Cuban, "History of Teaching in Social Studies," in *Handbook of Research on Social Studies Teaching and Learning*, ed. James Shaver (New York: Macmillan, 1992), 197–209; Suzanne Wilson, "Research on History Teaching," in *Handbook of Research on Teaching*, ed. Virginia Richardson (New York: Macmillan, 2001), 527–544.

18. Cuban, "History of Teaching in Social Studies."

19. For instance, Roger Beck et al., *Modern World History* (Dumfries, N.C: Holt McDougal, 2005) and Edward Ayers, *American Anthem* (New York: Holt, Rinehart, and Winston, 2007).

20. Jackson Spielvogel, *World History: Modern Times* (New York: Glencoe McGraw-Hill, 2005).

21. *The American Vision: Modern Times* (New York: Glencoe McGraw-Hill, 2005).

22. A question arises that cannot be answered by the available data I have compiled. Why did the all three Cardozo teachers use different versions of the New, New History? There was no evidence that the three received direct training in teaching students to read, think, and write like historians. It would be a stretch to attribute this to working closely together (they did not), happenstance (a possibility), or a carryover from the Cardozo Project in Urban Teaching a half-century earlier (very unlikely). One possibility, however, is that the district's focus on standards—particularly the new Common Core ones—and the link between teacher evaluation and sticking to standards influenced what these teachers did.

The IMPACT evaluation scheme and visits by master educators (particularly those with a background in social studies) with follow-up conferences may have tilted history teachers toward the DC schools' Social Studies Standards, which include many references to historical evidence, use of primary and secondary sources, critical thinking skills, etc. See "District of Columbia Social Studies, Pre-K through Grade 12," p. 29 for grades 3–5, p. 48 for grades 6–8, p. 88 for grades 9–12, at http://osse.dc.gov/sites/default/files/dc/ sites/osse/publication/attachments/DCPS-horiz-soc_studies.pdf. This is all guesswork, of course. But the sharp difference between Cardozo and Glenville teachers in using the NHH approach does raise such questions.

23. Beth Morton et al., "Education and Certification Qualifications of Departmentalized Public High School-Level Teachers of Core Subjects," NCES-338, (Washington, DC: US Department of Education, 2008), v, 18.

24. Cuban, "History of Teaching in Social Studies."

25. Robin Henke, *What Happens in Classrooms? 1994–1995*, NCES 1999-348 (Washington, DC: US Department of Education, National Center for Education Statistics, 1999), 4, 8, 13, 16.

26. James Leming et al., *A National Random Survey of High School Social Studies Teachers' Professional Opinions, Values, and Classroom Practices* (Storrs, CT: The Center for Survey Research and Analysis, University of Connecticut, January 2009), 28, 31. I did not include responses to prompts that asked whether teachers engaged students in "critical thinking skills" (80 percent) and "problem solving" (71 percent) in "every class" or "almost every class" because these phrases went undefined in either the questions asked of teachers or the responses teachers made.

27. I attended a TAH grant workshop in the Oakland (California) Unified School District in 2005 and worked with a group of experienced teachers on identifying patterns of teacher- and student-centered activities in US history classes. In listening to the teachers, many pointed out to me how they use primary and secondary sources and have their students search for bias in closely reading these sources. This project under the leadership of Stan Pesick and Shelley Weintraub had worked for nearly a decade earlier on historical thinking with Oakland teachers and librarians. See Stan Pesick and Shelley Weintraub, "DeTocqueville's Ghost: Examining the Struggle for Democracy in America," *History Teacher* 36, no. 2 (2003): 231–251. For an example of another TAH grant see "Northern Nevada Teaching American History Project," http:// teachinghistory.org/tah-grants/project-spotlight/25191.

28. Mike Henry, "The DBQ Change: Returning to the Original Intent," *College Board AP Central for Educators*, http://apcentral.collegeboard.com/apc/ members/homepage/10467_print.html?type=popup; also see Luther Spoehr, "Advanced Placement United States History: A Fifty-Year Perspective," *History News Network*, September 3, 2014.

29. Email from Joel Breakstone to Larry Cuban, January 23, 2015; Theresa Johnston, "Stanford-developed History Lessons for Grades 6–12 Adopted Worldwide," *GSE News*, March 17, 2014, https://ed.stanford.edu/news/ stanford-developed-history-lessons-grades-6-12-adopted-worldwide. There are, of course, other districts that have been using the Thinking Like a Historian approach well before SHEG was founded. See, for example, the work in Oakland (California) Unified School District that began in the early 2000s at: https://sites.google.com/a/ousd.k12.ca.us/history/home.

30. Thus far, New York State has included document-based questions into its statewide assessment of social studies (including the Regents exam). When more states include such items in their tests, I expect increases in the number of teachers who build into their daily lessons how to analyze primary sources, bias, and corroborating sources. See http://www.archives.nysed.gov/ education/showcase/dbq.shtml.

31. David Hicks et al., "Social Studies Teachers' Use of Classroom-Based and Web-Based Use Historical Primary Sources," *Theory and Research in Social Education* 32, no. 2 (2004): 213–247. The response rate to this random sample was 40 percent.

32. John Lee et al., "Social Studies and History Teachers' Uses of Non-Digital and Digital Historical Resources," *Social Studies Research and Practice* 1, no. 3 (2006): 291–311. Response rate from teachers was 70 percent. There are other limited studies showing that small fractions of social studies teachers use primary sources or have class discussions that go in depth into historical issues; see Abby Reisman, "Entering the Historical Problem Space: Whole-Class Text-Based Discussion in History Class, *Teachers College Record*,117 (February 2015): 1–44; John Saye et al., "Authentic Pedagogy: Its Presence in Social Studies Classrooms and Relationship to Student Performance on State-Mandated Tests," *Theory and Research in Social Studies* 41, no. 1, (2013): 89–132.

33. I observed nine lessons from six teachers at Gunderson High School in San Jose Unified School District during 2009–2010; one lesson of a teacher at Mission High School in San Francisco Unified School District in 2013; two lessons of one teacher at Roosevelt High School in the Washington, DC Public Schools; four lessons of four teachers at Aragon High School in the San Mateo Union High School District in 2014; three lessons from one teacher at John F. Kennedy High School in the Fremont Unified School District in 2014, and two lessons from two teachers at Los Altos High School and Mountain View High School in the Mountain View-Los Altos High School District in 2015.

34. A sampling of individual case studies and collections of cases that describe teachers using inquiry to investigate the past in ways that historians do: Robert Bain, "They Thought The World Was Flat? Applying the Principles of *How People Learn* in Teaching High School History," in *How Students Learn: History, Mathematics, and Science in the Classroom*, ed. Suzanne Donovan and John Bransford (Washington, DC: The National Academies Press, 2005): 179–213; Bruce

Lesh, *"Why Won't You Just Tell Us the Answer?" Teaching Historical Thinking in Grades 7–12* (Portland, ME: Stenhouse Publishers, 2011); Bruce VanSledright, *The Challenge of Rethinking History Education* New York: Routledge, 2011); Sam Wineburg and Suzanne Wilson, "Models of Wisdom in the Teaching of History," *Historical Thinking and Other Unnatural Acts*, ed. Sam Wineburg (Philadelphia: Temple University Press, 2001), 155–172.

35. To make this informed guess, I relied on analogies to earlier movements where coalitions of policy elites, academics, and researchers worked hard to adopt reform-driven policies that sought major changes in the prevailing teacher-centered patterns of teaching. There were the pedagogical progressives who worked for student-centered pedagogy focusing on the "whole child," interdisciplinary curriculum, the "project method," and real-world tasks to replace the text-bound, recitation-driven, whole-group pedagogy that governed schools in the early twentieth century. Then there were the Cold War warrior academics of the mid-1950s who designed new curricula in the sciences, math, and the social studies to produce skilled graduates who would become engineers, scientists, and mathematicians and thereby compete more effectively with the Soviet Union. Finally, there was the "Open Classroom" movement where a model of child-centered teaching and curriculum was imported from the United Kingdom and flourished from the mid-1960s through the mid-1970s in the United States. In these three instances, major reform efforts were made, some funded by the federal government and foundations, to alter what teachers taught and how.

   In *How Teachers Taught*, I examined these reform efforts to determine to what degree the adopted policies had changed classroom practices. I found between 20 and 25 percent of teachers in elementary schools adopting various versions of the intended reform for part of their classroom practice, and far less adoption—10 to 15 percent—by high school teachers. Those fractions of teachers who did adopt reforms created hybrids of both teacher- and student-centered practices. The vast majority, though, continued with the dominant lecture, textbook, worksheets, homework and test routines that had marked US classrooms in the twentieth century. See pp. 112, 173, and 202.

36. John Dewey, cited in Tyack and Tobin, "The 'Grammar of Schooling,'" 454.

37. Avishag Reisman, "The 'Document-Based Lesson': Bringing Disciplinary Inquiry into High School History Classrooms with Adolescent Struggling Readers," *Journal of Curriculum Studies* 44, no. 2 (2012): 233–264; interview with Sam Wineburg, January 15, 2015.

38. On November 21, 2014, a high school teacher in the Fremont Unified District in Northern California made this comment to a post on my blog, https://larrycuban.wordpress.com/2014/11/21/content-vs-skills-again-and-again-part-2/.

39. The history teacher at the private college prep high school made this comment to a post on my blog on April 21, 2015, https://larrycuban.wordpress.com/2015/04/21/how-many-teachers-teach-a-new-kind-of-history/.

APPENDIX A

1. Jaume Aurell, "Autobiography as Unconventional History: Construct-
   ing the Author," *Rethinking History: The Journal of Theory and Practice* 10, no. 3
   (2006): 433–449.

2. Patrick Hutton, quoted in James Young, "Between History and Memory: The
   Uncanny Voices of Historian and Survivor," *History and Memory* 9, nos. 1/2
   (1997): 47–58.

3. See Larry Cuban, *How Teachers Taught*, 2nd ed. (New York: Teachers College Press,
   1993); David Tyack and Larry Cuban, *Tinkering Toward Utopia* (Cambridge, MA:
   Harvard University Press, 1995); *Hugging the Middle: How Teachers Teach in an Era
   of Testing and Accountability* (New York: Teachers College Press, 2008).

Acknowledgments

No book is an island. Like every book I have written over the years, this one depended on many people who helped me in the conception and execution of the project. I want to thank Diana Hess, who kick-started this project through a Spencer Foundation small grant. She saw the uniqueness of a historian who was a former high school history teacher examining his teaching a half-century ago and returning to the same high schools to assess the teaching of history today. She saw, as I did, how such an inquiry into the past is connected to important policy issues facing today's decision makers. Without her support, the project and this book would not have been launched and the journey completed. Thank you, Diana.

The grant got me started, but I could not have completed the study without the help of others in the schools. Glenville High School principal Jacqueline Bell, librarian Kimberly Smith, and the four history teachers I observed and interviewed (who asked for confidentiality) permitted me to enter their professional lives. At Cardozo High School, Frazier O'Leary, a veteran English teacher and passionate observer of the DC school scene, helped me traverse the half-century of Cardozo history after I left in the late-1960s. He took me around the newly renovated building and, most important, introduced me to two of the three teachers I interviewed and observed (who also asked for confidentiality). He was both gracious and charming and, above all, knowledgeable and dedicated to his students. Thank you, Frazier.

Jack Schneider took the time to read the penultimate draft of this book and gave me constructive advice, much of which I took. I am grateful for that help, Jack.

Finally, I thank Doug Clayton at Harvard Education Press, who saw the policy implications of a then-and-now study of history teaching in urban high schools.

While no book may be an island, I do take responsibility for any errors that remain.

About the Author

LARRY CUBAN is professor emeritus of education at Stanford University. He has taught courses in the methods of teaching social studies; the history of school reform, curriculum, and instruction; and leadership.

His background in the field of education before becoming a professor included fourteen years of teaching high school social studies in big-city schools, directing a teacher education program that prepared returning Peace Corps volunteers to teach in inner-city schools, and serving seven years as a district superintendent.

His most recent books are *Inside the Black Box of Classroom Practice: Change Without Reform in American Education* (2013), *As Good as It Gets: What School Reform Brought to Austin* (2010); *Hugging the Middle: How Teachers Teach in an Era of Testing and Accountability* (2009); *Partners in Literacy* (with Sondra Cuban, 2007); *Against the Odds: Insights from One District's Small School Reform* (coauthor, 2010); and *Cutting Through the Hype: The Essential Guide to School Reform* (with Jane David, 2010).